GLOBAL SHADOWS

Global Shadows

AFRICA IN THE NEOLIBERAL WORLD ORDER

James Ferguson

DUKE UNIVERSITY PRESS   Durham and London   2006

Global Shadows

AFRICA IN THE NEOLIBERAL WORLD ORDER

James Ferguson

DUKE UNIVERSITY PRESS   Durham and London   2006

© 2006 Duke University Press

All rights reserved

Printed in the United States

of America on acid-free paper ∞

Designed by C. H. Westmoreland

Typeset in Galliard

by Tseng Information Systems, Inc.

Library of Congress Cataloging-in-

Publication Data appear on the last

printed page of this book.

Contents

Acknowledgments

The essays in this volume were written at various times over the course of the last decade. They treat a range of subjects, and each can be read on its own, as an independent essay. But they converge on certain broad themes and together amount to a single book-long argument for a certain perspective on anthropology and "Africa." I have, for the most part, left the several previously published essays in the form in which they originally appeared, in recognition of the way each responded to a particular set of circumstances in the world and reflected a certain waypoint in the development of my own ideas. I have, however, tried to correct any errors and to update references, where appropriate.

Apart from the introduction and chapter 1, which introduce the volume, the chapters appear in the order they were originally written. Chapter 2, "Paradoxes of Sovereignty and Independence," was published in *Siting Culture*, edited by Karen Fog Olwig (Routledge, 1996). Chapter 3, "De-moralizing Economies," was originally published (in a shorter form) in *Moralizing States*, edited by Sally Falk Moore (AES Monograph Series, 1993). Chapter 4, "Transnational Topographies of Power," was published in a slightly different version (and with a slightly different title) in *A Companion to the Anthropology of Politics*, edited by David Nugent and Joan Vincent (Blackwell, 2004). Chapter 5, "Chrysalis," appeared (in an abridged version) in *Global Networks* (3, no. 3 [2003]: 271–98). Chapter 6, "Of Mimicry and Membership," appeared in *Cultural Anthropology* (17, no. 4 [2002]: 551–69). Chapters 7 and 8, along with the introduction and chapter 1, have not appeared previously.

Unusually for an anthropologist, I have not written these chapters about people and places of which I have intimate knowledge through fieldwork. Instead, I have tried to speak about larger issues —concerning, broadly, "Africa" and its place in the world—that can be addressed only by venturing beyond the kinds of knowledge claims that can be firmly "grounded" in any specific ethnographically known case. I believe that there are compelling reasons for attempting this, as I explain in the introduction. But given the strong disciplinary commitment of contemporary anthropology to ethnographic specificity, it is perhaps appropriate to note to the anthropological reader that my experiment here is meant as a way not of discarding (still less of disparaging) ethnography but, rather, of pointing out some directions in which it might turn. Engaging with discussions and projects that are framed at levels of scale and abstraction ("Africa," "the West," "the globe," "the world") clearly not amenable to ethnographic study in the traditional sense undoubtedly poses a challenge for ethnographic practice. But it seems to me that this challenge is being met as a new generation of researchers is starting successfully to bring recognizably ethnographic methods of social and cultural contextualization to bear on projects and processes that are evidently (and often self-consciously) non-local. I am thinking of such examples as (to choose a largely arbitrary handful from a much larger field) Erica Bornstein's study of "Christian development" agencies in Zimbabwe (2003), Gillian Hart's analysis of the movement of transnational capital (in the form of Taiwanese family firms) to South Africa (2002), Annelise Riles's ethnographic exploration of global networks of women's organizations (2001), or Anna Tsing's account of speculative mining investment in Indonesia (2001)—all studies that convincingly link "global" projects and processes to specific, and ethnographically knowable, social and cultural contexts. In such a rich intellectual environment, there can be no question of "turning away" from ethnography; rather, the point of the free-ranging, speculative essays that follow is to pose a challenge to established anthropological ways of knowing "Africa" by identifying certain conceptual (and, in the broadest sense, political) issues that forms of scholarship rooted in a commitment to particularity have up to now too often ignored, avoided, or simply felt unequal to. Given the current (and, it seems to me, extremely vital) state of the field of anthropology at present, there is every reason to be hopeful that such a provocation will be answered with new and innovative forms of ethnographic practice that can push the sorts of questions I have tried to raise in this book in productive and intellectually rewarding directions.

More than anything I have written before, this book has been shaped by the institutional and professional settings within which its chapters took form. Most of the chapters began as seminar papers, presented at conferences, workshops, and invited lectures at dozens of different universities in the United States and elsewhere. It is perhaps too easy to be cynical about the "circuit" of seminars and colloquia that are so much a part of academic life in the United States. My own experience, at least, is of having been enormously enriched by my encounters with hundreds of serious, thoughtful faculty and student colleagues in such settings—colleagues whose questions, insights, and suggestions played a truly germinal part in forming my ideas, shaping the contours of my arguments, and pushing me toward greater clarity in my writing. I cannot thank all of these colleagues individually, but I am profoundly in their debt.

Much of the work on this book was done while I was a member of the Department of Anthropology at the University of California, Irvine (UCI). The Irvine Department provided a wonderfully stimulating and supportive environment for my intellectual development over the years, and I am deeply grateful to my anthropology colleagues (especially Victoria Bernal, Tom Boellstorff, Mike Burton, Teresa Caldeira, Frank Cancian, Leo Chavez, Susan Greenhalgh, Karen Leonard, Bill Maurer, and Mei Zhan), as well as to the members of UCI's Critical Theory Institute, and to the many wonderful students I worked with over the years at Irvine. Since 2003, I have enjoyed an equally delightful academic home in the Department of Cultural and Social Anthropology at Stanford University, which provided an environment amazingly rich in both intellectual excitement and warm collegiality for the final round of work on the book. Portions of the book were also written during a fellowship year (2000–01) at the Center for Advanced Study in the Behavioral Sciences, whose support is gratefully acknowledged. Conversations with other fellows at the center—especially Ute Frevert, Tom Haskell, David Holloway, Jean Lave, Steve Lansing, David Nirenberg, and Mary Louise Pratt—were a source of pleasure and stimulation as I worked on the book that year.

Several colleagues have helped me by providing answers to specific questions and queries; in particular, I thank Tony Simpson for his help with chapter 5, Michael Lambert for assistance with chapter 6, and Kristin Reed for providing valuable information and corrections for chapter 8. I am also grateful to the Chrysalis authors Mjumo Mzyece, Brian Mulenga, and, most of all, Chanda Chisala for helpful and stimulating feedback on my analysis of their writings in chapter 5.

Many other people have read chapters or sections of the manuscript, and I am grateful to all of them. Especially helpful readings, with very useful suggestions for improvement, came from Homi Bhabha, Tom Boellstorff, Teresa Caldeira, John Comaroff, Peter Geschiere, Jeremy Gould, Sean Hanretta, Ian Hodder, Bill Maurer, Charlie Piot, Richard Roberts, and Blair Rutherford. I also owe a special debt to the students in my 2004 course "The Anthropology of Neoliberalism" at Stanford, who read several of the essays and helped me to sharpen and clarify my arguments. Akhil Gupta has read or heard many of the chapters of the book, at various stages of preparation, and my thinking in many areas (most of all, the argument in chapter 4, "Transnational Topographies of Power") has been powerfully shaped by discussions with him. I have benefited enormously from our shared intellectual exchanges, work in common, and friendship over the years.

Finally, as always, my greatest intellectual debt is to Liisa Malkki. Her insights and suggestions inform every chapter, and the creativity, originality, and courage of her thought have been a continuing inspiration to me.

Introduction:

Global Shadows

AFRICA AND THE WORLD

What kind of place is Africa? The question, on the face of it, is an improbable one. "Africa" is a huge continent, covering one fifth of the world's land surface, where over 800 million people live an extraordinary variety of lives. Is there any meaningful sense in which we can speak of this as a "place"? Looking at the range of empirical differences internal to the continent—different natural environments, historical experiences, religious traditions, forms of government, languages, livelihoods, and so on—the unity of a thing called "Africa," its status as a single "place," however the continental descriptor may be qualified geographically or racially ("Sub-Saharan," "black," "tropical," or what have you) seems dubious. Certainly, one may reasonably doubt whether national situations as different as, say, those of Botswana and Liberia are greatly illuminated by treating them as two examples of a generic Africanness, just as one is entitled to question the extent to which, say, Somalia and Namibia partake in a civilizational sameness. Indeed, it has often been suggested that the very category of "Sub-Saharan Africa," with its conventional separation from a "Middle East" that would include North Africa, is as much a product of modern race thinking as it is an obvious cultural or historical unity.

Yet the world is (perhaps now more than ever) full of talk, not of specific African nations, societies, or localities, but of "Africa" itself. And this "Africa" talk—both on the continent and off—seems to have a certain intensity, full of anguished energy and (often vague) moral concern. When we hear about "Africa" today, it is usually in urgent and troubled tones. It is never just Africa, but always the crisis in Africa, the problems of Africa, the failure of Africa, the moral challenge of Africa to "the international community," even (in British Prime Minister Tony Blair's memorable phrase) Africa as "a scar on the conscience of the world." What is at stake in current discussions about "Africa," its problems, and its place in the world? And what should be the response of those of us who have, over the years, sought to understand not "Africa in general" (that unlikely object) but specific places and social realities "in" Africa?

Historically, Western societies have found in "Africa" a radical other for their own constructions of civilization, enlightenment, progress, development, modernity, and, indeed, history. As Achille Mbembe (2001: 2) puts it, "Africa as an idea, a concept, has historically served, and continues to serve, as a polemical argument for the West's desperate desire to assert its difference from the rest of the world." "Africa" in this sense has served as a metaphor of absence—a "dark continent" against which the lightness and whiteness of "Western civilization" can be pictured. It is in this sense that Africa, as a category, enters Western knowledge and imagination first of all, as Mbembe says, as "an absent object," set always in relation to the full presence of the West. Today, for all that has changed, "Africa" continues to be described through a series of lacks and absences, failings and problems, plagues and catastrophes.

The discipline of anthropology is, of course, historically implicated in Western constructions of Africa. The importance of the role played by anthropology in this process is easily overstated, and broad-brush accounts of anthropology as "handmaiden to imperialism" have sometimes been insufficiently attentive to the diversity of theoretical and political currents within the discipline (and to the similar imbrication of other disciplines in colonial apparatuses of knowledge). But there is no doubt that anthropology was one of a number of sites for the elaboration of ideas of Africa as a continent defined by "tradition," "simple societies," and "societies without history," even as "Africa" itself was a central site for the development of key ideas in anthropology (Moore 1994).[1] Yet in spite of the substantial disciplinary investment in the idea of "Africa," anthropology has in recent decades turned away from the very category, perhaps hoping to avoid repeating the conceptual and political errors of colonial-era anthropology (cf. Asad 1973). Anthropological work on the continent has continued, of course, but neither descriptive nor theoretical claims are normally ventured at the level of "Africa." The odd result is that the discipline that contributed more than any other to what V. Y. Mudimbe (1988) has termed "the invention of Africa" has had almost nothing to say about "Africa" in its time of crisis.

This is perhaps, in part, a consequence of anthropology's twentieth-century disciplinary commitment to the detailed observation of spatially delimited areas through localized fieldwork (for a critical overview, see Gupta and Ferguson 1997b). If one starts with the premise that "real" knowledge of Africa is "grounded" in detailed ethnographic knowledge of local communities, then the likely response to a question about, say, "the crisis in Africa" is only too predictable. "Africa," the traditional anthropologist will reply, "is, after all, an enormous and diverse continent. Conditions are really very different from country to country, and from locality to locality. So, I don't know about 'Africa,' but let me tell you about where I worked. . . ." The reply is a principled one, but it is also a strikingly ineffective way of responding to the question. The result is that detailed anthropological knowledge seems to have very little impact on broader discussions about "Africa" (in the world of policy and practice or that of popular representations). Journalistic and policy visions of "Africa" thus continue to rely on narratives that anthropologists readily recognize as misleading, factually incorrect, and often racist; meanwhile, the scrupulously localized "Africa" that appears in the ethnographic accounts in professional anthropology journals becomes ever more difficult to relate to the "Africa" we read about in the *New York Times*. Refusing the very category of "Africa" as empirically problematic, anthropologists and other scholars devoted to particularity have thus allowed themselves to remain bystanders in the wider arena of discussions about "Africa."[2]

Out of dissatisfaction with this state of affairs, I have in recent years tried to work toward a different sort of writing. The essays in this book are all attempts to speak, in an explicitly non- or supraethnographic way, about broader questions concerning the category that is "Africa" and its place in the world. I use the essay form as a way to move across analytic and scalar levels more freely than is usual in ethnographic accounts, and to move swiftly—indeed, speculatively—from particular observations to some very general and abstract, broad questions to which I seek to relate them. I do so not to present a synthetic view of an empirical object, but simply to try out ("essay") certain ways of thinking about a continental predicament, and a discursive and imaginative object, that cannot be grasped simply as the sum of a series of localities. The essays, some previously published, are meant to be independent of each other, and each can be read as a single, stand-alone piece. But they converge around the question of "Africa" as a place-in-the-world, and they all in one way or another seek to use a consideration of this question as a way to think about such large-scale issues as globalization, modernity, worldwide inequality, and social justice.

My aim in doing this is emphatically *not* to define a historical or cultural region of "Africa" (or "Sub-Saharan Africa," "black Africa," "tropical Africa," or what have you), and then identify features of that history or culture that would explain "the crisis in Africa." There have been a number of recent attempts to do this by tracing causal relations between certain features of the historical experience or cultural heritage of "Africa" (normally, Sub-Saharan Africa, often excluding South Africa) and certain features of contemporary African societies or (especially) states that confound developmentalist expectations. Some such authors have focused on the relatively recent historical experience of colonialism, with its legacies of authoritarian rule (Ake 1997), pseudo-traditional rural despotism (Mamdani 1996), "weak states" (Clapham 1996; Reno 1999), "artificial" boundaries (Engelbert 2002), and enclave export production (Leonard and Straus 2003). Others refuse to give so much weight or power to the colonial era and consider a longer historical horizon. Some point to long-term considerations of geography and population density (Herbst 2000); others, to distinctive enduring features of African social and political organization and the way that colonial and postcolonial African states, as Mbembe (2001: 40) has put it, "rested on eminently indigenous social bases." The most ambitious of such authors seek to identify a Sub-Saharan civilizational trajectory characterized in terms that range from the impressively Braudelian, broad-brushed historical sociology of African "extroversion" of Jean-François Bayart (1993, 2000) to the dubious recent culturology of Patrick Chabal and Jean-Pascal Deloz (1999).

Whatever one may think of such attempts, they are very different from the project undertaken here. The essays that follow make no attempt to identify historical or cultural features shared by all of "Africa" that would explain its distinctive and troubled historical encounter with "development." They do, of course, refer at various points to specific regional social patterns that have been identified by empirical research (my own and, much more importantly, that of innumerable others, without which the book could not have been written). Indeed, it is only by drawing on and attempting to synthesize a vast regional literature that I am able to speak, for instance, of the spread of what I term "nongovernmental states" in chapters 1 and 8, or of a regional cultural "repertoire" of ways of understanding wealth in chapter 3. But my fundamental concern in this book is less with Africa as empirical territory (that "geographical accident," as Mbembe [2002b: 630] has called it), culture region, or historical civilization than with "Africa" as a category through which a "world" is structured—a category that (like all categories) is historically and socially constructed (indeed, in some sense arbitrary), but also a category that is "real," that is imposed with force, that has a mandatory quality; a category within which, and according to which, people must live. I want to focus attention on how a vast, complicated, heterogeneous region of the planet has come to occupy a place-in-the-world called "Africa" that is nowadays nearly synonymous with failure and poverty. I want to ask both how that place-in-the-world functions in a wider categorical system and what this means for the way we understand an increasingly transnational political, economic, and social "global order."

Risks are undoubtedly involved in taking up, rather than simply critiquing or refusing, such a categorical "Africa" as a meaningful object of scholarship. Given the mischief that has been done by depictions of "Africa" (especially, but not only, those propagated by foreign Western "experts"), some skepticism is appropriate. As Mbembe (2001: 241–42) has provocatively suggested, "There is no description of Africa that does not involve destructive and mendacious functions." Yet a wide range of social actors on the continent understand their own situations, and construct their strategies for improving them, in terms of an imagined "Africa" and its place in a wider world. In chapter 6, for instance, we encounter the case of two impoverished Guinean boys who write a letter seeking help from "the members and officials of Europe" on behalf of "we the children and the youth of Africa," and who use the word "Africa" or "African" no fewer than eleven times in their brief, one-page letter; in chapter 5 we see a group of highly educated young Zambian nationalists move from an optimistic discussion of a new Zambian national culture to an anguished debate over whether "Africans" suffer from a generic cultural inferiority. Such instances serve to remind us that it is not only scholars who give credence to a constructed African "geo-body" (as Thongchai Winichakul [1994] might put it) that is at once dubiously artificial and powerfully real. For as Mbembe (2001: 241–42) observes, when it comes to the category of "Africa," the "oscillation between the real and the imaginary, the imaginary realized and the real imagined, does not take place solely in writing. This interweaving also takes place in life."

As will become more clear in the pages to follow, I wish to suggest that recent thinking about "the globe" and "the global" often evokes an image of a planetary network of connected points, and that "Africa" is marginal to, and often even completely absent from, such dominant imaginations of "the global" (see especially chapter 1). The "globe" in "globalization," in this respect, is not simply a synonym for "the world." "The world," in my usage, refers to a more encompassing categorical system within which countries and geographical regions have their "places," with a "place" understood as both a location in space and a rank in a system of social categories (as in the expression "knowing your place")—what I term, in shorthand, a "place-in-the-world."

That "Africa" (however heterogeneous or incoherent such a category may be in the eyes of scholars) is a such a "place"—that is, a socially meaningful, only too real, and forcefully imposed position in the contemporary world—is easily visible if we notice how fantasies of a categorical "Africa" (normally, "Sub-Saharan" or "black" Africa) and "real" political-economic processes on the continent are interrelated. Consider, for instance, a recent major study of private capital flows to Africa, which found that "negative perceptions of Africa are a major cause of under-investment" (Bhinda et al. 1999: 72). The team discovered that "even successful [African] countries suffer from negative information about the continent as a whole: 'potential investors lump them together with other countries, as part of a *continent* that is considered not to be attractive'" (emphasis added). Indeed, the researchers found that investors are sometimes "unable to distinguish among countries" and tend "to attribute negative performance to the whole region" (Bhinda et al. 1999: 55). As one foreign investor put it, "The basic rule for black Africa is to get your money back as soon as possible, or don't do it. Who knows what's going to happen next year?" (Bhinda et al. 1999: 49). Such perceptions don't just misunderstand social reality; they also shape it. The effect on African economies, according to the study, is "a vicious circle of poor information, low expectations, and low investment" (Bhinda et al. 1999: 72). As the authors point out, "If caution reduces investment in a given year, the resulting decline in productive capacity then fulfils their negative expectations, resulting in a low investment equilibrium" (Bhinda et al. 1999: 49). It is "complex investor perceptions rather than objective data" that guide many such investment decisions (Bhinda et al. 1999:15), and it is clear that the spectral category "Africa" looms large in these perceptions, with powerfully consequential results.[3]

This brief example is perhaps enough to suggest just how real the category of "Africa" is in today's global economy, and how short is the path linking the meanings and fantasies of words and images with what likes to imagine itself as the "real" world of global investment and capital flows (cf. Tsing 2001). This—the consequential power and mandatory force of regional categorization—is why we can no longer avoid talking about "Africa" if we want to understand the wider ordering of the "world" within which such a category has come to acquire its distinctive contemporary meaning.[4]

In most accounts, scholarly as well as popular, Africa is understood in relentlessly negative terms. In relation to the global political economy, Africa is inevitably characterized by reference to a series of lacks, failures, problems, and crises. Its states are "weak," "poorly consolidated," "failed," and "dysfunctional"; its economies, "underdeveloped," "collapsing," and increasingly "marginal" to the world. Its people appear as victims many times over: victims of poverty, of war, and above all of AIDS—all the modern plagues that seem to have a kind of perverse affinity for the African continent. Such accounts can be rightly faulted for seeing Africa only in negative relation to normative standards ("proper states," "good economies," etc.) that are external to it (see later). But it would be difficult to argue that they are, in any simple way, mistaken. On the contrary, there appears to be an unfortunate abundance of evidence in support of such characterizations.

A recent literature makes clear that most African states today are indeed "failing" to perform most of the tasks that they are, in the terms of almost any normative political theory, "supposed to do," and that much of the continent suffers from levels of insecurity and violence (if not outright civil war) that Africans and Africanists alike regard as terrifying. At the same time, it is equally clear that the latest round of worldwide capitalist restructuring, with its frenzied construction of "the global economy," has left little or no place for Africa outside of its old colonial role as provider of raw materials (especially mineral wealth). Mass poverty—that long-standing continental curse—is not only not improving but, in many areas, actually getting worse. The AIDS situation on the continent, meanwhile, has become so grim that it is difficult to overstate the magnitude of the tragedy. With only 10 percent of the world's population, Sub-Saharan Africa has fully two thirds of all the world's people living with HIV/AIDS (some 25 million), and in 2003, some 2.2 million Africans died of the disease (some three quarters of the world total), a rate of some 6,000 every day (UNAIDS 2004). Estimated life expectancies at birth in a number of African countries have now dropped to the mid 30s and even lower (UNDP 2004), even as life spans almost everywhere else in the world continue to lengthen.

Economically, Sub-Saharan Africa in recent years has suffered from increasing marginalization, low or negative rates of economic growth, and a striking failure to attract foreign investment. In a recent worldwide ranking of "human poverty" (using an index composed of economic and "quality of life" measures), the lowest-ranking twenty countries were all in Africa, and of the lowest ranking fifty, thirty-nine were African.[5] The region's share of world gross national product (GNP), world trade, and foreign direct investment all have fallen sharply in the last thirty years. Giovanni Arrighi has characterized the situation as "the African tragedy" and noted that from the mid-1970s onward, African economies suffered "a true collapse—a plunge followed by continuing decline in the 1980s and 1990s" (Arrighi 2002: 16). He cites statistics showing that the regional per capita GNP of Sub-Saharan Africa, which in 1975 stood at 17.6 percent of the world average, had dropped by 1999 to just 10.5 percent, while "Sub-Saharan health, mortality and adult-literacy levels have deteriorated at comparable rates" (Arrighi 2002: 5). Africa's economic collapse, Arrighi observes, has had "disastrous consequences not only for the welfare of its people but also for their status in the world at large" (Arrighi 2002: 17). From a very different theoretical and political location, Nicholas van de Walle has given a similar account of Africa's "progressive marginalization from the world economy" (van de Walle 2001: 5). He cites figures showing that the average African country's GNP per capita actually shrank between 1970 and 1998, with GNP in 1998 just 91 percent of the figure for 1970 (van de Walle 2001: 277). Africa's share of global economic activity, meanwhile, he describes as "small and declining," with the region accounting for 10 percent of the world's population, but only 1.1 percent of world gross domestic product (GDP) and 0.6 percent of world foreign direct investment (van de Walle 2001: 5–6). Reviewing similar statistics on the declining African share of world trade, Susan George has remarked, "One can almost hear the sound of sub-Saharan Africa sliding off the world map" (George 1993: 66).[6]

Politically, the continent has been racked by a series of civil and interstate wars, with a number of countries having endured year after year of endemic instability and violence and, along with that, the killing, maiming, and masses of refugees that so often dominate the world's imagination of "Africa." Political elites have found ways to capitalize on conditions of insecurity and private violence, with the result that the bureaucratic state has in many parts of Africa been "hollowed out" (Clapham 1996), while what William Reno (1999) has termed "warlord politics" has become increasingly entrenched. Even in countries that have enjoyed relative peace, practices of personal rule, clientelism, and "corruption" have left states increasingly unable or unwilling to provide basic levels of public order, infrastructure, and social services. Indeed, rather than even seeking to impose law, at least some African rulers have secured for themselves a niche in the global economy through organized illegality—what Jean-Francois Bayart, Stephen Ellis, and Béatrice Hibou (1999) have termed "the criminalization of the state in Africa."

A dark picture, undoubtedly. Suspiciously dark, perhaps, given the apparent continuity here with old Western myths of African failure, African savagery, African darkness. Do accounts that cast Africa as a land of failed states, uncontrollable violence, horrific disease, and unending poverty simply recycle old clichés of Western presence and eternal African absence—as if the earth, like the moon, had a permanently darkened half, a shadowed land fated never to receive its turn to come into the "light" of peace and prosperity? We are surely right to be suspicious of accounts that see in Africa only a lack or an incompleteness, and of authoritative announcements that, as Mbembe (2001: 9) has pointedly observed, tell us "nearly everything that African states, societies, and economies *are not*" while telling us little or nothing about what they actually *are*. But while it is appropriate to maintain a certain skepticism for discourses of African lack and failure, it would be a mistake to dismiss or to deny the bleakness of the continental picture that emerges from recent studies of "Africa" or to suppose wishfully that the ugliness and horror depicted in the empirical studies are simply the projection of a Western fantasy. The gloomy assessments cited earlier tell an important truth about Africa's contemporary place-in-the-world. They cannot be dismissed as an "Afro-pessimism" that could, by an act of will, be discarded in favor of a sunny "Afro-optimism."[7]

This is especially clear when we consider that the policy measures and reforms of recent years that were supposed to provide the grounds for "Afro-optimism" by reversing Africa's economic marginalization and reining in its often predatory governments are now widely recognized as having failed to achieve their stated purposes. "Structural-adjustment" policies, imposed on African states by international lenders in the 1980s and 1990s, were supposed to achieve "stabilization" and economic growth through the devaluation of currencies, the deregulation of markets (including agricultural markets), the reduction of state bureaucracies, and the privatization of state and parastatal industries.[8] In keeping with the economic philosophy of "neoliberalism," it was preached that removing state "distortions" of markets would create the conditions for economic growth, while rapid privatization would yield a flood of new private capital investment. The effects of these measures on economic growth, and the extent to which they were or were not actually implemented in particular countries, remain hotly debated.[9] But this much is clear: The idea that deregulation and privatization would prove a panacea for African economic stagnation was a dangerous and destructive illusion. Instead of economic recovery, the structural-adjustment era has seen the lowest rates of economic growth ever recorded in Africa (actually negative, in many cases), along with increasing inequality and marginalization (cf. chapter 3).

Equally destructive has been the effect of so-called structural adjustment on African states. As van de Walle has argued, structural-adjustment loans have had "a negative impact on central state capacity, and have actually reinforced neopatrimonial tendencies in the region" (van de Walle 2001: 14). Austerity measures meant to "roll back the state" to make room for markets and "civil society" have led instead to "a noted increase in corruption and rent-seeking" (van de Walle 2001: 275–76) and to what Hibou has termed "the privatization of the state" (Hibou 2004). Alongside this, the "reform" process has, according to van de Walle,

> motivated a progressive withdrawal of governments from key developmental functions they had espoused in an earlier era. All over Africa, the withdrawal from social services is patent, particularly

outside the capital. In the poorest countries of the region, donors and NGOs have increasingly replaced governments, which now provide a minor proportion of these services. Even in the richest countries, the state's ability and willingness to service rural constituencies has atrophied. Paradoxically, many of the states in the region are both more centralized and bigger, and yet they appear to do less development work than they did before adjustment. (van de Walle 2001: 276)

The formal democratization of many African states in the 1990s, which many took to mark an optimistic new beginning for the continent, has in a number of countries transformed the political terrain in important ways. But multiparty elections, where they have occurred, have done little to alter the fundamental dynamic of "weak" and predatory states. For one thing, many elections on the continent have been little more than elaborately staged ceremonies through which authoritarian leaders have sought to ratify their rule. Even genuinely multiparty elections, pronounced "free and fair" by international observers, have often been sites for the exercise of clientelistic power and organized violence. Such observations would seem to support the prediction of one leading political scientist who speculated a decade ago that formal democratization was unlikely to alter a "bedrock political form" in the region that would remain "weak, authoritarian, clientelistic, and inefficient" (Callaghy 1995: 150). But perhaps the more important point is that the promise of democracy has been held out to African publics at just the moment in history when key matters of macroeconomic policy were taken out of the hands of African states, inviting Ankie Hoogvelt's skeptical conclusion that "it must have been thought in international policy circles that the pain of [structural] adjustment would be easier to bear if the people felt that they had voted for it themselves" (Hoogvelt 2002: 24). Democratization, in an ironic twist, became a way of placing the blame for the structural problems of African economies squarely on the shoulders of African governments—and by implication on African voters themselves (see chapter 3). Meanwhile, substantial matters involving the policies of external donors have tended to be insulated from processes of representative democracy, often via the use of nongovernmental organizations (NGOs), glossed as "civil society," as a kind of surrogate *demos*. The result is what Jeremy Gould and Julia Ojanen, in their stimulating study of poverty politics in Tanzania, have termed "a depoliticized mode of technocratic governance" (Gould and Ojanen 2003: 7; cf. chapters 3 and 4).

The economic and political reforms of the last two decades were meant to bring African states and economies into line with a standard global model. But the ironic result of the structural-adjustment era has been the creation of an Africa that is actually more different than ever from the imagined global standard, more of a "problem case" than ever before. As discussed in several of the chapters to follow, neoliberal Africa has in recent years seen a proliferation of collapsed states or states whose presence barely extends beyond the boundaries of their capital cities. Vast areas of the continent have been effectively abandoned by their national states, subject instead to the tense and shifting authority of warlords and private armies and to the economic predations of resource-extracting multinational firms operating in secured economic enclaves (Reno 1999, 2001a; chapter 8). Modern social and medical services, where they exist at all, are more likely to be provided by transnational NGOs than by states (see chapter 4)—and this at a time that the AIDS epidemic is creating unprecedented need for such services. Endemic violence, "weak" states, and resource-extracting enclave production are hardly new features of the African political economy, of course. But there does appear to be a new extremity in the way that many African states have withdrawn from their putative national societies, leaving export production concentrated in guarded enclaves that are increasingly detached from their surrounding societies.[10]

The links between resource-extraction enclaves, chronic warfare, and predatory states have been much discussed recently (Leonard and Straus 2003; Reno 1999, 2001a; see also chapter 8). But it is worth noting how such enclaves participate not only in the destruction of national economic spaces but also in the construction of "global" ones. For just as enclaves of, say, mining production are often fenced off (literally and metaphorically) from their surrounding societies, they are at the same time linked up, with a "flexibility" that is exemplary of the most up-to-date, "post-Fordist" neoliberalism, both with giant transnational corporations and with networks of small contractors and subcontractors that span thousands of miles and link nodes across multiple continents (see Reno 2001a; chap. 8).

As I argue in chapter 1, "Globalizing Africa?" such a geography finds its place in a world where much is indeed "globally connected," but such "global" links connect in a selective, discontinuous, and point-to-point fashion. This is true not only of the economic connections of transnational capital, but also of the "global" networks of NGOs that increasingly dominate the space of politics on the continent. Such networks of political and economic connection do indeed "span the globe," as is often claimed, but they do not cover it. Instead, they hop over (rather than flowing through) the territories inhabited by the vast majority of the African population. This leaves most Africans with only a tenuous and indirect connection to "the global economy," as critics have often observed. But this is not simply a matter of exclusion. The same processes that produce exclusion, marginalization, and abjection are also producing new forms of non-national economic spaces (see chapters 1 and 8), new forms of government by NGO and transnational networks (see chapter 4), and new kinds of more or less desperate claims to membership and recognition at a supranational level (see chapter 6).

Africa's participation in "globalization," then, has certainly not been a matter simply of "joining the world economy"; perversely, it has instead been a matter of highly selective and spatially encapsulated forms of global connection combined with widespread disconnection and exclusion. Any attempt to understand the position in the world that is Africa must take into account both this bleak political economic predicament and its broader implications with respect to Africa's "rank" in an imagined (and real) "world." That a purportedly universalizing movement of "globalization" should have the effect of rendering Africa once again "dark" in the eyes of the wider world suggests the intimate link, in this respect, between the question of economic marginalization in a global economy and that of membership in a global society.

It is difficult to avoid noticing an abundance of shadows in recent discussions of Africa's political economy. Economic analysts of Africa have long spoken of a "shadow economy," of course, an "informal sector" where goods and services not officially reckoned are traded on the "black market." While the "shadow economy" exists everywhere, Africa is perhaps distinctive in that, on much of the continent, it is generally reckoned to be larger than the formal sector (of which it is presumably the shadow). Meanwhile, Ali Mazrui has complained that, in adopting the Western profit motive but not the entrepreneurial spirit, Africans have borrowed "the shadow, not the substance" of a Western capitalist economy (as cited in Hecht and Simone 1994: 107). By analogy with the shadow economy, Reno (1999) has recently developed the idea of the "shadow state" as a way to describe the way that state officials in "weak states" may gain power not through their control of a state bureaucracy, but through more or less concealed alliances with local power brokers or warlords, arms traders, and multinational firms. Carolyn Nordstrom (2001), meanwhile, has proposed an "ethnography of the shadows" that would explore the international networks that emerge in African war zones outside but alongside the forms of trade formally recognized by states. Similarly, Mark Duffield (2001) finds a key to African civil conflict in what he calls "shadow networks," while the private security forces that play a leading role in African conflicts go by such names as "shadow armies" and "shadow soldiers" (*New York Times* 2004). Globalization theorists, meanwhile, have shadowy metaphors of their own when it comes to Africa, describing the continent as revealing the "dark side" (Stiglitz 2001) or "Satanic geographies" (Smith 1997) of globalization or as constituting a "black hole of the information economy" (Castells 2000).

To read all this, it is hard to avoid remembering once again the legacy of Africa's historical role, in the eyes of the West, as the "dark continent," the land of shady goings-on. No doubt the old colonial version of African "darkness" as simply an absence of the bright light of reason still lingers in some quarters, especially in popular and journalistic accounts. But the dominant tone of recent scholarly writings on Africa suggests a different sort of darkness—not so much a continent defined by a lack of enlightenment as a place where much is unknown, hard to make out, perhaps even unknowable. This speaks, perhaps, to the methodological difficulties and limitations of the research endeavor as much as it does to the "African" social realities being described.

But there is more to the prevalent "shadow" imagery than simply darkness or poor visibility. Beyond mere uncertainty or lack of clarity, the "shadow" idea usually also implies also a kind of *doubling*. Alongside the official economy, the "shadow economy" is an "informal" one that is "parallel" to it. Doubling the formal state as it appears or pretends to be, we find the "shadow state" lurking beside it. Alongside the uniformed troops of the "legitimate" national army are the private "shadow soldiers" of private or "irregular" armies. In all of these figurations, the first version is the "official," and implicitly Western, model, while its uncanny dark double is the "African" version thereof. This leads to a cluster of now tired questions, all turning on the uncertainty about whether such "African" doubles are "really" what they pretend to be. (Are African states really states at all? Are African elections real elections? Are African working classes really working classes? and so on.) And, complementarily, this leads to the cultural nationalist question, Do institutions and cultural forms that are copied (however "imperfectly") from a Western model retain their status as "really" (i.e., authentically) "African"? (For a recent critical discussion, see Mbembe 2002a.)

African aspirations to "development" and "modernity" have always been shadowed by such questions surrounding the authenticity of the copy. The twin fears are that the copy is either too different from the original or not different enough. The fear that the copy is too different is the fear that "modern" African institutions and practices are failed copies, faint copies, mere shadows of the original—indeed, such imperfect likenesses that they are unable to function as that which they pretend to be or ought to be (thus, Africa as a continent of failed states, faux nations, and "basketcase" economies). The converse fear is that the copy is not different enough, that it is merely derivative and therefore empty; that modern Africa has lost its relation to itself and ceased to be properly "African"; that it has (through the distortions of imperialism, racism, and globalization) become a mere bad copy, a negative image of someone else's positivity.[11] Africans, in this view, should reject the false value placed on things Western and value "their own" cultures instead. But both worries ignore the fact that a shadow is not only a dim or empty likeness. It also implies a bond and a relationship. A shadow, after all, is not a copy but an attached twin—a shadow is what sticks with you. Likeness here implies not only resemblance but also a connection, a proximity, an equivalence, even an identity. A shadow, in this sense, is not simply a negative space, a space of absence; it is a likeness, an inseparable other-who-is-also-oneself to whom one is bound.

Highlighting this last dimension of the shadowy nature of Africa's place-in-the-world is a way of insisting on the fundamental *relationality* (as Mary Louise Pratt [2002] has put it) of the position in the world that is "Africa" (cf. Simone 2001). Independence formally broke the colonial shadow relation between "Africa" and "the West," declaring that African nations would henceforth "stand on their own." An ironic result was the localization of responsibility for "African poverty" in the policies and programs of African nation-states. As I show in chapter 2, a comparison of the depoliticization of poverty in the internationally recognized nation-state of Lesotho with the fiercely "relational" contestations over economic inequality in the discussion of the South African "Bantustan" (and would-be nation-state) of Transkei reveals how the political form of the independent nation-state has obscured the continuing transnational relations that help to produce "African poverty." More recently, neoliberal restructuring has brought its own disconnections and disavowals, with the reduction of official aid and an emphasis on "African responsibility for African problems" (see chapters 3 and 5). But as the essays in the latter part of this book seek to show, the shadows of an Africa-in-the-world keep creeping in, insisting on an ongoing relationship between "Africa" and "the West" and ongoing responsibilities as a consequence thereof. Claims of likeness, in this context, constitute not a copying, but a shadowing, even a haunting—a declaration of comparability, an aspiration to membership and inclusion in the world, and sometimes also an assertion of a responsibility.

I began to think about this during my first fieldwork in Africa in a village in the mountains of Lesotho in 1983. I was talking to an older man whom I knew well (I will call him Mr. Lebona) about his plans to build a new house for himself and his family. He proudly declared his intention to build what he called a "European-style" house, by which he meant a small rectangular house with a cement floor and a galvanized steel roof. Such houses were newly in fashion at that time, and most of the newer houses in the area were of this kind, replacing the old-style Sesotho round houses, which were built with stone walls and thatched grass roofs. I was living in a rented Sesotho-style house and had developed an appreciation for the virtues of the local architecture. The round houses were, thanks to their thick mud-and-stone walls, admirably insulated, staying cool in the summer and warm in the winter. They were built entirely with local materials and local labor, and they nestled beautifully into the hills from which their rock walls were dug. The cattle-dung plaster used on the walls and floors was even said to have naturally antiseptic properties. The Sesotho round houses seemed to me, in the language of the times, an "appropriate technology." The "European" rectangular houses, in contrast, were (thanks to their metal roofs) hot in the summer and cold in the winter. They were also unnecessarily expensive, requiring imported materials, and conspicuously ugly. I made the case to Mr. Lebona in just these terms. Why did he want to build a rectangular "European" house, when the "local," Sesotho traditional house had all these virtues?

Mr. Lebona looked amused. His response, which came quickly and forcefully, gave me pause, and still does. Looking me carefully in the eye, he asked, "What kind of house does your father have, there in America?" (I was at the time young enough to be regarded as a mere "student," so the use of my father as the point of comparison was logical). "Is it round?" No, I confessed; it was rectangular. "Does it have a grass roof?" No, it did not. "Does it have cattle dung for a floor?" No. And then: "How many rooms does your father's house have?" Here, I had to stop and think—which Mr. Lebona appeared to find amazing, as rectangular houses in his experience had either two or three rooms. Finally, I mumbled, "About ten, I think." After pausing to let this sink in, he said only: "That is the direction we would like to move in."

The shift that Mr. Lebona forced in my line of thinking is instructive. Starting from the premise that "Sesotho culture" was in no way inferior, I began by defending the virtues of traditional architecture. Why, when one has a valuable culture of one's own, would one seek a copy (a bad copy, at that) of the culture of the colonizer? Mr. Lebona interrupted that argument with questions about material inequality. Was it not true that my father's house was a finer house? That it was bigger? Made of more expensive materials? And was it not true that, once my fieldwork was over, I would go home to live in a house like my father's, not a one-room structure made of rocks and dung? The aspiration to a "European" house, he forced me to see, was not a matter of blind copying; it was a powerful claim to a chance for transformed conditions of life—a place-in-the-world, a standard of living, a "direction we would like to move in."

The lesson I draw from this is not that analysts of Africa ought to focus on "political economy" instead of "culture" (as if economic inequalities were somehow non-cultural or cultural differences were somehow immaterial or apolitical). It is, rather, that the question of cultural difference itself is (everywhere, no doubt, but perhaps especially in contemporary Africa) tightly bound up with questions of inequality, aspiration, and rank in an imagined "world." While a relativizing anthropology has, out of a well-intentioned but misplaced sense of "respect," tried to treat different cultural traditions as "equal," real cultural differences always take on meaning within contexts of sharp social and economic inequality. Inequality is thus not only a matter of "political economy"; cultural differences (e.g., in dress, language, or, indeed, styles of house construction) may in practice be just as "stratified" (i.e., ranked from "high" to "low") as income or wealth.

The theme of the "copying" of Western forms and its relation to questions of standing in the world is developed in two of the essays that follow. Chapter 5, "Chrysalis," uses an analysis of discussions that emerged in a Zambian on-line magazine to explore the problems and limits of nationalism in neoliberal times. The magazine *Chrysalis* was a bold attempt by a group of young, highly educated, cosmopolitan elites to craft a new Zambian nationalism for the information age. But their discussion of a new "national culture" was quickly overtaken by the scandalous suggestion (made by a Zambian columnist) that the only "culture" Zambia needed for the information age was "the culture of the whites," which should therefore be simply "copied." The storm of controversy raised by this suggestion and its surprising resolution sheds light, I suggest, on the difficulties in creating national culture and nationalist discourses of legitimation under conditions of neoliberalism. Chapter 6, "Mimicry and Membership," begins with a reading of an open letter written by two Guinean boys who lost their lives trying to get to Europe, a letter that appeals to the "members of Europe" to (among other things) "help us to become like you." Again, the scandal of an apparent mimicry helps us to think about what is really at stake in contemporary assertions of African difference and likeness and allows us to see how the idea of cultural difference has sometimes helped to disguise relations of inequality and to deflect claims for "Western" recognition of, and responsibility for, "Africa."

My claim is that taking a hard, and sometimes uncomfortable, look at African aspirations to "likeness" with real and imagined Western standards can help to point out serious gaps in some of our most cherished understandings of cultural diversity and global order. For in each of the cases I discuss, the question of likeness forces an unsettling shift from the question of cultural *difference* to the question of material *inequality*—just as Mr. Lebona shifted my attention from a regard for cultural difference (a Sesotho-style house) to an acknowledgement of extreme inequality (a one-room house versus a ten-room house). The connection of cultural difference to social inequality is a theme that is insufficiently appreciated in much recent thinking about what is sometimes called global culture. For cultural practices are not just a matter of flow and diffusion or of consumer choices made by individuals. Instead, they index membership in different and unequal social groups, globally as well as locally. In this sense, yearnings for cultural convergence with an imagined global standard (like Mr. Lebona's wish for a rectangular house) can mark not simply mental colonization or capitulation to cultural imperialism, but an aspiration to overcome categorical subordination. The persistence of cultural difference, meanwhile (however inventive and hybrid it may be), can come to appear as the token not (as it often appears to the anthropologist) of brave cultural resistance, but of social and economic subjection (where a "traditional African way of life" is simply a polite name for poverty).

Perhaps this is why so much of the critical literature on globalization seems oddly out of place in Africa. Most Africans can hardly feel that they are being dominated by being forced to take on the goods and forms of a homogenizing global culture when those goods and forms are, in fact, largely unavailable to them. "Globalization" has not brought a global consumer culture within the reach of most Africans, and still less has it imposed a homogenization of lifestyles with a global norm. Rather, it has brought an increasingly acute awareness of the semiotic and material goods of the global rich, even as economic pauperization and the loss of faith in the promises of development have made the chances of actually attaining such goods seem more remote than ever. Under such circumstances, the problems of homogenization that loom large in many accounts of globalization's evils (such as the "McDonaldization" of cuisine or the "culture-eroding" effects of American television) can hardly appear to be burning problems to those who are largely unable to act as consumers of the goods of the global consumer society. That such people find other ways of getting by, that they concoct "local" ways both of "coping" and asserting global membership, often through a brilliantly inventive bricolage of scraps and leftovers, is a fact more likely to be celebrated by the cultural analyst than by the "locals" themselves, who may see such practices more as signs of weakness than of strength.

Contrary examples are also readily available. History is littered with instances of social oppression taking the form of forced cultural assimilation, when the defense of cultural difference and the resistance of foreign domination have been neatly aligned. But there is no fixed or inevitable link between oppression or colonization and cultural strategies that seek similarity rather than difference. Anthropologists in particular have often supposed that the maintenance of cultural difference somehow naturally stands on the side of what is vaguely specified as "resistance" to "power." But we must allow that cherished link to be put into question if we are to grasp a range of African attempts to assert membership and equality through likeness and to claim what Homi Bhabha

(2001) has termed a "semblant solidarity." If such strategies (like Mr. Lebona's plans for a rectangular house) can appear as a certain sort of "shadow" of that to which they aspire, it is a shadow that marks not simply a silhouette of darkness and absence but a haunting figure of resemblance—a "shade" that, through its uncanny combination of likeness and difference, claims a connection, a relationship, and sometimes an aspirational equality. As African societies have long recognized, a shade is not an absence, an emptiness, or a derivative image. It is a kind of relative.

This suggests the need for a modest skepticism toward the commonly taken for granted values of independence (the aim of traditional African nationalism) and "local autonomy" (the value animating a good deal of current "antiglobalization" politics). For the claim that looms largest, in the essays that follow—a claim that is rendered incomprehensible, if not actually contemptible, by a paradigm that equates liberation with national independence—is the claim of worldly connection and membership, the claim that explicitly contests the separation and segmentation that have so far been the principal fruit of "globalization" for Africa. It is a claim that to consider "Africa" is to consider relationships and responsibilities in a larger system; to consider, as part and parcel of "the global," the question of membership and its criteria. A place-in-the-world is a place in a system of dependencies and responsibilities, rights and obligations. It is all too easy to attenuate these relationships, to replace the real relations of inequality and dependence with a merely formal relation of equality among independent entities (see chapter 2). But the most challenging current political demands go beyond the claims of political independence and instead involve demands for connection, and for relationship, even under conditions of inequality and dependence (see chapter 6).

Does such a move threaten the claim of a proud equality among nations that once made national independence such a compelling political program? On the face of it, yes, since it insists on foregrounding the continuing inequalities that independence was, in the ideal version of things, supposed to abolish. But if there is one thing that we should have learned from the history of the new nations in the post–World War II era, it is that substantive inequality does not go away through setting up formally equal flags, embassies, etc. (see chapter 2)—no more than the substantive inequality among citizens in liberal capitalism goes away when each has the right to equality under the law (the law that, as Anatole France famously wrote in *Le Lys Rouge* in 1894, "in its majestic equality forbids the rich as well as the poor to sleep under bridges, to beg in the streets, and to steal bread").[12] The re-emergent question of supranational membership—of Africans as, in some yet to be defined sense, "citizens of the world"—puts the question of the unequal relation between Africa and the West back on the table in a radical way, after decolonization and national independence had channeled it, for a time, into the question of national development.

At this point, we can see the emergence of forms of new politics that are not captured in the old frameworks of nationalism and development. These include the emergence of a politics of "international civil society" (see chapter 4), claims of transnational moral accountability (see chapter 3), claims to an imagined supranational authority that might recognize rights that are denied at the level of the nation-state (see chapter 6), and attempts to assert transnational responsibility directly, often via desperate forms of migration (see chapters 6 and 7). Analysis of these newly emergent politics is only beginning, but those seeking to understand contemporary African politics, in the widest sense, will need new habits of thinking if we are to grasp their true originality and importance.

The questions raised by considering Africa's place-in-the-world, then, are indeed "global" ones, but not in the way that most discussions of globalization would imply. Instead, they point to the need for a new framing of discussions of the global: centered less on transnational flows and images of unfettered connection than on the social relations that selectively constitute global society; the statuses and ranks that it comprises; and the relations, rights, and obligations that characterize it. To take seriously African experiences of the global requires that any discussion of "globalization" and "new world orders" must first of all be a discussion of social relations of membership, responsibility, and inequality on a truly planetary scale.

Globalizing Africa?

OBSERVATIONS FROM AN

INCONVENIENT CONTINENT

The enormous recent literature on globalization so far has had remarkably little to say about Africa. Astonishingly, the entire continent is often simply ignored altogether, even in the most ambitious
and ostensibly all-encompassing narratives. Popular bestsellers that
seek to explain the new "global" world—whether in celebration or
critique—have much to say about the newly industrializing countries of Asia, the manufacturing boom in China, the European
Union, the causes of Middle Eastern "terrorism," jobs gained and
lost in the United States, the North American Free Trade Agreement (NAFTA) and its effects in Mexico, and the spread of Dis-
neyland and McDonald's to France. But they manage to characterize "the globe" and "the entire world" in ways that say almost
nothing at all about a continent of some 800 million people that
takes up fully 20 percent of the planet's land mass. Academic block-
busters have not been very different in this respect. Saskia Sassen's
Globalization and Its Discontents (1999), for instance, has nothing to
say about Africa, except to note that African migrants sometimes
show up in "global cities" like London and New York. Joseph Stiglitz's influential book, also titled *Globalization and Its Discontents*
(2003), deals almost entirely with the operations of the International Monetary Fund (IMF) and World Bank in Asia and Eastern
Europe, with only a few pages devoted to the African countries

that have arguably suffered the most from the lethal IMF dogmatism he is concerned about documenting.[1] From the self-described radical left, meanwhile, Michael Hardt and Antonion Negri's celebrated tome *Empire* (2001), despite its nearly 500 pages of text and abundant concern for what the authors term "the multitude," cannot muster even a paragraph's worth of analysis concerning the continent. Again and again, it seems, when it comes to globalization, Africa just doesn't fit the story line. It is an inconvenient case.

This neglect is perhaps understandable at the level of real-world politics. Defenders of neoliberal structural-adjustment programs naturally find Africa an inconvenient example; they prefer to talk about Asian tigers and Southeast Asian dragons, since they have a hard time finding any lions among the many African nations that have taken the IMF medicine and liberalized their economies in recent years. But African examples are equally awkward for those termed "anti-globalization" critics, who often equate globalization with an expanding capitalism in search of new cheap labor for its factories and new markets for its consumer goods (stereotypically, Nike sweatshops and McDonald's hamburgers). Here, of course, the inconvenient fact is that Africa's hardships have very little to do with being overrun with Western factories and consumer goods. It is hard to find evidence of the depredations of runaway capitalist expansion in countries that are begging in vain for foreign investment of any kind and unable to provide a significant market for the consumer goods stereotypically associated with globalization.

But if Africa is an awkward case for globalization's polemical boosters and detractors, it seems equally inconvenient for more analytical theorists of globalization, who aspire to planetary "coverage" but somehow do not quite know what to do with Africa (cf. Paolini 1997). Here, Anthony Giddens's approach is typical. He begins his short book of lectures on globalization (Giddens 2002) with an anecdote that claims a planetwide scope for the analysis to follow. A friend, he explains, was conducting fieldwork in a village whose location he describes only as a "remote area" of "central Africa." She was invited to a home for an evening of entertainment, but instead of the traditional pastimes she expected, she discovered that the family was to watch a video of a new Hollywood movie that at that point "hadn't even reached the cinemas in London" (Giddens 2002: 24). The point, clearly, is that even the ends of the earth—that is, the remotest villages of (what is identified only as) "central Africa"—are today swept up within a globalized social order. Yet the rest of Giddens's book does not make so much as a passing reference to Africa. Instead, the narrative repeatedly describes the world in terms of a traditional "before" and a globalized "after" that leaves no place for most contemporary African social realities except in the putative past. The collaborative volume on globalization by David Held, Anthony McGrew, David Goldblatt, and Jonathan Perraton (1999) is a more scholarly account, but it builds on a similar slippage. The volume's introduction claims to explicate a globalization explicitly defined by what the authors term "*worldwide* interconnectedness" (Held et al. 1999: 2; emphasis mine), but this is followed by substantive chapters that are explicitly restricted to what they call "states in advanced capitalist societies" (and it soon becomes clear that African societies are not "advanced" enough to qualify). Interconnectedness among six rich countries is documented most effectively, but the reader is left to wonder what, exactly, is "worldwide" about it.

Africa's inconvenience is not surprising if we consider that most of the dominant theories of globalization have been theories about worldwide *convergence* of one sort or another. From the earliest European projects of colonization to the latest structural-adjustment programs, Africa has proved remarkably resistant to a range of externally imposed projects that have aimed to bring it into conformity with Western or "global" models. It is striking that Africa today is the only world region where one will find huge populated swaths of the earth that are under the effective authority of no central, nation-state government (including most of the Democratic Republic of the Congo [DRC] at present, huge areas of southern Sudan, and nearly all of Somalia). It is worth emphasizing that these are not odd little patches but truly vast areas. As I like to remind undergraduate students, if you put the map of Europe inside the DRC, with London at the west coast, Moscow would lie within the eastern border; in southern Sudan, the area that was until recently out of the reach of even major relief agencies spanned an area bigger than France. Nor is this a question of brief or transitory political circumstances. The weak grip of the central state in countries like the Congo and Angola goes back for many decades, while much of southern Sudan has been out of the control of its national government almost continuously since it became independent in 1956. Even where nation-states *do* enjoy some measure of effective control of their hinterlands, formal similarities in political institutions betray stark differences in actual modes of functioning, as recent work on African states (discussed later) shows. Meanwhile, the property laws that are sometimes taken for granted as the bedrock of capitalism in its most familiar form are only very precariously institutionalized in many African settings (as might be attested by a foreign investor in Nigeria or a commercial farmer in Zimbabwe). Finally, as we know, in perhaps a score of African countries, a host of standard development indicators—from GDP per capita to access to health care and schooling to life expectancy—have in recent years been falling, not rising. This is true not only of countries wracked by war but also of many that have seen nothing but peace. In Zambia, for instance—the country I have studied most—poverty rates are today reckoned at some 73 percent. Diseases like malaria, cholera, and measles are resurgent as public-health countermeasures have collapsed. School attendance has dropped below 50 percent in some areas, and the population is said to be less educated than at any time since independence in 1964. Estimated life expectancy at birth, meanwhile, has fallen—mostly, but not entirely, due to AIDS—from around 50 in 1980 to just 32.4 years, the lowest in the world.[2]

All of this poses a profound challenge for global convergence narratives. It does not necessarily mean that such accounts are in any simple way "wrong." Indeed, in many domains, convergence arguments are often stronger than anthropologists (perhaps wishfully) allow. But the recent history of Africa does pose a profound challenge to ideas of global economic and political convergence. If the world's societies are truly converging on a single, "global" model, how is it possible to account for Africa's different, difficult trajectory? Is it simply a "development failure," to be placed at the door of morally culpable elites? A "lag" that we need only wait to see overcome? A horrible accident, predicated on contingencies such as the AIDS pandemic? What is the meaning—*theoretically*—of what presents itself as a vast continental anomaly?

Where recent globalization theorists have addressed Africa, it has typically been as a negative case: an example of the price of the failure to globalize, as the IMF would have it; a "global ghetto" abandoned by capitalism, as the geographer Neil Smith (1997) would insist; a continent of "wasted lives" of no use to the capitalist world economy, as Zygmunt Bauman (2004) has recently suggested; or "the black hole of the information society," as Manuel Castells (2000) would have it. Such negative characterizations risk ignoring the social, political, and institutional specificity of Africa and reinventing Africa as a twenty-first-century "dark continent." For contemporary Africa is clearly *not* a featureless void defined only by its exclusion from the benefits of global capitalism, nor is it an informational "black hole."

Instead, I suggest that a reading of recent interdisciplinary scholarship on Africa can help to reveal the quite specific ways in which Africa is, and is not, "global" and thereby shed surprising new light on our understanding of what "globalization" may mean at present. What we see (as anthropologists have long insisted) depends on where we are looking from. Looking at "globalization" from the vantage point provided by recent research focused on Africa brings into visibility things that might otherwise be overlooked and forces us to think harder about issues that might otherwise be passed over or left unresolved.

In a highly schematic way, then, this essay reviews insights from recent Africanist scholarship concerning three elements usually identified as central aspects of "globalization": first, the question of culture (and the related question of alternative modernities); second, "flows" of private capital (especially foreign direct investment); and third, transformations in governance and the changing role of the nation-state. It argues that attention to the undoubtedly extreme situation in some parts of Africa can help to clarify what is, and is not, "global" about the contemporary transnational political economy.

Anthropologists first confronted notions of cultural globalization in relation to the question (or, for anthropologists, the specter) of cultural homogenization. What was the fate of cultural difference in a world where fewer and fewer people lived in conditions that could be understood as those of pristine isolation; a world where ever increasing proportions of people lived in cities, drove cars, and watched television; a world where such emblems of an expanding U.S. culture as the English language, pop music, blue jeans, and McDonald's seemed to be expanding across the globe? Was the cultural future of the world a sort of Westernized or Americanized global monoculture—the "Coca-Cola-ization" of the entire planet? And if so, what was the fate of the discipline of anthropology itself in such a uniform cultural world?

Fortunately—at least for the field of anthropology—it soon emerged that cultural globalization was not a simple matter of homogenization. As anthropologists like Ulf Hannerz (1987, 1992, 1996) began to remind us, transnational exchanges of cultural products, forms, and ideas were hardly a new phenomenon, and experience showed that such traffic in meaning was not incompatible with enduring forms of cultural difference. Cultural differences were produced, thrived, and took on their significance within social relations of interconnection, not in primordial isolation. For people in Calcutta to drink Coca-Cola would no more spell the end of Indian culture than the colonial adoption of the Indian drink tea by Londoners abolished Englishness. And one was entitled to wonder, as Clifford Geertz (1994) pointed out, whether the great cuisines of Asia were really in mortal danger of being outcompeted by the likes of Kentucky Fried Chicken. In fact, a host of local studies began to show that transnational traffic in meaning led not to a global monoculture, but to complex forms of cultural creativity—what Hannerz called "creolization"—whose result was not a numbing uniformity but a dynamic "cut-and-mix" world of surprising borrowings, ironic reinventions, and dazzling resignifications.

The idea that logically emerged from this was that societies and cultures were not to be understood as located along a continuum

30   Globalizing Africa?

between a "premodern" tradition, on the one hand, and a Euro-centrically conceived modernity on the other. Instead, Arjun Appadurai and others suggested that it was necessary to rethink our understandings of modernity to take account of the many different sorts of *modern* cultural trajectories that anthropologists were documenting. If non-Western cultures were not necessarily non-modern ones, then it would be necessary to develop a more pluralized understanding of modernity: not modernity in the singular (where the question is, Are you there yet or not?) but modernities in the plural, a variety of different *ways* of being modern: "alternative modernities" (see Appadurai 1996; *Daedalus* 2000; Gaonkar 2001; Holston 1999).

This is undoubtedly a very appealing idea, but it immediately raises a number of problems, which critics have not failed to point out. One problem is the meaning of the term "modernity." Once we give up the benchmark of a singular modernity, then what does the term mean, analytically? If Cameroonians practicing witchcraft are in fact being "modern," as Peter Geschiere (1997) has recently suggested, then one wonders: What would count as non-modern? Or is every aspect of the contemporary world by definition modern — in which case, the term risks losing all meaning by encompassing everything. Another set of criticisms has pointed out that the focus on cultural flows and their creative reinterpretation can lead to an insufficient appreciation of the force of global norms and of institutional and organizational domains where one does indeed find, if not homogenization, at least a high degree of standardization. Sociologists of education, for instance, have shown such standardization in at least the formal aspects of schooling (see, e.g., Boli and Ramirez 1986; Meyer et al. 1992). Here I want to point to a slightly different problem with the idea, which derives from the way that *regions* matter for the modernity discussion.

In East and Southeast Asia, the idea of multiple or "alternative" tracks through modernity has for some years had considerable currency, even outside of academic discussions. There, the pluralization of modernity has been linked to the possibility of a parallel track along which Asian nations might develop in a way that would be economically analogous to the West but culturally distinctive. Such newly industrializing Asian countries as Malaysia, Singapore, and Taiwan, in this view, can achieve "First World" economies, and the superhighways, skyscrapers, and consumer conveniences that come with them, without thereby becoming "Westernized." They can thus retain what are sometimes thought of as cultural or even racial virtues that the West lacks, while making their own, "alternative" way through modernity and enjoying a standard of living equal to or better than that of "the West" (Ong 1999: 55–83).

In Africa, however, such an economic convergence with "First World" living standards hardly seems to be in the offing. For this reason, a recent tendency for scholars of Africa to adopt the language of "modernities" in the plural has very different implications and proceeds from different motives.[3] In the face of decades of scholarship that insisted on seeing African societies as in some sense located in the "primitive" or "traditional" past, contemporary Africanists are understandably drawn to a way of thinking that insists on placing African societies in the same ("coeval") time as the West (Fabian 1983) and on understanding African ways of life not as an ahistorical "tradition," but as part and parcel of the modern world. It is this that leads Geschiere to insist on "the modernity of witchcraft": the desire to show that what is called "witchcraft" is *not* simply a holdover from the past but, rather, a set of contemporary practices that respond to such "modern" contemporary forces as the cash economy, class formation, and the state. Mamadou Diouf (2000) makes a related, and similarly convincing, argument for the "modernity" of the transnational networks of Senegalese Mourid traders.

Yet in Africa, modernity has always been a matter not simply of past and present, but also of up and down. The aspiration to modernity has been an aspiration to rise in the world in economic and political terms; to improve one's way of life, one's standing, one's place-in-the-world. Modernity has thus been a way of talking about global inequality and about material needs and how they might be met. In particular, it has indexed specific aspirations to such primary "modern" goods as improved housing, health care, and education. Yet now, anthropologists, having declared modernization theory defunct and development discourse passé, proudly announce that Africa, notwithstanding all its problems, is in fact just as modern as anyplace else. It just has its own, "alternative" version of modernity.

As I point out in chapter 7, Africans are often puzzled by such claims. Africa's *lack* of modernity seems, to many people there, all too palpable in the conditions that surround them—in the bad roads, poor health care, crumbling buildings, and precariously improvised livelihoods that one cannot avoid encountering in the continent's "less developed" countries. Where anthropologists proclaim Africa always already modern, local discourses on modernity more often insist on seeing a continuing lack (see chapter 5 and chapter 7)—a lack that is understood in terms not of a cultural inferiority but of a political-economic inequality. For this reason, the question of modernity is widely apprehended in Africa in relation to the concept of "development" and the issue of social and economic standards of living. For all their manifold failings, the developmental narratives that have long dominated thinking about Africa's place-in-the-world—narratives that explicitly rank countries from high to low, from more to less "developed"—do at least acknowledge (and promise to remedy) the grievances of political-economic inequality and low global status in relation to other places. The anthropologist's evenhanded assessment of "modernities," however, by pluralizing without ranking the different relations to "modernity" of different world regions, runs the risk of deemphasizing or overlooking the socioeconomic inequalities and questions of global rank that loom so large in African understandings of the modern. In this way, a well-meaning anthropological urge to treat modernity as a cultural formation whose different versions may be understood as both coeval and of equal value ends up looking like an evasion of the demands of those who instead see modernity as a privileged and desired socioeconomic condition that is actively contrasted with their own radically unequal way of life.

The point I want to make here (one that is elaborated more fully in chapter 7) is not that anthropologists have been wrong to historicize cultural practices or to call into question the assumed linearities of Eurocentric progress narratives. It is, rather, that there is an unappreciated danger—which becomes especially visible in the African context—that a culturalized and relativized notion of modernity tends to allow the material and social inequalities that have long been at the heart of African aspirations to modernity to drop out of the picture. In their eagerness to treat African people as (cultural) equals, Western anthropologists have sometimes too easily sidestepped the harder discussion about the economic *inequalities* and disillusionments that threaten to make any such equality a merely ideal or sentimental one.

Let us turn to the economic domain and consider the question of the continent's relation to what is often called "global capital." It is striking how easy it is for Africa to figure in accounts of a globalized cultural world, in contrast to its near absence from most pictures of a global economy. No survey of world music, for instance, would be conceivable without a major section on Africa, yet it is common for surveys of the global economy to contain only the most cursory reference to Sub-Saharan Africa. Yet one of the key claims of dominant accounts of globalization is that deregulated markets and footloose capital today roam the entire globe. How does Africa figure in this? Consider the question of private capital flows.

CAPITAL FLOWS

It was one of the orthodoxies of post–World War II development theory that the poorest countries would naturally serve as magnets for capital, and that investment in those countries would yield such high rates of economic growth that they would soon converge economically with the rich industrial countries. Both assumptions, it is now widely agreed, proved to be wrong. The poorest countries today attract very little private capital of any kind. According to the former World Bank economist William Easterly, the countries that make up the richest 20 percent of the world population received 88 percent of private gross capital inflows in 1990; those countries making up the poorest 20 percent received 1 percent (Easterly 2001: 58–59).[4] The increase in transnational capital flows, of which we have heard much in recent years, has been "mostly a rich–rich affair," as the economists Maurice Obstfeld and Alan Taylor have put it, a matter less of "development" than of diversification. Indeed, they go on to observe that "today's foreign investment in the poorest developing countries lags far behind the levels attained at the start of the last century" (Obstfeld and Taylor 2002: 59).

As for economic growth, recent studies show no tendency for the poorest countries to converge toward the rich ones. On the contrary, the data appear to show a strong tendency for the gap to widen, as rich countries have grown rapidly while most of the poorest have, in terms of economic growth, stood still or even lost ground. It is not a story about economic convergence, then, but—as the economist Lant Pritchett put it in the title of an influential paper—"Divergence, Big Time" (Pritchett 1997). In recent years, many of the poorest African countries have put in place IMF-sponsored reforms (chiefly, opening markets and privatizing state assets) that were intended to produce a flood of capital investment. But the result for most has not been a boom in foreign investment. More often, it has been a collapse of basic institutions (including major industries as well as social infrastructure such as schools and health care) and an explosion of official illegality.

When capital *has* come to Africa in recent years, it has been overwhelmingly in the area of mineral-resource extraction. In the midst of what generally have been very hard times on most of the continent, mining and oil extraction have boomed in several countries. Again, this is a matter that is discussed at some length later in this volume (see chapter 8). What needs to be highlighted for the present is only the extent to which this economic investment has been concentrated in secured enclaves, often with little impact on the wider society. The clearest case (and no doubt the most attractive for the foreign investor) is provided by off-shore oil extraction, as in Angola, where neither the oil nor most of the money it brings in ever touches Angolan soil. But even non-petroleum mineral extraction today very often takes place in capital-intensive enclaves that are substantially insulated from the local economy, or even in guarded fiefdoms protected by private armies and security forces (see chapter 8).

In an earlier period, mining investment often brought with it a far-reaching social investment. In the Zambian Copperbelt, for instance, investment in copper mining brought the construction of vast "company towns" for nearly 100,000 workers. These towns eventually came to include not only company-provided housing, schools, and hospitals, but even social workers, recreational amenities, and domestic-education programs (Ferguson 1999). Here, the business of mining involved not only extraction, but also a broader long-term social project. Its presence was, we might say, socially "*thick.*" But nowadays, mining (and even more so, oil production) is socially *thin*; it has become much more capital intensive and relies on much smaller groups of highly skilled workers (sometimes foreign workers on short-term contracts). It depends ever less on wider societal investments. Today, enclaves of mineral-extracting investment in Africa are usually tightly integrated with the head offices of multinational corporations and metropolitan centers but sharply walled off from their own national societies (often literally walled off with bricks, razor wire, and security guards).

Consider the case of gold mining in Ghana. The privatization of the gold mines in that country, combined with generous tax incentives, has done just what it was supposed to do: bring in large amounts of private investment. Thanks to such investment, Ghana's gold industry has undergone a massive transformation since the mid-1980s. Foreign direct investment (FDI) of about $5 billion has flowed in, probably exceeding the value of FDI in all other sectors combined, while production has risen from 300,000 ounces in 1985 to 2,336,000 ounces in 2001 (World Bank 2003: 2). Gold has now replaced cocoa as Ghana's main export. Yet a recent World Bank report voices doubt about what the "true net benefits" of this "development" might be. As the report points out, capital-intensive mining by foreign firms has a high import content and produces "only modest amounts of net foreign exchange for Ghana after accounting for all its outflows" (World Bank 2003: 23). Tax revenues are also slight, due to the "various fiscal incentives" offered to attract foreign investors in the first place. Most important (and in contrast to earlier, more labor-intensive mining ventures), there has been little creation of employment for Ghanaians because of the "highly capital intensive nature of modern surface mining techniques" (World Bank 2003: 23).[5]

The report tellingly describes a "field visit" by World Bank staff to the center of the gold-mining country in Wassa District, which found "competition between mining and agriculture for arable land, [a] poor state of local infrastructure, inadequate public services, and high unemployment" (World Bank 2003: 21). It concludes that "the local economy . . . does not appear to have benefited from large-scale mining through sustained economic growth and improved public services," and that "local people feel no perceptible benefit from the resources extracted from 'their' land" (World Bank 2003: 21). Unemployed youth, the report notes, had recently attacked local chiefs and destroyed their palaces out of frustration over "lack of jobs and insufficient access to land for cultivation" (World Bank 2003: 21).

Some other forms of mining on the continent—notably, for alluvial diamonds—are both less capital intensive and less spatially concentrated and thus harder to insulate from the wider society through enclave methods. But that does not stop a variety of powerful and well-armed interests from attempting (with mixed success) to carve out such exclusionary spatial enclaves. In the rich diamond-producing region of Mbuji-Mayi in the DRC, for instance, private companies routinely use military force in efforts to monopolize the collection of alluvial diamonds. The partly state-owned firm Société minière de Bakwanga (known as MIBA) uses both private security firms and what are termed DRC "police officers" (who nonetheless report to MIBA's head of security, not to any police superiors) to shoot, arrest, and beat up "trespassers." The partly Zimbabwean-owned firm Sengamines enjoys similar protection from the Zimbabwean armed forces. It is unclear, as a recent human-rights report notes, "what legal framework, if any, they are operating within" (Amnesty International 2002: 8). Both companies habitually shoot and kill local people unfortunate enough to attempt to dig diamonds on the companies' claimed "concessions," even though both the boundaries of the concessions and their legal basis are often highly unclear (see Amnesty International 2002; see also Global Witness 2004, which provides a useful overview of the use of violence to secure natural resources in the DRC in recent years).

Much more could be said about all this (see chapter 8), but here I emphasize only two points. First, the movement of capital that such enterprises entail does indeed crisscross the globe, but it does not encompass or cover it. The movements of capital cross national borders, but they jump from point to point, and huge regions are simply bypassed. Capital does not "flow" from New York to Angola's oil fields, or from London to Ghana's gold mines; it hops, neatly skipping over most of what lies in between. Second, where capital has been coming to Africa at all, it has largely been concentrated in spatially segregated, socially "thin" mineral-extraction enclaves. Again, the "movement of capital" here does not cover the globe; it connects discrete points on it. Capital is *globe-hopping*, not *globe-covering*. The significance of this social fact for understanding patterns of political order and disorder on the continent is discussed in the next section.

GOVERNANCE

The reforms demanded by "structural adjustment" were—according to their neoliberal proponents—supposed to roll back oppressive and overbearing states and to liberate a newly vital "civil society." The result was to be a new sort of "governance" that would be both more democratic and more economically efficient. Formal democratization has indeed swept over much of the continent (though far from all of it), and multiparty elections have invigorated the political life of a number of countries. At the same time, swarms of new "nongovernmental organizations" (NGOs) have arisen, taking advantage of the shift in donor policies that moved funding for projects away from mistrusted state bureaucracies and into what were understood as more "direct" or "grassroots" channels of implementation (see chapter 4).

But rather than setting in motion a general liberation, the best scholarship on recent African politics (as noted in the introduction) suggests that this "rolling back" of the state has provoked or exacerbated a far-reaching political crisis. As more and more of the functions of the state have been effectively "outsourced" to NGOs, state capacity has deteriorated rapidly—unsurprisingly, as Joseph Hanlon has pointed out, since the higher salaries and better terms of employment offered by NGOs quickly "decapacitated" governments by luring all the best civil servants out of the government ministries (Hanlon 2000). Those who remained were often paid less than subsistence salaries, with the inevitable consequences of corruption and an explosion of "parallel businesses." Deprived both of capable staff and of economic resources, states quickly became "hollowed out," in the words of Christopher Clapham (1996), and state officials set about on a "privatization plan" of their own—what Jean-François Bayart, Stephen Ellis, and Béatrice Hibou (1999) have called "the criminalization of the state." Alongside, and interpenetrated with, the formal institutions of the state, informal networks of officials, local power brokers or warlords, arms traders, and international firms in many countries form what Reno (1999) has termed a "shadow state" that leaves the formal institutions of government little more than an empty shell. In such environments, it has been easy to mobilize irregular armies for private economic gain, and a vigorous transnational trade in arms has been one of the few economic areas of consistent growth. It is not that states have disappeared, or even simply that they are, as it is often put, "weak." It is, rather, that they have increasingly gotten out of the business of governing, even as they (or, rather, the politicians and bureaucrats who occupy their offices) retain a lively interest in other sorts of business. In this new era, it is not the organizations of "civil society" that are "nongovernmental"—it is the state itself.

For much of Africa, such a new political order has meant not "less state interference and inefficiency," as Western neoliberal reformers imagined, but simply less order, less peace, and less security. In a number of countries (now including even such traditionally "stable" states as Côte d'Ivoire), it has meant civil war. At the same time, the role of private security companies and professional mercenaries in securing economically valuable enclaves has mushroomed, as is now increasingly well documented (Lock 1998; Musah and Fayemi 2000; Reno 2001a, 2001b, 2004; Singer 2003; see also chapter 8).

In fact, the picture that seems to emerge from the recent scholarly literature is of two quite different kinds of governance, applied to the two different Africas that French colonialism once distinguished as "*Afrique utile*" and "*Afrique inutile*"—or "usable/useful Africa" and "unusable/useless Africa," as Reno (1999) has reminded us. Usable Africa gets secure enclaves—noncontiguous "useful" bits that are secured, policed, and, in a minimal sense, governed through private or semiprivate means. These enclaves are increasingly linked up, not in a national grid, but in transnational networks that connect economically valued spaces dispersed around the world in a point-to-point fashion.

The rest—the vast terrain of "unusable Africa"—gets increasingly nongovernmental states, and an array of extra-state forms of control and regulation that range from revitalized forms of local political authority (often styled "traditional") to open banditry and warlordism. This state of affairs is often violent and disorderly, but it should not be understood simply as an absence of government. As Janet Roitman has recently pointed out for the Chad Basin (2004), even banditry has its own intricate forms of social and moral order, and its forms of "regulation" often find points of attachment with the interests of both state officials and variously militarized illegal traffickers (for whom the "*inutile*" areas that are of little interest to foreign investors may turn out to be quite "*utile*" indeed). At the same time, areas in which states no longer project bureaucratic control are often effectively "governed" in a transnational humanitarian or developmental mode, as a hodgepodge of transnational private voluntary organizations carry out the day-to-day work of providing rudimentary governmental and social services, especially in regions of crisis and conflict. I have elsewhere described such "government-by-NGO" as a form of "transnational governmentality" (Ferguson and Gupta 2002). Like the privately secured mineral extraction enclave, the humanitarian emergency zone is subject to a form of government that cannot be located within a national grid, but is instead spread across a patchwork of transnationally networked, noncontiguous bits. (See chapter 4.)

Perhaps the most surprising finding of the recent literature concerns the relation between the World Bank and International Monetary Fund (IMF) projects for political reform and the desired goal of attracting capital and achieving economic growth. For the fact is that the countries that are (in the terms of World Bank and IMF "governance" reformers) the biggest "failures" have been among the *most* successful at developing capital-attracting enclaves. African countries where peace, democracy, and some measure of the rule of law obtain have had very mixed records of drawing capital investment in recent years. (Zambia is unfortunately a prime example.) But countries with the "weakest" and most corrupt states, and even raging civil wars, have often attracted very significant inflows. Reno's book on "warlord politics," for instance, picked four countries for study based on their "widespread violence and extremely weak state institutions": Liberia, Sierra Leone, Congo/ Zaire, and Nigeria (Reno 1999). Was capital fleeing from these lawless spaces? On the contrary: The four soaked up over half of private capital inflows to Sub-Saharan Africa (excluding South Africa) in his sample year of 1994–95. Indeed, countries with raging civil wars and spectacularly illiberal governments have on a number of occasions done surprisingly well, according to growth measures. Consider Angola, which during the war-torn 1980s boasted one of the better GDP growth rates on the continent, or Sudan, whose 8.1 percent annual GDP growth made it Africa's economic growth "star" of the 1990s, in spite of its horrific civil war and oppressive government.[6]

Such observations suggest that the picture of Africa as a place that has been simply abandoned by global capital has to be qualified. It is true that, as capital "hops" over "unusable Africa," alighting only in mineral-rich enclaves that are starkly disconnected from their national societies, much of Africa is indeed marginalized from the global economy, as several theorists of globalization have noted. But the situation that comes into view from recent scholarship is not exactly the featureless void that Castells (2000) evokes in his characterization of Africa as a "black hole" of the information society. On the contrary, specific forms of "global" integration on the continent coexist with specific—and equally "global"— forms of exclusion, marginalization, and disconnection. Indeed, it is worth asking whether Africa's combination of privately secured mineral-extraction enclaves and weakly governed humanitarian hinterlands might constitute not a lamentably immature form of globalization, but a quite "advanced" and sophisticated mutation of it. If so, the forms of "global economy" that have developed in some mineral-rich African countries in recent years might show us not just a theoretically interesting anomaly, but also a frightening sort of political-economic model for some other world regions that combine mineral wealth with political intractability. (This possibility is briefly explored in chapter 8.)

I have suggested that a survey of recent scholarship on Africa might not only illuminate the situation on the continent but also help us to think more critically about the meaning of the global. I will now illustrate this with a brief example from the domain of environmental politics.

Discussions of the environment often rely on a language of the "global." Global warming, the ozone layer, acid rain, ocean ecosystems, Chernobyl, desertification—all seem to show with overwhelming clarity that today's key environmental issues are global ones that demand to be addressed at what we call the "global level," not merely the national or the regional level. Such common-sense turns of phrase invoke the "global" as an encompassing, overarching spatial *level*, a notion that has come to be widespread both in popular and journalistic understandings and in the scholarly literature on "globalization."

The implication usually drawn from such invocations of the environment as a global issue is that the "national level" is inadequate for environmental regulation and protection, since environmental crises do not respect national borders. So environmentalism, we are told, must "go global." Now, it is undoubtedly true that environmental crises reveal the limitations of the nation-state system in a particularly vivid way. But if the global is not, as I have argued, an enveloping *level* of coverage superior to the national but, rather, a form of point-to-point connectivity that bypasses and short-circuits all scales based on contiguity, then the "global" may be just as inadequate to environmental problems as the national (indeed, possibly even more so). This is so because ecosystems do not work "point-to-point" any more than they work nationally.

A great deal of what passes for environmental regulation and protection in Africa works according to the point-to-point model (and is thus well and truly "global" in my sense). National parks, of course, are themselves guarded enclaves, existing in often fiercely combative relations with surrounding residents. Often fenced and militarily patrolled, these patches of internationally valued "nature" may be protected with "shoot-to-kill" policies against "poachers" who are often simply the local people who lost their land and their ancestral hunting rights when they were forcibly evicted to make way for the game park (see Adams and McShane 1996; Duffy 2000; Neumann 2001a).

More recent efforts in environmental protection and wildlife conservation in Africa have responded to the failures of the traditional "fortress conservation" approach by promoting a new approach based on "community participation." The idea is to involve members of "local communities" in the management of wildlife "resources," in the hope that they will be able to control poaching while also benefiting in some way from the existence of preserved wildlife (Hulme and Murphree 2001). Yet Roderick Neumann (2001b) has convincingly argued that the new model depends just as much as the old one on the coercive partitioning of space and the desire to "secure" selected rural areas as "resources" for internationally valued eco-tourism. In his case study of the Selous Conservation Programme in Tanzania, he shows that the creation of "buffer zones" for the use of villagers was designed to recruit villagers into a kind of anti-poaching self-surveillance. "Community participation" did not replace coercion; it supplemented it. Both state violence and the threat of it, Neumann argues, were essential to the working of the project. Indeed, his conclusion is that "community participation" and state violence worked together as "integrated forms of social control designed to meet the needs and goals of international conservation organizations and the tourism industry" (Neumann 2001b: 324). There is thus no contradiction in the fact that wildlife management in Tanzania has seen both increasing "community participation" and increasing militarization in recent years—as illustrated in a recent reported incident in the famed Serengeti Park in which game rangers allegedly arrested, lined up, and shot to death some fifty famine-stricken villagers who had entered the park armed with bows and arrows in search of small game (Neumann 2001b: 305).

Such spatial enclaving in the service of "nature" is not only the work of states. Environmental NGOs, too, often carve out their own spatial enclaves or turfs, perhaps targeting "hot spots" of biodiversity or seeking to preserve specific environmental "treasures" or endangered species. Such NGOs are indeed often "globally" networked (i.e., linked with similar organizations around the world), but it is a network of points, with most of what lies in between simply bypassed or ignored. Meanwhile, the generalized destitution, the undermining of state authority, and the spread of civil war on the continent pose fundamental threats to ecosystems that no system of protected enclaves can mitigate for long.

Consider the work of an environmental NGO called Africa Rainforest and River Conservation (ARRC). According to the group's Web site, its aim is to help preserve life that "has flourished in Africa's darkest regions" for millions of years but that today "is collapsing at the hands of man."[7] Its main work to date has been in the Chinko River basin of the Central African Republic (CAR), where President Ange-Felix Patasse reportedly authorized the group to create a wildlife preserve while developing a "counter-poaching program" to prevent the destruction of game by groups of armed poachers from across the Sudanese border.

A revealing article by a journalist writing for the *Observer* magazine, published by the British newspaper the *Guardian*, provides the details on how the conservation project in the CAR is being carried out (Clynes 2002). Apparently, the ARRC, led by its founder, the Wyoming physician Bruce Hayse, has hired mercenaries to attack the Sudanese poachers and to try to form a 400-strong local anti-poaching militia to patrol the Chinko River basin. The ARRC's "director of operations" is reportedly a former Rhodesian mercenary and a veteran of the South African private military firm Executive Outcomes who uses the alias Dave Bryant. In previous jobs in South Africa, Mozambique, and Malawi, Bryant moved easily across the "often blurry" line separating paramilitary and anti-poaching work (Clynes 2002: 5). He sees no conflict between military work and the task of conservation: "People don't like the fact that I'm ex-military, but who better to do this job?"[8]

Other activists in the field of African wildlife conservation appear uneasy with the idea of a foreign NGO using conservation funds to create a nongovernmental military force. "We wouldn't do it," said Richard Carroll of the World Wildlife Fund (wwf). "Can you imagine the headlines? 'wwf supporting South African mercenaries to kill Central Africans'?" (Clynes 2002: 6). But in a recent interview, Hayse defended the operation by claiming, "What we're doing is really not that extreme by African standards in terms of game parks," and noting (correctly) that shoot-to-kill policies have been used in nationally administered parks in countries like Kenya and Zimbabwe. While people will certainly be killed, he noted reassuringly, "We're not proposing to go out and do any kind of widespread massacre."9

Asked for comment during this interview, an official named Peter Knights from WildAid, another conservation NGO, agreed that "extreme measures" had been used in wildlife conservation for some time on the continent. "And it's not just about wildlife," he continued:

> It's about resources in general, and it's unfortunately the scenario we find in Africa, where there's so many of these small civil wars. You often don't hear about it, especially not here in the United States, but there's a lot of wars, a lot of conflicts going on, and sometimes it's about wildlife. Sometimes it's about other commodities.

Indeed, those "other commodities" appear to be a part of the ARRC story, as well. According to the *Observer* article, the ARRC has responded to a funding crunch by seeking to raise its own money by selling diamonds dug in "its" area. The journalist Tom Clynes observed Bryant and others negotiating the acquisition and sale of the stones (though without great success, at least initially), and Hayse openly defended the new funding device: "Diamonds looked like a way to develop the project with some kind of secure financial foundation, and to provide a more equitable means for the local people to sell the diamonds they pick up" (Clynes 2002: 7). With a "flexibility" reminiscent of other actors in the region, the ARRC is apparently seeking to put its "conservation" enclave to multiple uses.

The ARRC is undoubtedly an extreme case in its explicit commitment to privatized violence in support of conservation. It is not unique, however. Deborah Avant (2004) has recently given a fascinating account of the process through which local officials of the wwf and the International Rhino Fund (IRF) ended up deciding to hire mercenaries to protect the Garamba National Park in the DRC. The WWF's national leadership eventually repudiated the effort, but the IRF (together with the WWF's local officers) has continued to pursue hired protection via private security firms, as well as via Ugandan troops operating near the park (Avant 2004: 376).

Mainstream conservation organizations like the WWF have kept their distance from such practices, at least in public—probably because (as Avant rightly observes) they derive much of their power from a perception of moral authority that could easily be eroded by such things as involvement with mercenaries. But many officials of these organizations are, by some accounts, more supportive of such measures in private. Indeed, according to the *Observer* report, the president and founder of the well-known Rainforest Action Network, Randy Hayes, was present on the ARRC's Chinko River expedition, and some officials are apparently glad that someone is willing to do this sort of "dirty work." According to one mainstream conservationist (as quoted in Clynes 2002: 6), "It's probably better that the WWF isn't involved. This is the side of conservation that the organizations with the panda-bear logos don't want to deal with. It's dirty, filthy work. And if you want to succeed, you don't put a choirboy in charge."

Perhaps the more important point, however, is that the practice of the ARRC is only a particularly uncompromising manifestation of a vision of nature and its relation to the "global" that is much more widespread. After all, it is not only environmental extremists who take as their object of intervention what they imagine to be pristine pockets of asocial nature. (The "hot spots" approach to biodiversity has been endorsed by many mainstream conservation organizations, including Conservation International and the WWF.) And it is not only wild-eyed "eco-mercenaries" who believe that a "we" group of well-funded First World activists can and should claim the moral authority of a planetary conscience in support of their own very particular interventions. Indeed, more "mainstream" environmental NGOs also appear very much a part of the larger "global" landscape that I have sketched here, operating as they do in a world of fragmented spaces, deteriorating state authority, enclaved environmental "resources," and privatized security.

This is assuredly not to say that transnational NGOs seeking to conserve wildlife and ecosystems deserve only our scorn and condemnation for their efforts. Their work is often extremely valuable and sometimes very sensitive to the sorts of concerns that I have highlighted. My point is not to dismiss the project of wildlife conservation but to point out the way that even such important and undoubtedly well-intentioned transnational projects, often driven by altruistic motives, have increasingly, through a logic of pragmatic adaptation to circumstance, taken on some of the forms of spatial organization that we more readily associate with the exploitation of enclaves for mineral extraction. The same could be said about humanitarian and relief agencies on the continent, which have also become increasingly reliant on extra-state mechanisms to establish patchworks of political order where states have become nongovernmental. As a worker for Save the Children observed of the private military companies in Sierra Leone, "They bang heads very efficiently, the fighting stops—and that's when babies get fed" (as quoted in Reno 2001a: 212). Saving rhinos, like feeding babies, is surely a noble cause. But a close look at the means by which such causes are pursued would seem to have much to tell us about how Africa is linked up with a variety of contemporary "global" projects.

We have grown accustomed to a language of global "flows" in thinking about "globalization," but flow is a peculiarly poor metaphor for the point-to-point connectivity and networking of enclaves that confront us when we examine Africa's experience of globalization (cf. Tsing 2001). Such language literally *naturalizes* globalization by making it analogous to the natural process of flowing water. Rivers really do flow. Like so many ecologically significant processes, a river's flow works via spatial contiguity—a river goes from point A to point B only by traversing, watering, and connecting the territory that lies between the two points. But as the contemporary African material shows so vividly, the "global" does not "flow," thereby connecting and watering contiguous spaces; it hops instead, efficiently connecting the enclaved points in the network while excluding (with equal efficiency) the spaces that lie between the points. Ecological processes that depend on spatial contiguity are, to be sure, not exclusively "local"—often they are regional and, indeed, sometimes even planetary. But neither the regional nor the planetary scale is easily addressed via today's "globe-hopping" political and economic forms.

If this is so, then so-called global forms of economy, politics, and regulation have no inherent advantage in dealing with environmental issues. Indeed, insofar as contemporary "global" interventions on behalf of "the environment" rely on the existence of protected enclaves subject to radically distinct and spatially discontinuous modes of policing and government, they reveal with great clarity the way that apparently universal and planetary projects in fact rely on sharp spatial divisions and violently policed zones of exclusion. Such interventions are indeed "global" in that they rely on the transnational organization of funding, institutions, and moral concern, but their very mode of operation reveals the selectively disordered and starkly divided landscape that, I have argued, is a foundational feature of Africa's contemporary mode of integration into "global society."

CONCLUSION

A review of recent scholarship on the political economy of Africa suggests that a continent that is widely understood to be simply backward or excluded vis-à-vis the newly emergent forms of global society may in fact reveal key features of how the "global" works today, and how it might work in the future. As I observed at the start: What we see depends on where we are looking from. What do we see about the "global" today from the vantage point of these recent studies?

The global, as seen from Africa, is not a seamless, shiny, round, and all-encompassing totality (as the word seems to imply). Nor is it a higher level of planetary unity, interconnection, and communication. Rather, the "global" we see in recent studies of Africa has sharp, jagged edges; rich and dangerous traffic amid zones of generalized abjection; razor-wired enclaves next to abandoned hinterlands. It features entire countries with estimated life expectancies in the mid-thirties and dropping; warfare seemingly without end; and the steepest economic inequalities seen in human history to date. It is a global where capital flows and markets are at once lightning fast and patchy and incomplete; where the globally networked enclave sits right beside the ungovernable humanitarian disaster zone. It is a global not of planetary communion, but of disconnection, segmentation, and segregation—not a seamless world without borders, but a patchwork of discontinuous and hierarchically ranked spaces, whose edges are carefully delimited, guarded, and enforced.

Such an Africa-centered view does not show us the "true nature" of globalization—as if previous totalizing accounts of a globalized world could now be simply dismissed or replaced with a new one. Rather, the view developed here represents an attempt—an "essay"—to show the possibility of taking another perspective on the "global" and to insist that there is no view of "globalization" that simply "covers it all," that all views (even the most apparently all-inclusive and authoritative ones) are in fact views "from somewhere" (cf. Tsing 2000). The fact that an Africa-focused picture of globalization looks so unlike what most global theories lead us to expect does not mean that other accounts, "from" other "places," can simply be dismissed. But neither is it simply a matter adding a new piece to an otherwise intact picture (as in the old cliché about the five blind men and the elephant)—as if we could simply "add Africa and stir" and thus arrive at a truly all-inclusive picture. Instead, the view from Africa challenges us to develop new, more situated understandings of emerging global patterns, understandings that attend more adequately not only to exciting new interconnections, but also to the material inequalities and spatial and scalar disjunctures that such interconnections both depend on and, in some ways, help to produce. Above all, what the inconvenient questions coming out of Africa show us is how much more thinking, and how much more empirical social research, remains to be done before we can really understand a globalization that divides the planet as much as it unites it.

Paradoxes of Sovereignty
and Independence

"REAL" AND "PSEUDO-" NATION-STATES AND

THE DEPOLITICIZATION OF POVERTY

There is a joke, which is said to be told (in various versions) by residents of Tijuana, Mexico. A "gringo" tourist walks into a Tijuana bar and finds himself getting the cold shoulder from the locals who are drinking there. He approaches a Mexican drinking at the bar for an explanation, asking if they could not have a beer together. The Mexican refuses, saying: "Look, you gringos came here in 1840 and stole half our country. Now you sit up there with your cars and your swimming pools and your skyscrapers, while we sit here in our poverty. Why should I have a drink with you?" The gringo responds: "You mean, 150 years later, you still can't forgive us for taking half of your country?" "No," the Mexican replies. "I can forgive that. It is not easy, but I can forgive that you took half of our country. But there is one thing that I can't forgive." "What is that?" asks the gringo. "What I *can't* forgive, is that you didn't take the other half, too."[1]

The joke is not very funny. Even when told by Mexicans, it is vaguely embarrassing to a liberal political sensibility. At the end of a century dominated by anticolonial nationalist struggles for sovereignty and independence, we can hardly help but see national independence as almost synonymous with dignity, freedom, and empowerment. This, I will suggest here, may be in some respects a trap. A comparison drawn from the recent political history of southern Africa may be a way of illuminating this.

In particular, I will briefly describe the way poverty and power-lessness have been apprehended and written about in Lesotho, a nation-state whose political independence and territorial sovereignty are universally acknowledged. I will then compare this with the way that very similar realities have been apprehended in the pseudo–nation-state of Transkei, a South African "Bantu-stan" whose claims to national independence and sovereignty were fiercely contested, and ultimately denied (see map). I will argue that the very weakness of Transkei's claims for sovereignty facilitated a radical, politicizing analysis of the roots of poverty and under-development that can usefully be extended to the predicaments of the impoverished "real" nation-states of the world. Particularly at a time when the nation-state form is under unprecedented strain all around the world, with naturalized national mappings of peoples onto places more and more widely challenged and contested both in scholarship and in the wider world, there may be much to be gained from exploring political and analytical alternatives to the sovereign nation-state frame of reference. A close look at the south-ern African experience may help us to do just that.

In a final note, I will also reflect on some parallels between the dominant anthropological vision of the world as an assemblage of separate and unique "cultures" or "societies" and the dominant "development" vision of the world as an assemblage of "national economies." I will argue that anthropological ideas of culture, so-ciety, and "the field" tend to localize and depoliticize our under-standings of global inequality and cultural difference in the same way that the idea of the sovereign nation-state localizes and de-politicizes our perceptions of poverty.

LESOTHO: A "REAL" NATION-STATE

As I first prepared to travel to Lesotho for field research in 1982, it was necessary to assure many friends and acquaintances in the United States that Lesotho was, as I said, "a real country." With much discussion in the press of South Africa's attempt to establish bogus ethnic "Bantustans" as supposedly independent states, it was necessary to insist on this. Given Lesotho's precarious position as a small enclave completely surrounded by South Africa, confusion was perhaps understandable. In any case, it was necessary to emphasize that Lesotho was not a phony ethnic "homeland" but a former British colony that had received its internationally recognized independence in 1966. And that, to me and to my friends, made all the difference.

It was history that had made Lesotho "a real country." Through the resistance of its people and the canny diplomacy of its nineteenth-century founder, King Moshoeshoe I, Lesotho was not incorporated within South Africa but was (like Swaziland and Botswana) brought into the British Empire as a so-called protectorate (then known as Basutoland) under the jurisdiction of a High Commission. Spared the overrule of the South African settler state, Lesotho and the other so-called High Commission territories attained independence in the mid-1960s, along with the rest of the British-held colonies in Africa. Free and independent, one of the "front-line states" in the struggle against apartheid, Lesotho stood proudly apart from South Africa and its ethnic Bantustans (whose supposed independence Lesotho defiantly refused to recognize).

When I arrived in Lesotho, however, this categorical difference began to seem less absolute. Thoroughly dominated by South Africa economically and politically, Lesotho's "independence" proved difficult to locate. Migrant labor to South Africa was the predominant form of employment; South African firms dominated local banking, manufacture, and commerce; and the South African rand was the everyday currency. One of the few gestures toward economic independence (if only a symbolic one) was in fact the introduction of a Lesotho currency, the maloti, at par with the rand. Yet few seemed to take to the nationalist gesture; currency continued to be insistently spoken of as "rand," and South African notes were actively preferred. Worse still, many informants compared their own situation unfavorably with that of the residents of South African Bantustans like the Transkei. Indeed, one of my most articulate and politically sophisticated informants shocked me by wishing openly that Lesotho might become a Bantustan—

for in the Bantustans, he insisted, taxes were lower, and government services were better, than in Lesotho. The distinction between "real" and "pseudo" nation-states, so important back in the United States, seemed much less so here on the ground.

To an economic historian, this would perhaps be unsurprising. For in economic terms, there is not a great deal to distinguish Lesotho's history from that of the "Native Reserves" within South Africa (i.e., the territories reserved for "native" black South Africans, which would later become the foundation of the supposedly independent "Bantustans"). To begin with, the Basotho subjects of King Moshoeshoe, like other African farmers in the region, lost most of their best agricultural land in a series of wars with encroaching white settlers between 1840 and 1869. On this diminished land area, the peasant farmers of Basutoland nonetheless managed to respond to new markets with the production of surprisingly large crops of surplus grain throughout the late nineteenth century (Murray 1981), a pattern which has also been documented for black peasant farmers in the South African "Native Reserves" (Bundy 1979; Wilson and Thompson 1971). At the same time, increasing numbers of Basotho traveled to work in South Africa after the discovery there of diamonds in 1867 and gold in 1886. Over the years, however, agricultural production slumped as more and more people cultivated a small and deteriorating land base and as the once lucrative South African markets for agricultural produce were closed off. More and more, families came to depend on cash remittances from men employed in South Africa, most commonly in the mines. By the time of independence in 1966, Lesotho was little more than a labor reserve for the South African economy (Murray 1981). This economic trajectory displays striking parallels with that of the "Native Reserves" of South Africa and of the Transkei in particular[2] (Wilson and Thompson 1971: 69).[3]

Yet if Lesotho's economic history was surprisingly similar to that of "Native Reserves" like the Transkei, its political trajectory was dramatically different. For when the British decolonized in the 1960s, Lesotho, along with the other southern African protectorates, achieved the status of an internationally recognized, sovereign nation-state, notwithstanding its precarious geographical position entirely encircled by South Africa (see map).

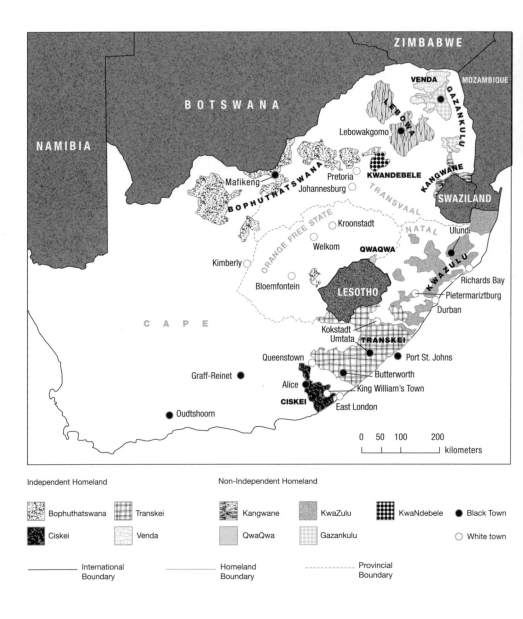

MAP. SOUTH AFRICA'S "HOMELANDS," ALSO SHOWING LESOTHO,
BOTSWANA, AND SWAZILAND. AFTER OMOND 1985: 7–8.

As a small, economically dependent, geographically surrounded labor reserve, British Basutoland was perhaps an odd candidate for national independence. In the debates surrounding decolonization, certainly, there were some who claimed that such a territory would be economically neither independent nor (as it was said) "viable" (Spence 1968). Politically, too, it was not clear how "independent" an independent Lesotho could be, being completely surrounded by such a powerful and domineering neighbor. Indeed, such fears proved well founded in the early years of independent Lesotho, which saw not only continuing economic dependence, but repeated and unsubtle South African interference in electoral processes and a substantial presence of white South Africans in key government positions.[4]

Yet such reservations never seriously challenged Lesotho's legitimacy and acceptance within the international community. The new nation-state was received as simply one of a number of former British colonial territories acceding to independence. Indeed, it seems clear that Lesotho's sovereign status was accepted by the international community more as a response to its status as a British ex-colony than as an endorsement of any internal capabilities to function economically or politically. Unlike the case of Transkei, Lesotho's accession to statehood was received as a routine decolonization, not as part of a cynical ploy to strip black South Africans of their citizenship (see later). It was this political context, rather than any objective features of the territories involved, that made Lesotho, but not Transkei, a "real country."

TRANSKEI: CHRONICLE OF A PSEUDO-NATION-STATE

The roots of the apartheid-era attempt to create ethnic "homelands" or "Bantustans" in South Africa are to be found in the old "Native Reserves" formally established under the terms of the Land Act of 1913, which reserved about 7 percent of South Africa's land (later increased to 13 percent) for exclusive African settlement, while setting aside the rest—the overwhelming majority—for the whites. These provided the territorial base for the infamous migrant labor system, functioning as "labor reserves" for the South African economy while keeping (at least in theory) the families and dependents of migrant workers on the land and out of the cities (Wolpe 1972). With the rise of the Nationalist Party and its policy of "apartheid" in 1948, the rural reserves acquired a new political importance. For as the master plan of apartheid unfolded through the 1950s and 1960s, it became clear that its central strategy was to translate the facts of racial domination and segregation (already well established in South Africa) into the terms of *national* difference. With discrimination on the basis of color rapidly losing legitimacy both inside and outside South Africa, the planners of apartheid aimed to redefine black South Africans as ethnic citizens of "their own" (as they said) "national states" or "homelands" to be constructed and consolidated mainly out of the pieces of the old Native Reserves. As these new "Bantu states," or Bantustans, attained "independence," their "African" citizens would indeed enjoy the political rights and voting privileges that the world was demanding—but only *within* those states. There they would be free (as it was usually put) to "develop freely along their own lines." But within the 87 percent of the country designated "white South Africa," black Africans would be foreign citizens. Even Africans born and raised in so-called white areas would be assigned citizenship on the basis of their ethnicity in one of the Bantu states, thus becoming foreigners in their own land. Citizens of the Bantustans might, of course, be allowed within "white South Africa" as workers, with the proper permissions, but they would be no more entitled to political rights there than are foreign workers in other countries (such as Turks in Germany or Mexicans in the United States). Through this sinister and ingenious plan, the race problem (so-called) would be solved at a stroke, for there would *be* no more black South Africans. Instead, the problem would be re-posed as a problem of nationality and of migration between independent national states.

A considerable amount of energy and money was put into this improbable plan. Millions of people, as is now well established, were forcibly relocated and dumped within the boundaries of the new Bantustans-to-be (Platzky and Walker 1985). Supposedly independent governments were indeed set up, starting in 1976, for the Bantustans of Transkei, Bophutatswana, Venda, and Ciskei. Ultimately, it was envisaged that all ten ethnic "homelands" (see map) would become independent, to be linked together with so-called white South Africa in what South African President P. W. Botha liked to call a "constellation of states" something like the British Commonwealth. Planners also harbored hopes (from as early as 1954) that the former High Commission territories of Lesotho, Swaziland, and Botswana might also eventually be brought into such a constellation (Spence 1968: 74).

As all this was happening, an extraordinary effort was being made to establish the legitimacy of the supposed national states both within South Africa and beyond. National governments were established with all the trappings, complete with ambassadors, embassies, and limousines. Moreover, national symbols were self-consciously fashioned for the new states. Anthems, flags, crests, mottos—all were being churned out at a record clip in the early 1970s by Pretoria's Department of Bantu Administration and Development. The new "Republic of Transkei" was given not only a national flag, but also a national crest (in the incongruous style of medieval European heraldry) displaying a bull's head (said to symbolize "not only the vital role of animal husbandry but also the importance of bulls in the ritual life of the Xhosa people"), along with the unintentionally ironic motto, "Unity Is Strength" (Malan and Hattingh 1976). Transkei's supposed independence in 1976 was accompanied by a tremendous flurry of such nationalist symbol-waving, including an elaborate and expensive independence ceremony and the publication of a glossy coffee-table book celebrating the new "Republic of Transkei" and its cultural heritage. Never was Hobsbawm's and Ranger's somewhat cynical phrase "the invention of tradition" (Hobsbawm and Ranger 1983) more literally appropriate.[5]

In the end, of course, these various attempts to secure legitimacy for the Bantustans were a more or less complete failure. In spite of vigorous lobbying, no nation outside of South Africa ever extended formal diplomatic recognition to the supposedly independent states. And in spite of a dizzying combination of carrots and sticks thrust at them, the supposed citizens of the Bantustans were never well sold on the idea that "independence" for impoverished and scattered patches of African reserves constituted their political deliverance. Eventually, the Bantustan strategy was abandoned as a total failure. Today, in a democratic South Africa, the former homelands have been completely reincorporated within a unitary South Africa, with a provincial structure that preserves none of the old homeland boundaries or institutional structures. The era of independent Bantustans ended up being a short one.

But it is worth remembering that such an outcome was not always obvious or inevitable. When Transkei was put forward as the first of the new "independent" Bantu states, many observers—black as well as white—regarded it as a not implausible new entry into the world of nation-states. It was, as its defenders noted, larger, richer, and more populous than its internationally recognized neighbors, Lesotho and Swaziland (see map). It was better consolidated, as well as larger, than the other proposed "national states," and if its territory was not entirely contiguous, well, neither was that of many other well-established nation-states, including the United States, among many other examples. Moreover, the legal case for Transkeian statehood (in formal, constitutional terms) turned out to be surprisingly strong (Southall 1982: 5–6). Transkei's poverty and lack of resources made it vulnerable to arguments about its economic "viability," but, as Mlahleni Njisane (who would later become Transkei's non-accredited ambassador to the United States), correctly observed, Transkei was "neither the smallest nor the poorest of countries in Africa." On the contrary, he claimed, "The simple fact is that Transkei will not be any worse off than half the Third World" (BCP 1976: 16–17).

Internationally, too, it was not immediately obvious that the Transkei's independence would fail. The Republic of Transkei, let us remember, appeared on *National Geographic*'s world maps as an independent country from 1976 until at least 1981.[6] Although formal diplomatic recognition was withheld, many informal and business contacts were established with foreign countries, especially with such internationally spurned states as Israel and Taiwan. And we may never know how close the Reagan administration may have come to extending formal recognition to the Bantustans.

Some Reagan advisers, at least, were not prepared to dismiss the "independent national states."

Ultimately, the legitimacy of Transkei was arbitrated both in the international "community of nations" and in vigorous domestic political debate. Arrayed against the formidable propaganda apparatus of the South African state were powerful oppositional political movements (ironically, "anti-independence" movements), which stripped away the coating of flags and anthems and nationalist rhetoric to attack the underlying political maneuver they concealed. A few quotations will give a bit of the flavor of the anti-independence campaigns.

The Black People's Convention, in 1975, declared:

> The Independence of Transkei is a cunning manoeuvre by the racist regime of Vorster to give National and International credibility to the abhorrent policy of apartheid, precisely at a time when the process of liberation has shown itself to be inevitable in Africa, and also at a time when the subcontinent has dramatically changed in favour of the struggle for National liberation. . . . The so-called independence is nothing but yet another manoeuvre to "legalize" the alienation of the people of the Transkei from the rest of Azania, which is their motherland, so as to give the denial of their rights in Azania a legal and constitutional backing. (BCP 1976: 39)

For Steve Biko, the Bantustans were "the greatest single fraud ever invented by white politicians" (Biko 1978: 83). Some black politicians thought they could use Bantustan independence to press for black liberation—"quick," as Biko said, "to see a loophole even in a two-foot-thick iron wall" (Biko 1978: 36). "But if you want to fight your enemy you do not accept from him the unloaded of his two guns and then challenge him to a duel" (Biko 1978: 85).

> These tribal cocoons called "homelands" are nothing else but sophisticated concentration camps where black people are allowed to "suffer peacefully." . . . [W]e black people should all the time keep in mind that South Africa is our country and that all of it belongs to us. The arrogance that makes white people travel all the way from Holland to come and balkanise our country and shift us around has to be destroyed. Our kindness has been misused and our hospitality

turned against us. Whereas whites were mere guests to us on their arrival in this country they have now pushed us out to a 13% corner of the land and are acting as bad hosts in the rest of the country. This we must put right. Down with bantustans!!! (Biko 1978:86).

POLITICS AND POVERTY: TWO DISCURSIVE LANDSCAPES

The difference in the positions of Lesotho and Transkei in the world of legitimate nation-states resulted in strikingly different treatments of the realities of poverty and powerlessness that the two territories so evidently share. In the "development" discourse that has long dominated discussions of Lesotho, poverty has inevitably been treated as an attribute of Lesotho's *national economy*. As I have shown elsewhere (Ferguson 1994), historical and structural causes of Lesotho's predicament have been largely obscured from view as the "nation-state" frame of reference has displaced a wider, regional perspective. Through what I have called the "antipolitics machine" of "development," persistent poverty has been constructed as a product of Lesotho's rather unfortunate geography and lack of resources (taken as givens), together with the technical fact that these meager resources have not been fully "developed." The actual causes of poverty in Lesotho were, as I have suggested, very much like those in the Transkei, but discussions of poverty in Lesotho have rarely made any reference to South African state policy, enforced low wages, influx control, or apartheid. Poverty in the independent nation-state of Lesotho has long been formulated in insistently national terms, as "*Lesotho's* poverty"— and, thus, implicitly, Lesotho's problem (Ferguson 1994).

The apartheid experiment involved, among other things, an attempt to deploy this same maneuver internally: to transform the political problem of poor and racially oppressed South Africans into a question of international relations with "developing countries." Indeed, South African planners always claimed that "apartheid" really only meant "separate development" and that they were eager to help "the Bantu" to "develop" within their own independent "Bantu-states" (Bantustans). Along with the invention of national flags and crests, then, went a parallel emphasis on the "development" of each homeland, guided by its own government but with the paternalistic assistance of the South African state. National development plans were solemnly drawn up for each homeland, even the tiniest ones like Lebowa and QwaQwa. Consultants and academics argued earnestly over the merits of different "national development strategies." Development projects were drawn up and implemented; their failures were analyzed and lamented.

Transkei was thus very much caught up in the web of "development" discourse. Like Lesotho, it was the object of a distinctive mode of knowledge that sought to identify "problems" within the national economy and to prescribe technical solutions to them. In at least some respects, then, the "illegitimate" and internationally despised "development" activities in Transkei and the "legitimate," internationally beloved "development" initiatives in Lesotho—so different in the view from afar—looked a good deal alike when seen closer up.

But beyond these similarities lies a crucial difference. For the *reception* of the "developmental" constructions I have described, both inside and outside of the territories in question, was strikingly different in Transkei than was the case in Lesotho. "Development" discourse in Lesotho largely succeeded in depoliticizing poverty, constructing it in technical (and national) terms as a lack of some combination of skills, inputs, and resources. In the case of Transkei, by contrast, "development" discourse encountered an acute, vigorously politicizing critique. Rather than accepting "Transkei" as a bounded economic unit, critics from the start relentlessly insisted on connecting the Transkei's economic predicament with a wider economic order and on linking, in a quite direct way, rural black poverty with urban white wealth.

Hector Ncokazi, who led the resistance to Transkei's independence until his detention by security forces in 1976, declared, for instance:

> The people of the Transkei who are so shabbily and callously ill-treated by the South African socio-political system are the self-same people, who have built the South African economy which the government boasts of abroad. They have suffered most as a result of mine disasters that have riddled this country in the past. They now

want the fruits of their labours and compensation, by the granting of human rights, for their sufferings. (BCP 1976: 22)

Hlaku Rachidi of the Black People's Convention observed:

[In the Bantustan plan], Blacks must be pushed off and made so-called citizens of dummy states all around South Africa, to reduce their claim in broader metropolitan South Africa. One notices immediately that this is a sophisticated version of the same "Native Reserves" created during the Smuts era. The so-called dummy black states now envisaged will have no elaborate industrial infrastructure calculated to give jobs to the millions of Blacks who are supposedly their citizens. Neither are they seriously meant to have this by their white creators because the white man has decided that although he certainly does not want the black man's vote in the broader metropolitan South Africa, he certainly wants the black man's labour to man the white man's factories, to build for him, to sweep his streets, to make his garden and to care for his babies. Thus migratory labour will eventually be at the heart of the entire relationship between the so-called dummy states and the broader metropolitan South Africa.... [The Bantustans] will be used as dumping grounds for the unwanted black vote ... [and] will serve as convenient labour reservoirs without the other complicating factors arising out of having to recognise the permanence of black labour in metropolitan South Africa. (BCP 1976: 42–43)

Such radical political critique, coupled with effective political mobilization, eventually had its effects at the level of policy discourse, as well, as the whole Bantustan strategy began to be more and more seriously questioned in the mid-1980s. The Development Bank of Southern Africa (DBSA), for instance, was an official lending agency charged with "development" investment in the homelands. The early issues of the DBSA's house journal, *Development Southern Africa*, reveal a broad acceptance of the "separate development" framework and showcase various attempts to hammer out "development" policy for the new "national states" (e.g., for Transkei [Nkhulu 1984]). By 1986, however, it is possible to find quite fundamental questioning of this framework within this policy discourse. Thus, one author critiqued a proposed "Rural Development Strategy for Lebowa," observing that its authors had "failed to examine the nature and circumstances of poverty in Lebowa and, in particular, the structural dependence of Lebowa, with its largely 'locked in' population, within the South African political economy" (Cobbett 1986: 309–10). On the contrary, he claimed,

> by treating Lebowa in effect as a self-contained country and not critically examining its position within the South African economy, the authors have chosen to wear ideological blinkers. Thus, for example, the impact and implications of the migrant labour system on the development options for Lebowa are not examined. The document studiously avoids any political analysis both of the causes of rural poverty and of the possibilities which political reform might or could present. (Cobbett 1986: 317)

Another author writing at about the same time finds that discussions in the journal have come to a broad agreement on the existence of "one functional integrated South African economy" (as opposed to a set of distinct "national" economies corresponding to discrete "homelands"). He proceeds to argue that the "acceptance of a functional integrated economy and its implications for policy is so totally 'opposite' from previous thinking, that a simple adaptation of existing structures and strategies to this 'new' paradigm may lead to somewhat muddled thinking" (van der Merwe 1986: 464).

This sort of rejection of the idea that a small, dependent labor reserve could be analyzed as a national economy, and the questioning of the whole ethnic-national frame of reference, was—as I have argued at length elsewhere (Ferguson 1994)—conspicuously absent from official "development" discourse in Lesotho during this same period. Precisely because the legitimacy of Lesotho as a sovereign, independent nation-state was not in question, economic structures were insistently conceived in national terms ("Lesotho's economy"), and questions of poverty, growth, wages, and so on were treated as matters of national policy ("Lesotho's development problems"). In the case of Transkei, by contrast, the formidable political challenges to the very existence of the Bantustans created a very different discursive landscape in which questions of poverty, economic policy, and "development" could be posed in a way that made questions of wider regional economic and political structures more visible. This was true both of radical oppositional political discourse and, at a later stage and in a watered-down form, of some official development discourse.

DEPOLITICIZING POVERTY: A CONSTELLATION OF STATES

The apartheid regime's Bantustan strategy attempted to depoliticize the disempowerment of rural Africans by hiving them off in independent states. But the refusal of critics inside and outside South Africa to accept this spurious separation repoliticized the poverty of the rural reserves by reconnecting it to the system that created it.

The insistence on maintaining a strict distinction between this situation and the case of Lesotho—insisting on treating Lesotho as a "real" (i.e., sovereign and independent) nation—ironically depoliticized its powerlessness by unintentionally performing a similar separation. Through its very international respectability, Lesotho was rescued from P. W. Botha's envisioned "constellation of states" but simultaneously incorporated into a much larger constellation: the world community of nations, within which it occupies an equally powerless position (cf. Malkki 1994). This may suggest the relevance of the joke with which I began, which is in fact very serious. For the joke suggests that—as in the case of South Africa's magnanimous acceptance of Lesotho's formal independence—there may be a certain cunning involved in "taking only half." After all, is it not precisely by *acknowledging* Mexico's sovereignty, even while economically dominating the country, that the United States manages to contain the political implications of the massive poverty of *its* labor reserve within the ideological borders of "Mexico's problems"?[7]

I emphasize here that I do not mean to deny that national independence, in southern Africa and elsewhere, has often had progressive and empowering consequences. I mean only to point out that conceiving liberation in terms of national independence has had certain ideological effects that we would do well to keep within sight. In particular, where the national frame of reference has enjoyed an unquestioned legitimacy, economic grievances have tended to be seen as "problems" that are essentially local and internal to a national economy, and economic critique has been largely channeled into discussion of whether or not "the nation" is pursuing "the right policies." In this way, the wider system of economic relations that is constitutive of many of these "problems" is removed from view, thus localizing and depoliticizing the discussion in a very fundamental way from the start. This fact becomes especially visible, I have suggested, when the politics of poverty in a legitimate nation-state like Lesotho is contrasted with a case like that of Transkei, where an imposed national frame never achieved legitimacy, and a much more radical critique was thus enabled.

The history of South Africa's Bantustan experiment provides a highly instructive lesson in the treacherous traps of national sovereignty. The politicization that ensued through the debate over the Bantustans and associated antiapartheid critique resulted in the wide dissemination of a radical and clear-sighted analysis of the systemic roots of poverty in the region. Lesotho stands out as a clear counter-case, in which the introduction of an uncontested national sovereignty largely succeeded in obscuring regional connections and localizing responsibility for poverty within national borders.

But Lesotho, even if it is a particularly clear case, is not unique. None of the impoverished nations of the world are truly "sovereign" or "independent," and nowhere do we find a true "national economy." By being all too respectful of nationalist myths of sovereignty and independence, we who study the Third World have often unwittingly aided at a global level that very depoliticization that P. W. Botha failed to accomplish at the regional level through his envisioned "constellation of states." For what is the international order of nations if not just such a "constellation of states" that segments off the exploited and impoverished regions within discrete national compartments with "their own problems," thereby masking the relations that link the rich and poor regions behind the false fronts of a sovereignty and independence that have never existed?

The line between "real" and "pseudo-" nation-states is more fragile than we have yet realized, and South Africa's experience with ethnic "homelands" has more to teach us than we have yet acknowledged. There may be much to be gained by bringing the conceptual and political clarity that characterized critical analysis of South Africa's apartheid-era "pseudo-nation states" to our understanding of the contemporary international constellation of so-called real nation-states, as well.[8]

EPILOGUE: ANTHROPOLOGICAL APARTHEID?
A CONSTELLATION OF CULTURES

In this brief final section, I suggest some parallels between the way the idea of a national economy works to localize and depoliticize perceptions of poverty and the way conventional anthropological ideas about "cultures," "societies," and "the field" act to do the same to our understanding of cultural differences.

Let me begin by suggesting, uncontroversially, that just as there is no "national economy of Lesotho" separate from an encompassing set of relations with a wider South African (and ultimately global) system, so, too, there can be no local "cultures" apart from the wider and encompassing relations within which they are defined. Just as the economies of what world-system theorists refer to as "core" and "periphery" demand to be understood via their interrelations, so, too, the forms of life and systems of meaning that are found in the different parts of the postcolonial world demand to be understood relationally, as they inflect and constitute one another. Postcolonial theorists (e.g., Bhabha 1994; Gilroy 1991, 1993; Wright 1985) have shown that such things as Englishness and Europeanness require to be understood in relation to the colonial encounter: that whiteness is constructed on the ground of colonial non-whiteness; that rationality is built against the presumed irrationality of the savage native; that Enlightenment is pictured against the imagined blackness and ignorance of the Dark Continent. Cultures of the colonized, meanwhile, are constructed in a similar, if inverse, fashion. Thus, "*Sesotho* culture" in Lesotho is explicitly built up as a contrast and point of resistance against a dominant "white culture," locally styled "*Sekhooa*"[9]—and that which counts as "local culture" (thus, that which is "anthropological" enough to get into most ethnographic accounts) is constituted by this uneven encounter.

The conventional anthropological idea of "a culture" that forms "a system" that can be known "holistically," however, tends to push such constitutive relations from view.[10] The holistic vision of culture as system is usually based on some sort of analogy with language, where language is presumed to be uncomplicatedly unitary and systemic. Yet even for language, this may be a dubious way of proceeding, as Mary Louise Pratt (1987) has argued. Pratt contends that dominant models of language (in structural linguistics and elsewhere) rely on the fiction of a homogeneous and undifferentiated "speech community" in which all speakers are equal players and all share a set of common meanings and codes. Since actual speech situations are more often characterized by *partial* sharings, hierarchical power relations, and different and conflicting understandings on the part of differently situated actors, Pratt refers to the counterfactual linguistic model as a "linguistic utopia," serving to imagine a very particular type of community. Against this "linguistics of community," Pratt counterpoises what she calls a "linguistics of contact"—"linguistics that place(s) at its centre the workings of language across rather than within lines of social differentiation, of class, race, gender, age" (1987: 61).

Anthropological conceptions of "the field," too, I have argued elsewhere,[11] help to reinforce the anthropological weakness for seeing cultures as the property of separate "societies" or "communities" rather than as phenomena of hierarchical relation and interconnection.[12] The ethnographer's still familiar tropes of entry to and exit from "the field," the images of "heading out to" or "coming back from" the field, powerfully suggest two separate worlds, bridged only at the initiative of the intrepid anthropologist. Such images, of course, push to the margins of the anthropological picture precisely those connections that link the two places and situate them within a common, shared world. Deborah D'Amico-Samuels has put it well:

> Because the notion of the field current in anthropology allows that removal to take place symbolically and physically, the real distancing effects of the field are masked in the term "back from the field." These words perpetuate the notion that ethnographers and those who provide their data live in worlds that are different and separate, rather

than different and unequal in ways which tie the subordination of one to the power of the other. (D'Amico-Samuels 1991:75)

The distancing and relativizing move that allows us to evenhandedly contrast one "culture" (the one we study) with another ("our own") thus has some of the same hidden dangers as the nationalist move that sets up formally symmetrical relations between substantively unequal and mutually constitutive national economies.[13] In this sense, the familiar anthropological claim that "they have their own culture" carries something of the same effect in cultural analysis as the development planner's claim that "they have their own economy" does in economic analysis—namely, the closing off from view of those connections and relations that would allow for a very different analysis.

Refusing the spatial localization and insulation that is created by a "fielded" concept of culture, however, does something analogous to what the challenging of the sovereign nation-state did in the case of Transkei: It problematizes the "givens" and demands an accounting of *why* cultures are "different," "exotic," "isolated," or what have you, and of how they got to be that way. Placing central analytic focus on the connections and relations that constitute national economies as national, or local cultures as local, can combat the dehistoricization and depoliticization that both developmentalist analyses of economies and anthropological analyses of cultures, in their different ways, promote.

De-moralizing Economies

AFRICAN SOCIALISM, SCIENTIFIC

CAPITALISM, AND THE MORAL POLITICS

OF STRUCTURAL ADJUSTMENT

Give us rain. Give us bananas. Give us sugar cane. Give us plantains. Give us meat. Give us food. You are our king, but if you do not feed us properly we will get rid of you. The country is yours; the people must have their stomachs filled. Give us rain. Give us food. — Ritual Shambaai greeting to their new king

I think the economic logic behind dumping a load of toxic waste in the lowest-wage country is impeccable and we should face up to that. — Lawrence Summers, 1992

The exploiters of Zimbabwe
were cannibals drinking the masses' blood,
Sucking and sapping their energy.
The gun stopped all this.
Grandmother Nehanda,
You prophesied.
— Song celebrating Zimbabwe's independence

In the summer of 1989, I traveled across a Zambia reeling from the effects of a newly imposed IMF structural-adjustment regime.[1] Prices of essential goods were skyrocketing, employment was declining, and real incomes were rapidly shrinking. Many wondered how they would manage to make ends meet. Many, indeed, were failing to make ends meet: with high food prices, many went hungry; with free medical care abolished, many sick people could not receive treatment. For my part, I was trying to buy blankets for a trip to the countryside, but everywhere I went blankets were either unavailable or selling for preposterously high prices. Finally, after days of looking in the major centers of Lusaka and Kitwe, I found abundant, cheap blankets at a shop in the provincial town of Mansa. I wondered how it was that this merchant had in such abundance what was in short supply throughout the country. My research assistant, a young, educated Zambian man, had the answer: this merchant was widely known as a powerful sorcerer. He obtained his supplies by making potent medicines from the organs of human beings whom he murdered. It was the hearts, in particular, that he was after; this was what gave him his special supply lines and had enabled him to grow very rich.

On 12 December 1991, Lawrence Summers, the chief economist of the World Bank (who would go on to serve as U.S. Secretary of the Treasury and is currently the president of Harvard University), sent an internal bank memorandum (later leaked to the press) in which he argued that the export of pollution and toxic waste to the Third World constituted an economically sound, "world-welfare enhancing trade" that should be actively encouraged by the World Bank. Since "the measurement of the costs of health-impairing pollution depends on the foregone earnings from increased morbidity and mortality," he wrote, "a given amount of health-impairing pollution should be done in the country with the lowest cost, which will be the country with the lowest wages." Furthermore, he suggested, carcinogens associated with, say, prostate cancer ought to be of less concern in countries where people are not likely to live long enough to develop such diseases. In economic terms, he suggested, "the under-populated countries in Africa are vastly *under*-polluted." Summers rejected criticisms of this position on the grounds that they were based on such things as "moral reasons" and "social concerns" that "could be turned around and used more or less effectively against every Bank proposal for liberalization" (*The Economist* 1992).

Summers was correct in this last assertion. The World Bank–IMF structural-adjustment programs that have been forced down the throats of African governments in recent years are based on precisely the sort of spurious economistic "proofs" and implausible suspension of moral and social values that are displayed so conspicuously in the memorandum. It is possible to show that these structural-adjustment programs have already had enormously destructive social consequences and human costs.[2] It is also possible to argue, as Henry Bernstein has in an incisive critique, that the World Bank's structural-adjustment project is "a fantasy" likely "to generate results that are as brutal as they are ineffectual in terms of its stated goals" (Bernstein 1990:3). But my concern here is with neither the effects nor the efficacy of structural adjustment but, rather, with the style in which it is legitimated. For the cold, technocratic, economistic reasoning deployed to justify dumping toxic waste in Africa is in reality just the raw form of a literally "*de-moralizing*" logic of legitimation that, I will show, is pervasive in "development" accounts of "structural adjustment."

And yet, as the story of the merchant with which I began hints, the social world into which this de-moralizing mode of legitimation is inserted is one in which economic realities are routinely apprehended in fundamentally moral terms. The question I want to ask, then, is what happens when such an economistic, technicizing style of legitimation meets the insistent moralizing that is so much a part of discourses on the economy across wide areas of Africa?

PROSPERITY, POWER, AND AFRICAN MORAL DISCOURSE

The relation between matters of wealth, production, and prosperity, on the one hand, and moral and cosmological order, on the other, has been a pervasive theme in the ethnography of Africa—or, at least, of southern and central Africa, which are the ethnographic regions I know best. Though the ethnographies mostly deal with local particularities, I will here try to draw out some broad themes that seem to be very widely shared over a broad culture region. In the process, many subtleties will be lost. But my point is not to describe accurately a local system; it is to sketch with a broad brush a set of moral themes that are widely distributed across a vast region. I emphasize that these themes constitute not a rigid and specific system of belief but a flexible repertoire of key metaphors, contrasts, and discursive themes that provide a rich moral vocabulary for talking and thinking about issues of wealth, prosperity, profit, and exploitation in a variety of specific contexts.

Most generally, the production of wealth throughout wide areas of southern and central Africa is understood to be inseparable from the production of social relations. Production of wealth can be understood as pro-social, morally valuable "work," "producing oneself by producing people, relations, and things" (Comaroff and Comaroff 1991:143). Alternatively, it can be understood as an antisocial, morally illegitimate appropriation that is exploitative and destructive of community. A common axis of contrast is an opposition between honest "sweat," which builds something shared and socially valued, and trickery or artifice through which one exploits or "eats the sweat" of another. The ubiquitous notion of sorcery or witchcraft can play a number of roles here. It can be the sanction that checks antisocial accumulation (the familiar "leveling" role), but it can just as well be understood as the fearsome power that makes it possible for exploiters to exploit with impunity.[3] There is no need to romanticize sorcery here. Even sanctions that enforce norms of generosity are not necessarily egalitarian in their effects, as Sally Falk Moore has pointed out. Because only the rich can afford generosity, "prescriptive altruism" may hit the poor hardest, by "translat[ing] the many manifestations of the stinginess and craftiness of poverty into moral faults" (Moore 1986: 301). What is important for my purposes, however, is simply the fact that the social meaning of production and accumulation is widely interpreted in fundamentally moral terms.[4]

The same is often true of exchange and consumption. Key domains of wealth such as cattle, lineage land, and bride-wealth are often at least partially blocked off from or sheltered from commodity exchange.[5] Along with such restrictions on exchange commonly come moral valuations; against a realm of cash and commodities conceived as intrinsically "selfish" and associated with individual acquisitiveness and exploitation stand specially valued domains of sociality and solidarity. Thus, for instance, wealth in cattle in Lesotho is understood as a uniquely social domain, ideally associated with sharing and helping the poor, whereas money, as one informant put it, "is just closed up there [in the bank]; it will work for you alone, and not for the mutual help of all us Basotho."

In all of this, it is often possible to discern an underlying contrast between powers that create social prosperity versus powers that destroy it. A number of recent studies of chiefship show a key contrast between two aspects or moments of chiefly power.[6] On the one hand, it can provide for the people and bring peace and prosperity; on the other, it can destroy the land and feed off the blood of the people. Key metaphors appear again and again: the chief as both man and lion, rainmaker and witch, feeder of the people and eater of the people. These two modalities of power usually correspond to two kinds of wealth—broadly, the kind that feeds the people and the kind that eats them. The first type is a kind of collective wealth bound up with a prosperity that is general and shared. Key metaphors for this kind of pro-social prosperity are rain and feeding the people (the key connection is well expressed in the Sotho trinity of chiefship: *khotso* [peace, product of a healthy chiefship], *pula* [rain], *nala* [prosperity]). The second kind of wealth is selfish, antisocial, exploitative. Key metaphors are cannibalism, bloodsucking, and witchcraft. Pro-social, collective wealth provides the basis for community and mutuality; antisocial, exploitative wealth is the dangerous and destructive temptation for which people's hearts may be cut out.[7]

Karl Marx had Africa in mind when he made his famous analogy between the savage's "fetishism," entailing belief in the magical powers of an object, and a capitalist "fetishism" that disguised the social origins of the value of the commodity, imputing value to the object itself as a natural property. The insight into capitalism was undoubtedly profound, but with respect to Africa Marx could not have been more wrong. For the idea that keeps cropping up in the ethnography of Africa is not that the human world is ruled by powerful objects, but that all of the world, even the natural, bears the traces of *human* agency.

The best-known example of such thinking, of course, remains E. E. Evans-Pritchard's account of Azande causal reasoning (Evans-Pritchard 1976). When a large granary fell on a man who happened to be walking beneath it, killing him, Evans-Pritchard's informants insisted that witchcraft had to have been involved. When Evans-Pritchard argued that it was simply termites that had caused the mishap, the Azande agreed that the termites were involved but insisted that the termites were only the means—they were *how* the granary had fallen. The important question, however, was *why* it fell. Why did it fall at that moment rather than another? Why did that man happen to be under it at just that second? Surely termites were present, but the real question was: Who *sent* the termites?

This famous anecdote is usually told in the context of arguments about rationality and so-called closed systems of thought. But my point here is rather different. For what is crucial to our purposes is neither the rationality nor the mysticism of the Azande line of thinking but, rather, the determination to arrive at specifically *human* causes. Capitalist fetishism is here neatly inverted—where capitalism naturalizes the human world by imputing powers to objects, the Azande were busy humanizing the natural. And what is true of mortal fate is also true of economic and political destinies. Not only among the Azande, but throughout the region, disparities of power and wealth, like fluke accidents, never "just happen"; they demand to be explained in terms of meaningful human agency.

Such apprehensions of issues of power and wealth in broadly social and moral (i.e., human) terms are not only found in popular understandings of precolonial or "traditional" systems. Recent scholarship shows that capitalist forms of accumulation and modern state economic activities are very widely understood in similar terms. Feierman's study of chiefship in Tanzania (Feierman 1990) reveals that key discursive themes concerning the healing and harming of the land, the bringing of rain, and the productive or destructive nature of central power continue to be brought to bear on the activities of the modern state. David Lan (1985) showed dramatically how an indigenous moral discourse on chiefship and power was central to the legitimacy of the Zimbabwean revolution. And Peter Geschiere (1982a, 1988, 1997; see also Fisiy and Geschiere 1991) has shown that fundamental moral ideas about sorcery and wealth are pervasive in the relations of state officials with villagers in Cameroon. Jean-François Bayart has made a compelling general argument that the power of the state and urban elites in Africa must be understood in terms of indigenous moral cosmology. His wonderfully evocative phrase, "*la politique du ventre* (the politics of the belly)," refers both to the material processes of elite appropriation and to the widespread symbolic association of "eating" with both political domination and sorcery. In this perspective, Bayart argues, the stereotypical figure of the big-bellied African bureaucrat takes on a special significance (Bayart 1993).[8]

In this context, I would add only that African socialism, as a language of legitimation, spoke in terms that drew on many of these key popular moral themes. Where European socialism often insisted on a language of "objective necessities" and "empirically observable contradictions" (so-called scientific socialism), socialism in Africa was distinguished by its insistently moralizing tone.

For Julius Nyerere of Tanzania, to take only the best-known example, socialism was first of all an attitude of mind. The key oppositions, for Nyerere, were not primarily between rival economic systems or modes of production, but between conflicting moral orientations: selfishness versus sharing, exploitation versus solidarity, individual acquisitiveness versus communal mutuality. Socialism, for Nyerere, was the rejection of selfishness; a capitalist, in contrast, was defined as "the man who uses wealth for the purpose of dominating any of his fellows" (Nyerere 1968: 1). Exploitation was thus understood as a moral fault rather than as an aspect of a mode of production or an economic structure; socialism, in response, constituted an ethical commitment to forswear the temptation to exploit one's fellow man. As the Arusha Declaration put it, "A genuine TANU [Tanganyika African National Union] leader will not live off the sweat of another man, nor commit any feudalistic or capitalistic actions" (Nyerere 1968: 17). The TANU creed drew not only on the rhetoric of international socialism, but also on central moral oppositions that would be familiar to any ethnographer of the region: selfishness versus sociality, sharing versus exploitation, benevolence versus malevolence. And given his avowed refusal to "eat" his fellow man, Nyerere's conspicuous lack of a belly was perhaps as symbolically potent as his rejection of material luxury.

Socialist discourses of legitimation were, if anything, even more explicitly oriented to morality in Zambia than they were in Tanzania. President Kenneth Kaunda's elaboration of African socialism, which he called Humanism, explicitly declared itself an ethics. The heart of socialism, for Kaunda, was the fight against "the exploitation of man by man." Such exploitation could take place in class terms, as powerful people abused their power, or it could occur in a geographical sense, as urbanites exploited rural villagers. In any case, however, the policies of the socialist state were largely justified as a way of preventing the selfish from engaging in such exploitation, preventing exploiters from getting fat off of their fellows (Kaunda 1968, 1974; cf Ferguson 1997).

Let there be no mistake here: I am in no way arguing that such exploitation was in practice prevented, or that such legitimating discourses can be taken at face value as accurate statements of policy. African socialism was from the start an ideology of rule, and state moralizing in Tanzania, Zambia, and elsewhere was intensely interested, self-serving, and very often fraudulent. The point is not that the African socialist state stamped out selfishness or did away with exploitation, but that it spoke in a comprehensible local moral vocabulary. Its economic arguments were always moral arguments, in a familiar popular idiom. It is in terms of these popular idioms that African socialism was both attacked and defended.

Mineworkers in Zambia during my fieldwork in 1985–86, for instance, attacked the government most vigorously not for specific policies or acts, but for its general "selfishness." Officials were faulted, often in highly personal terms, for immorality, exploitation, and enriching themselves at the expense of the people. What mineworkers said of their government officials largely echoed what Hutu refugees in Tanzania were saying, more economically, of government officials there: "they eat our sweat" (Malkki 1995). When government or party officials came to exhort Zambian mineworkers to accept wage increases far below inflation rates, the miners scoffed at the big-bellied parasites who lectured them on the national need for belt-tightening. And along with the focus on the "appetite" of the elites went a parallel emphasis on the "hunger" of the people. Hunger is an all too real phenomenon in contemporary Zambia, but it should be recognized that it is also a powerful metaphor for a failure of government—the ultimate political bankruptcy being the failure to "feed the people." It is in this context that we should understand the repeated claims of employed mineworkers (who, even today, are among the better-paid workers in Zambia) to be going hungry. Consider the following lament from a letter I received from a young mineworker in Kitwe, describing the aftermath of the Copperbelt food riots of 1986. Note that an explicit rejection of state ideology is here directly tied to questions of hunger, family mutuality, and morality:

> On the day of reverting to the old price of mealie meal all milling companies were nationalized under those two books he [Kaunda] has written under the heading Humanism parts I & II; but for god's sake this was not the root cause and all these books have not brought anything [for] a Zambian to enjoy. So personally, how dare we toil over a book which has brought hunger on my body—imagine I got two boys, not knowing what was to come. I am unable to meet their needs, then to hell with humanism or socialism and according from wherever they have been imposed on the people these ideologies just downgrade the moral freedom of its citizens and believe me they are bound not to succeed.

SCIENTIFIC CAPITALISM

The coerced adoption of "structural-adjustment" programs by African states since the 1980s has been accompanied by a fundamental shift in the way these states have sought to legitimate their policies. Leaving behind the moral language of legitimation that was shared by African socialism and its critics alike, African politicians and bureaucrats now seek to explain and justify their new policies (for audiences both foreign and domestic) in the economistic language of international technocracy (a shift inevitably recorded in the West as a move toward "pragmatism" and "moderation" in matters economic). "Structural-adjustment" policies, often adopted only under extreme duress, are thus rationalized retrospectively as "necessary" for "economic growth" and "efficiency." They are, in fact, rarely *justified* at all (in the sense of a developed argument that the policies are in fact just); they are claimed to be "right" only in the sense that they are claimed to be "economically correct." This regime of "economic correctness" is far more oppressive in its effects than any amount of the over-discussed "political correctness" on college campuses. Indeed, it is as rigid and dogmatic in its reasoning as any "scientific socialism" ever was. It is in acknowledgement of this fact that I speak of the late-twentieth-century regime of IMF–World Bank governance in Africa as "scientific capitalism."

I will illustrate the language of legitimation of "scientific capitalism" with the World Bank report of 1981 titled *Accelerated Development in Sub-Saharan Africa* (the so-called Berg Report [World Bank 1981]). I focus on this document not because it is an accurate guide to the bank's actual economic policies (it is not), but because it arguably has been the single most central text in a coordinated strategy of ideological legitimation (Bernstein 1990: 16).

What is most noteworthy in this report is the way that extremely controversial and widely disputed claims are blandly asserted as simple, incontestable, scientific facts. For example, many thoughtful analysts in and out of Africa are concerned about a loss of food production and food security associated with the expanded cultivation of export crops. Yet the Berg Report flatly declares, with all the authority of a high-school textbook, "Empirical evidence does not support the hypothesis that expanding export production leads to declines in food production" (World Bank 1981: 62). Moreover, even if export crops *are* produced at the expense of food, we are told, careful measurement of the "domestic resource costs" of different commodities *proves* that African countries' "comparative advantage" is in export crops and that the cultivation of food crops is "inefficient" (World Bank 1981: 64–65). There is no room for discussion, let alone political debate or moral contemplation. The statistics are clear: growing food is just economically incorrect.

"Efficiency" likewise demands that efforts at industrialization be dismantled. It is not economically correct for African countries to seek to escape the niche the world market has provided for them. What is "necessary" is for African economies to concentrate on their areas of comparative advantage, which are to be found mostly in shrinking and unstable agricultural export commodity markets (World Bank 1981: 91–97). (The report did not yet anticipate, of course, that hosting toxic-waste dumps might become another such area of comparative advantage.) Similar technical justification is offered for other drastic policy dictates, such as doubling and tripling urban food prices, scrapping free health care, abolishing scholarships for higher education, and so on (World Bank 1981: 64, 43–44).

The effectiveness of the whole package of prescribed policy changes is definitively demonstrated through a "simulation" projecting, with the Bank's usual fraudulent pseudo-precision ("Source: World Bank projections"), the exact percentage increases that the specified reforms will bring in GDP, agriculture, exports, and imports (World Bank 1981: 122). What is there to argue about, after all? It's right there in the numbers.

It is true that in recent years there has been some dissatisfaction even within the bank with purely economistic approaches. Indeed, the fashionable view now among enlightened insiders is that just as important as "getting the prices right" is "getting the politics right." Although this shift is an interesting one and worth analyzing in its own right (as discussed later), it is clear that it does not introduce any real break with the logic of "economic correctness." For it is all too obvious that in the quest to "get the politics right," "politics" is understood as just another technical "factor." It is not an arena for public participation and moral discussion but only another "input" to be fixed at a "correct" level.

REMORALIZING ECONOMIC DISCOURSE

The focus of the analysis is on the efficiency with which resources are used. Economic growth implies using a country's scarce resources—labor, capital, natural resources, administrative and managerial capacity—more efficiently. Improving efficiency requires, first, that a country produce those things which it can best produce as compared with other countries and, second, producing them with the least use of limited resources. . . . [T]he record of poor growth in most Sub-Saharan African countries suggests that inadequate attention has been given to policies to increase the efficiency of resource use and that action to correct this situation is urgently called for. — World Bank (1981: 24)

The masses knows just as them guys know, enough is enough. . . . Whoever is there to represent, is there to tow their system's policies, but the masses know the purposeful of this system — secure their status politically, economically and socially and leave the masses to poverty. . . . There is a gloom in the nation because of the lack of medicines in hospitals and children are dying like nobody's business and [there is a] scarcity of essentials since the IMF programs. — Zambian mineworker's letter, 1987

I have shown that scientific capitalism seeks to present itself as a non-moral order, in which neutral, technical principles of efficiency and pragmatism give "correct" answers to questions of public policy. Yet a whole set of moral premises are implicit in these technicizing arguments. Notions of the inviolate rights of individuals, the sanctity of private property, the nobility of capitalist accumulation, and the intrinsic value of "freedom" (understood as the freedom to engage in economic transactions) lie just below the surface of much of the discourse of scientific capitalism. Often, too, there seems to be a puritan undertone of austerity as punishment for past irresponsibility: having lived high on the hog for so long, say the stern bankers and economists (safely ensconced in their five-star hotels and six-figure incomes), it is time for Africans to pay for their sins.

But the larger point is that these moral premises on which the technicizing justifications of structural adjustment depend almost always remain *implicit*. The moral and cosmological assumptions on which ideological justifications of structural adjustment often rest are unacknowledged and even actively denied by those who hold them. Like Summers, the legitimizers of scientific capitalism in Africa scrupulously distance themselves from any explicitly moral or "value-laden" claims. It is all a matter, they insist, of objective economic correctness, of how the equations work out. This is not to say that capitalist ideologies are somehow incapable of speaking in a moralizing voice. In many times and places, they have done just that, and with great success. But in contemporary justifications of structural adjustment in Africa, the legitimizing discourse of technical economic expertise does not speak, as Ronald Reagan once did, of the glory of individual freedom and the shining city on the hill. It speaks instead in the gray language of economic "pragmatism." The morality of the market thus denies its own status as a morality, presenting itself as mere technique.

Recent experience shows, however, that the economic policies of scientific capitalism continue to be understood by Africans in moral terms and that they are received and sometimes resisted accordingly. In Zambia, the establishment of "correct prices" and "efficient" markets resulted, quite predictably, in a series of food riots and eventually in the fall of the government. Informants told me that the 1986 Copperbelt riots effectively had been popular uprisings in which a wide range of respectable people—including, in one account, policemen—had joined. Many of those who participated in the looting were unashamed, even proud. T-shirts were printed in the townships reading, "Looters Association of Zambia." For many Zambians, what was truly illegitimate was not the theft by the looters, but the rise in prices itself. Similar events have occurred all over the continent, where IMF-sponsored policies have provoked legitimation crises for African states. Scientific capitalism's claim that prices are "economically correct" apparently has little meaning when, as the mineworker quoted earlier remarked, "children are dying like nobody's business."

Such observations may serve to remind us that, as Bernstein has noted, however little democratic accountability African states may have, "they do have to confront the consequences of their actions—if only by the exercise of repression—in ways that the World Bank or IMF do not" (Bernstein 1990: 28). Technocratic reason may be good enough to sell World Bank—IMF dogma in the international arena. But someone, somewhere down the line, has to implement these policies, at which point questions of legitimacy and popular reception must be addressed. In Africa, capitalism will have to learn, as socialism learned, to drop its "scientific" pretensions and speak a local language of moral legitimation. How (and whether) what is going on in places like Zambia can in fact be legitimated in locally meaningful, moral terms must remain an open question.

Wealth in Africa has long been understood as first of all a question of relations among people. This, I would suggest, is a politically and theoretically rich understanding, vastly more so than the IMF–World Bank's impoverished conception of the economy as an amoral, technical system. Against the truly fetishized view that would see "the market" as a natural force to which human life simply *must* submit, the African insight that markets, prices, and wages are always *human* products is a powerful one. In the worst case, of course, the attribution of economic ills to human agency may degenerate into crude scapegoating and demonizing—blaming the "greed" of Indian traders for a rise in prices, for instance. But the fundamental perception that economic facts are moral and human facts may also provide a resource for a much deeper critique. After all, when one's society is being systematically destroyed by "the market," that old Azande question is an acute one: "Who *sent* the market?"

African traditions of moral discourse on questions of economic process may thus be understood not as backward relics to be overcome, but as intellectual and political resources for the future. Geschiere has rightly noted that a whole range of "forms of politics held in contempt by most Western observers can only be comprehended in relation to a rich world of images and conceptions" (Geschiere 1989). What needs to be added is that this rich world of images and conceptions may itself enable and energize a potent popular politics.

The claims of technical capitalistic reason, which seem to be so readily accepted (for the time being) in Eastern Europe and the former Soviet Union, may not win the day so easily in Africa. Instead, there is reason to believe that the issue of "structural adjustment" will eventually have to be taken up in a moral key in a way that recognizes the inevitable connection of social, economic, and cosmological orders. This may offer a ray of hope, in what is indeed a de-moralizing era, that Africans may yet find ways to do what neither socialist nor capitalist states have managed: to create an economic order genuinely responsive to popular moral sensibilities. As the IMF and World Bank fail (as they must) in their project of "de-moralizing" African economies, it is just possible that the seeds are being sown for a different kind of economic reform, another "structural adjustment" that would unabashedly speak a moral language; open an honest debate on economic priorities and moral values; and—who knows?—maybe even end up "feeding the people" instead of "eating" them.

POLITICS AND RESPONSIBILITY

I have thus far argued that the rhetoric of scientific capitalism does not provide effective legitimation for the imposition of structural adjustment in Africa and that the attempt to reduce questions of public policy to questions of economistic technique runs afoul of a well-developed African talent for understanding questions of poverty and wealth in a social and moral frame that foregrounds questions of human agency and responsibility. In this final section, I will attempt to sketch some of the implications of this analysis for thinking about practical political alternatives and effective strategies of resistance to IMF–World Bank rule.

First, it should be clear that such alternatives should not be expected to come from within the IMF–World Bank apparatus itself. Extraordinary amounts of ink have been spilled in recent years in advertising the emergence from within this apparatus of a "new paradigm" that focuses not only on economic growth and expansion of markets but also on such things as "governance," "participation," and "sustainability."9 This is supposed to be the "liberal" ("with a human face") version of structural adjustment—the velvet glove, as it were, over the iron fist of 1980s-style market discipline. Yet it is not clear that there is really much that is new in this "new" paradigm. It is easily enough demonstrated that the ideological program of "governance" (at least in its dominant versions) is little concerned with substantive democracy and still less with the "empowerment" of the poor (Schmitz 1995). But this can hardly be surprising, since what the new paradigm seems to be principally about is getting African governments to accept, implement, and legitimate policies made in Europe and North America largely in the interests of Western banks.

De-moralizing Economies   83

The very existence of this literature, however, shows that the IMF–World Bank planners have taken notice of the legitimation crisis I have described. In the first wave of criticisms of African governments (beginning with the Berg Report), Western governments and lenders sought to place the blame for the failure of "modernization" on the shoulders of "inefficient," "mismanaged," "corrupt" African states. As Bernstein (1990) has pointed out, the failed policies for which African governments were being blamed were themselves largely pressed on them by those same Western governments and lenders now denouncing them in a process that created much of the corruption and mismanagement being decried. Yet this denunciation of the African state provided an ideological charter for the first round of draconian structural-adjustment reforms enforced by the IMF and its associated capital cartel.

The second wave of criticism of African governments (associated with the idea of a crisis of governance) takes note of the fact that the governments responsible for imposing the IMF–World Bank "reforms" suffer from a crisis of legitimacy. This is then blamed on the fundamentally nondemocratic and unaccountable nature of African governments (with no mention made of the nondemocratic and unaccountable nature of the IMF and the World Bank). The crisis of structural adjustment thus becomes a crisis of governance, for which the appropriate remedy is a reform of African governments, with a new attention not only to "good management" and "good government" but also to "democracy" and "human rights."

What friends of democracy need to bear in mind in all of this is that however democratic an African government may be in formal terms, its scope for making policy is radically constrained by the *nondemocratic* international financial institutions themselves. No matter what party is elected to power in a country like Zambia, it will have to come to terms with the IMF, and the voice of the Zambian electorate will have precious little say over those terms. Effective IMF rule over huge areas of economic and social policy is thus papered over with an appearance of popular sovereignty. The current ideological frothing over "democracy in Africa" in this way ends up serving a profoundly antidemocratic end—that is, the simulation of popular legitimation for policies that in fact are made in the most undemocratic way imaginable.

Whether this cynical strategy for legitimating structural adjustment can succeed, however, is another matter. "Good government," as defined by the lending agencies, may help to legitimate IMF–World Bank policies in the West, but it is not at all clear that it will get to the heart of the crisis in Africa. For as I have argued, popular legitimacy in Africa requires a perception not simply of *"good government"* (efficient and technically functional institutions) but of *a government that is "good"* (morally benevolent and protective of its people). An efficient and effective government is not necessarily a "good" one in this second sense, and a regime that presides over the efficient and effective pauperization of its people is not likely to acquire much legitimacy, no matter how many elections are held.

What Rene Lemarchand (1992) has referred to as "the moral discredit incurred by the state, both as concept and institution" thus remains a potent political fact across most of Africa, one that current shifts in legitimation strategies do little to address. Africans continue to regard the state largely as a malevolent and ever hungry predator and to perceive it not as an expression of their collective will but as an instrument of the exploiters, the tool of those who get fat "eating" the sweat of honest working people. It would be difficult to argue that they are wholly mistaken.

Moreover, Africans are increasingly aware of the inability of national governments to control either macroeconomic processes or the day-to-day living conditions of the people. No longer do they expect that a new government will solve their problems or that a shift in regime will make much difference in the grim slippage in their standards of living. Increasingly, they seek to find expressions of collective solidarity, social order, and moral beneficence outside of the state altogether—for example, in local, kin-based social systems; in ethnic separatism; in religiously inspired social movements; in millenarian cults; and in various other movements aimed at cleansing the world of its only too evident corruption and evil. Thus, Zambia has seen a revival of witch-cleansing movements (Auslander 1993) and localist social identities (Ferguson 1999); Mozambique, a renewal of kin-based traditions of political leadership; Uganda, an extraordinary succession of millenarian cults (also evident in Mozambique); North and West Africa, powerful Islamic fundamentalist movements; and so on. All of these movements (for all their differences and whatever their political merits and demerits) address the fundamental moral questions that I have suggested are at the heart of the crisis of African societies today. And it is just these fundamental moral questions that the reformers and ideologists of "governance" have so conspicuously *not* addressed and, perhaps, cannot address.

What this suggests for progressive political strategy is quite complex. First, there is a clear need to insist on the "re-moralization" of political discourse at the national level. It will not be sufficient to settle for "good government" without an explicit and public discussion of what "goodness" consists of and what state policies would best serve the public "good." It will not be sufficient to combat "corruption" in government without asking the larger question of whether the very aims and purposes of state rule are not corrupt. Such an opening of political discourse probably will not lead to dramatic changes in public policy, since, as I have argued, the range of possible action of African states is severely constrained by the vise grip of international finance. But it would at least allow the real moral and ethical issues at stake in policy decisions—such as who will eat and who will go hungry; whose sickness will be treated and whose allowed to fester—to be openly aired and honestly considered. And it might ultimately result in a more radical questioning of the whole bank–state complex and even of the legitimacy of international debt itself. (Indeed, in the years since this essay was originally written, just such a radical questioning of debt has become a key rallying point for progressive forces in and out of Africa, reaching perhaps its most powerful expression in the Jubilee 2000 debt-cancellation campaign.)

On another level, however, the assessment of the political situation in Africa must move beyond the state-centered framework entirely. The question of alternatives must move past the stultifying form, "Well, then, what *should* Zambia do?"[10] For the cast of relevant political actors extends far beyond the roster of national governments and political parties. Indeed, many of the most important political processes on the continent are occurring, as I have suggested, at subnational and transnational levels. The local institutions and grassroots social movements referred to earlier must be taken seriously and understood not as regressions or throwbacks, but as potentially formidable political responses to contemporary realities. Where political legitimacy has been achieved by such non-state movements and institutions, it is crucial to understand how this has occurred and to see how the moralizing frames of reference I have analyzed here may be engaged with viable and effective political structures. It is possible, too, that a better understanding of these movements will contribute to the crucial tactical goal of forging links and alliances among them, suggesting a beginning to a real alternative form of "governance."

At the same time, attention must be paid to the formidable institutions that are "governing" Africa from afar: the transnational financial institutions (World Bank, IMF, foreign banks) and development agencies (USAID, UNDP, UNHCR, etc.), as well as the churches, missions, and so-called nongovernmental organizations. These transnational institutions continue to be very little studied, even though they clearly play a very central role in the de facto governance and administration of the continent today (see, e.g., Hanlon 1991). We will not have a balanced understanding of the actual processes through which Africa is governed until we move beyond the myth of the sovereign African nation-state to explore the powerful but almost wholly unaccountable transnational institutions that effectively (and often not so effectively) rule large domains of African economy and society.

Finally, a consideration of the moral politics of structural adjustment must make its way from the moral dilemmas facing African people and governments back to the moral questions the crisis in Africa raises for "the West" itself. It is not only Africans who have traditions of moral discourse capable of generating critique, cleansing, and renewal. As David Cohen has pointed out, the West has its own traditions of accounting for moral responsibility that might well be dusted off and put to work as we survey the landscape of the post–Cold War world. Rather than accepting the marginal status ascribed to Africa by much end-of-the-cold-war punditry, Cohen suggests that the historical moment calls instead for a sober assessment of responsibility:

Rather than lamenting the loss of an era of donors and investors interested in winning allies in a global struggle, one could begin to account the losses to those prospective allies of participation in four decades of this most costly global game, whose rules and results were largely conceived and tabulated elsewhere. (Cohen 1993: 4)

Just as contemporary Germans have had to assess their collective moral responsibility for the Holocaust, Cohen suggests, both sides of the Cold War will have to assess their responsibility for "the militarization and impoverization of three-quarters of the globe," as well as for the creation of "conditions, interests, orientations, institutions, routines, and cultures that define the possibilities of much of the globe" (Cohen 1993: 4). If African traditions of moral discourse are capable of posing profoundly moral questions of human agency and causation, as I have suggested, Western traditions may lead us to the equally profound question of historical responsibility. Where Africans may ask, drawing on an indigenous intellectual tradition, "Who sent the market?" it remains for us in the West —as we survey the carnage left in the wake of colonization, Cold War, and the forced march of "development"—to ask an equally profound moral question, itself also embedded in a local cultural tradition: "My God, what have we done?"

One may well be wary, as Cohen notes, of the historical tendency to reduce the causes of African social problems to the doings of outside powers. But the generally salutary emphasis in recent Africanist scholarship on the centrality of African actors must not be an excuse, either, for evading the complex ethical and historical question of transnational responsibility.

History, Cohen insists, is not "at its end" but at a beginning, "a new and critical moment of responsibility" (Cohen 1993: 4). What this responsibility means in the case of the crisis in Africa, and how it is to be translated into concrete political action and public policy, must be at the heart of the continuing battles over the moral politics of structural adjustment as they are fought both in Africa and outside of it.

Transnational Topographies of Power

BEYOND "THE STATE" AND "CIVIL SOCIETY"

IN THE STUDY OF AFRICAN POLITICS

If there is to be an anthropology of "globalization," it is evident that it will require analytical tools, concepts that will enable critical analysis and open new understandings. As is so often the case, however, in the anthropological study of modernity the analytical tools closest to hand are themselves *part* of the social and cultural reality we seek to grasp. There can be no neat separation of analytic categories from "folk" categories when the folk categories in question include such key items of the social-science lexicon as "culture," "transnational," "diversity," "flows," "hybridity," "network," and so on. Such a situation calls for a heightened level of reflexive scrutiny of our categories of analysis if we are to gain critical purchase on the emerging ideologies and world views of our era rather than simply (re)produce them.

This is an issue that arises immediately when one looks at the recent literature on "democratization" in Africa. Here, "civil society" has emerged as a keyword, ubiquitous in both scholarly analyses of "democratization" and the "real-world" practices they seek to describe and explain. The fad for civil society has perhaps been most in evidence among political scientists, who have been understandably eager to leave behind their Cold War paradigms for livelier topics such as democratization, social movements, and what they call "state-society relations." But anthropologists, too, have been bitten by the bug, finding in "civil society" a new and improved incarnation of their old disciplinary trademark, "the local." Rising numbers of students writing anthropology dissertations, it seems, are heading out to "the field" in search not of an intriguing culture or a promising village but of an interesting NGO. But if such anthropological engagements are to be fruitful, it will be necessary to devote some critical scrutiny to the common-sense mapping of political and social space that the state–civil society opposition takes for granted. Beginning with the category "civil society" itself, I will try to show how the state–civil society opposition forms part of an even more pervasive way of thinking about the analytic "levels" of local, national, and global—a way of thinking that rests on what I call the *vertical topography of power*. I will argue that calling into question this vertical topography of power brings into view the transnational character of both "state" and "civil society" and opens new ways of thinking about both social movements and states.

I will not attempt a genealogy of the term "civil society," but I will note a few aspects of the changes in its meaning. Its origins are customarily traced to eighteenth-century liberal thought, especially to Scottish Enlightenment thinkers such as Francis Hutcheson, Adam Ferguson, and, later, Adam Smith, in whose thought the term is associated both with the developing conceptualization of society as a self-regulating mechanism and with concepts of natural law. Better known to many is the Hegelian usage of the term to denote an intermediary domain between the universal ideal of the state and the concrete particularity of the family, a conception famously critiqued by Karl Marx and imaginatively reworked by Antonio Gramsci. Today, the term most often comes up in discussions of democracy, especially to refer to voluntary organizations and NGOs that seek to influence, or claim space from, the state.

The term "civil society" still had a rather antique cast to it when I first encountered it in graduate seminars on social theory. But since then it has gotten a new lease on life, chiefly thanks to the dramatic recent political history of Eastern Europe (Arato and Cohen 1994;

Keane 1988; Seligman 1992). There, of course, communism had promised to lead to the gradual demise of the state. But instead, the state seemed to have swallowed up everything in its path, leaving behind no social force—not private businesses, church, or political party—capable of checking its monstrous powers. It was not the state, it seemed, but civil society that had "withered away." In this historically specific context, the old term had a remarkable resonance, and it licensed otherwise unlikely coalitions between actors (from dissident writers to the Catholic church) who had in common only that they demanded some space, autonomy, and freedom from the totalitarian state.

Coming out of this rather peculiar and particular history, the term "civil society" came for many to be almost interchangeable with the concept of democracy itself—nearly reversing the terms of Marx's famous critique, which had revealed the imaginary freedoms of capitalism's democratic political realm as an illusion, to be contrasted to the real *unfreedom* of "civil society," conceived as the domain of alienation, economic domination, and the slavery of the workplace. But this new conception (of "civil society" as the road to democracy) not only met the political needs of the Eastern European struggle against communist statism; it also found a ready export market—both in the First World (where it was appropriated by conservative Ronald Reagan–Margaret Thatcher projects for "rolling back the state") and in the Third World (where it seemed to provide leverage both for battling dictatorships and for grounding a post-socialist mass democratic politics). With little regard for historical context or critical genealogy, and in the space of only a few years, "civil society" has thus been universalized. It has been appropriated, for different reasons (if equally uncritically), by both the right and the left. Indeed, it has become one of those things (like development, education, or the environment) that no reasonable person can be against. The only question to be asked of civil society today seems to be: How can we get more of it?

I will argue that the current (often ahistorical and uncritical) use of the concept of "civil society" in the study of African politics obscures more than it reveals, and, indeed, that it often serves to help legitimate a profoundly antidemocratic transnational politics. One of my aims in this essay, then, is to point out the analytic limitations of the state–civil society opposition and trace its antidemocratic political and ideological uses.

But I also have a second, and less reactive, aim in exploring the specifically African career of the civil-society concept. For in the course of criticizing the state-versus-civil society formula, I hope to arrive at some suggestions about other ways of thinking about contemporary politics in Africa and elsewhere. In particular, I will argue that the "state"–"civil society" opposition brings along with it a whole topography of power, revealed perhaps most economically in Hegel's famous conception of civil society as, in Mahmood Mamdani's phrase, "sandwiched between the patriarchal family and the universal state" (Mamdani 1996:14; cf. Gibbon 1993). This conception rests on an imaginary space that puts the state up high, the family low (on the ground), and a range of other institutions in between. In what sense is the state "above" society and the family "below" it? Many different meanings are characteristically blurred together in this vertical image. Is it a matter of scale? Abstraction? Generality? Social hierarchy? Distance from nature? The confusion here is a productive one, in the Foucauldian sense, constructing a common-sense state that simply *is* "up there" somewhere, operating at a "higher level." This common-sense perception has been a crucial part of the way that nation-states have sought (often very successfully) to secure their legitimacy through what Akhil Gupta and I (Ferguson and Gupta 2002) have termed "claims of vertical encompassment." These claims naturalize the authority of the state over "the local" by merging three analytically distinct ideas—superior spatial scope; supremacy in a hierarchy of power; and superior generality of interest, knowledge, and moral purpose—into a single figure, the "up there" state that encompasses the local and exists on a "higher level."[1]

Such an image, of course, underlies the familiar public–private split and the idea (of which Jürgen Habermas makes much) of a "public sphere" that mediates between state and citizen. Imagining the family as a natural ground or base of society, as feminists have pointed out, leaves the domestic out of the sphere of politics entirely. But this imagined topography also undergirds most of our images of political struggle, which we readily imagine as coming "from below" (as we say), as "grounded" in rooted and authentic "lives," "experiences," and "communities" (cf. Malkki 1992). The state itself, meanwhile, can be imagined as reaching down into communities, intervening, in (as we say) a "top-down" manner, to manipulate or plan "society." Civil society, in this vertical topography, may appear as the middle latitude, the zone of contact between the "up there" state and the "on the ground" people, snug in their communities. Whether this contact zone is conceived as the domain of pressure groups and pluralist politics (as in liberal political theory) or of class struggle in a war of position (as in Gramscian Marxism), this imaginary topography of power has been an enormously consequential one.

What would it mean to rethink this? What if we question the self-evident "verticality" of the relation of state to society, displace the primacy of the nation-state frame of analysis, and rearrange the imaginary space within which civil society can be so automatically "interposed between" higher and lower levels? As we will see, such a move entails rethinking "the state" and looking at transnational apparatuses of governmentality which I will suggest are of special significance in many parts of contemporary Africa, where states are, in significant ways, no longer able to exercise the range of powers we usually associate with a sovereign nation-state, or even (in a few cases) to function at all as states in any conventional sense of the term. But it also, and at the same time, entails rethinking received ideas of "community," "grassroots," and "the local," laden as these terms are with nostalgia and the aura of a "grounded" authenticity. Using the politics of structural adjustment in Zambia and the South African civic movement as examples, I will try to show that both the "top" and the "bottom" of the vertical picture today operate within a profoundly transnationalized global context that makes the constructed and fictive nature of the vertical topography of power increasingly visible and opens new possibilities for both research and political practice. First, however, I wish to continue the interrogation of the contemporary conceptualization of the problem of "state–civil society relations" by showing how much it shares, at the level of the topographic imagination, with the older "nation-building" paradigm that it has largely replaced.

I will begin by considering two views of African politics that, some-times in explicit opposition and often in implicit and confused combination, have dominated the intellectual scene in recent decades. The older paradigm sees nation-building as the central political process in postcolonial Africa, with a modernizing state in conflict with primordial ethnic loyalties. The newer view recommends the rollback of an overgrown and suffocating state and celebrates the resurgence of "civil society," often putatively linked to a process of "democratization." In deliberately presenting a highly schematic and simplified account of their distinctive features, my purpose is to reveal an underlying set of assumptions that they share.

"Nation-building"

The key premise of the "nation-building" approach to African politics is the existence of two different levels of political integration and a necessary and historic movement from one to the other. The first such level, logically and historically prior, is the local or subnational; this is the level of primordial social and political attachments left over from the premodern past. Originally referred to via such labels as tribal organization or traditional African society, these supposed "givens" of African political life were thought to include structures of kinship, community, and (in some formulations) ethnicity. Later, Goran Hyden would summarize such local "primordial affiliations" under the singularly unfortunate rubric, "the economy of affection" (Hyden 1983). Indeed, it should be noted that while such "primordialist" approaches to sub-national identities may fairly be described as out of date, they are very far from having vanished from the contemporary scene.[2]

The second level of integration in the "nation-building" scheme is, of course, the national. Emergent, new, modern nations were understood to be in the process of construction—stepping out, as it were, for the first time onto the stage of world history. With national structures of authority struggling to establish themselves in the face of "primordial" commitments, "nation-building" appeared to be both an urgent task and a historically inevitable process. Yet the generally hopeful tone of the work in this tradition is shadowed by the phantom that stalks "nation-building"—the specter of premodern resurgences such as "tribalism" or such manifestations of the lingering "economy of affection" as nepotism, corruption, and other banes of "good government." Failed nation-building, it follows, can mean only a resurgence of primordial affiliations (still the usual journalistic explanation for civil wars in Africa). State success, by contrast, means the construction of new bases of authority resting on nation-state citizenship. Above the national level, finally, appears the international, understood largely as (1) a source of "aid," a helping hand in nation-building; and (2) a utopian image of the union of nation-states, with the key symbol of the United Nations as the promise of the universality of the nation form (cf. Malkki 1994).

"Development," in such a view, is the natural reward for successful national integration, just as nation-building is the characteristic rhetoric of the developmental state. The strong, activist state thus naturally becomes the protagonist in the optimistic narratives of "national development" that flourish within this paradigm. This view of the world is perhaps sufficiently familiar as to make it possible to move ahead without further elaboration.

"State and Society"

"State and society"—the "new paradigm" in the study of African politics that emerged at the end of the 1980s to rival the old nation-building approach[3]—regards the state and its projects with new skepticism and rediscovers the local as the site of civil society, a vigorous, dynamic field of possibilities too long suffocated by the state. In place of a modernizing national state bravely struggling against premodern ethnic fragmentation, the image now is of a despotic and overbearing state that monopolizes political and economic space, stifling both democracy and economic growth. Instead of the main protagonist of development, the state (now conceived as flabby, bureaucratic, and corrupt) begins to appear as the chief obstacle to it. What are called "governance" reforms are needed to reduce the role of the state and bring it into "balance" with civil society (see, e.g., Carter Center 1990; Hydén and Bratton 1992; World Bank 1989, 1992).

The local level, meanwhile, is no longer understood as necessarily backward, ethnic, or rural. New attention is paid to such non-"primordial" manifestations of the local as voluntary associations and "grassroots" organizations through which Africans meet their own needs and may even press their interests against the state. There is, in much of this newer research, an unmistakable tone of approval and even celebration—not of the nation-building state, but of a liberated and liberatory civil society. Left to its own devices, it seems, society might make political and economic progress; the problem now is how to induce the state to get out of the way and to make it more responsive to civil society's demands. Hence, the connection, repeatedly asserted in the "governance" literature, between democratization (conceived as making space for civil society) and development (conceived as getting the state out of the way of a dynamic non-state sector). It is such a link, too, that accounts for the otherwise peculiar idea of a natural affinity between the draconian and decidedly unpopular measures of structural adjustment, on the one hand, and populist demands for democratization on the other (a point I will return to shortly).

The "new" state-and-society approach is often posed as a simple opposition to the "old" nation-building (or "statist") model. But the two paradigms are not as different as they might at first appear. In particular, the state-and-society paradigm uses the very same division of politics into analytic "levels" as does the "nation-building" one, altering only the valuation of their roles. The "national" level is now called "the state"; the "local" level, "civil society." But where the older view had a new, dynamic, progressive national level energizing and overcoming an old, stagnant, reactionary local level, the new view reverses these values. Now the national level (the state) is corrupt, patrimonial, stagnant, out of date, and holding back needed change; while the local level (civil society) is understood as neither ethnic nor archaic, but as a dynamic, emerging, bustling assemblage of progressive civic organizations that could bring about democracy and development if only the state would get out of the way.

The international, too, appears in both paradigms, but with

largely opposite functions. International agencies, especially financial ones, appear in the state-and-society view less as state benefactors and providers of "aid" than as the policemen of states—regulating their functioning and rolling back their excesses through "structural adjustment." If the nation-building view imagined the international in the form of an idealistic United Nations, the state-and-society paradigm pictures a no-nonsense IMF: stern, real-world bankers speaking what I call in chapter 3 the language of economic correctness.

The implications for "development" are clear and, again, nearly the reverse of those of the nation-building approach. For the state-and-society paradigm sees development not as the project of a developmentalist state, but as a societal process that is held back by the stifling hold of the state. Structural adjustment is needed to liberate market forces to work their development magic. Where the first paradigm saw the development problem as too much society and not enough state, the second sees it as too much state and not enough society.

The two views, it should by now be clear, bear a remarkable resemblance to one another, even as they are manifestly opposed. Indeed, everything happens as if the second model were, as Claude Lévi-Strauss might say, a very simple transformation of the first. Through a structural inversion more familiar perhaps to analysts of myth than of politics, we are left with two paradigms that are simultaneously completely opposed to one another and almost identical (see figure 1).

THE TOPOGRAPHY OF "STATE AND CIVIL SOCIETY"

It is obvious that a range of phenomena exist in contemporary Africa that are not captured in the old nation-building optic that saw politics as a battle between a modernizing state and primordial ethnic groups—hence, the recourse to the idea of civil society to encompass a disparate hodgepodge of social groups and institutions that have in common only that they exist in some way outside of or beyond the state. Indeed, while the term "civil society" is often not defined at all in contemporary Africanist literature, most authors

FIGURE 1. TWO PARADIGMS, TWO ANALYTIC LEVELS

	NATION-BUILDING	STATE AND SOCIETY
NATIONAL	national integration modernity: + democracy: + development: + progress: +	the state modernity: − democracy: − development: − progress: −
LOCAL	tribal, primordial attachments modernity: − democracy: − development: − progress: −	civil society modernity: + democracy: + development: + progress: +

Key:
modernity (+/−): up-to-date, new / backward, old
democracy (+/−): promotes democracy / inhibits democracy
development (+/−): creates economic growth / obstacle to growth
progress (+/−): dynamic, progressive / stagnant, anti-progress

seem to intend the classical Hegelian usage that, as I pointed out, imagines a middle zone of "society" interposed between family and state. Others speak more specifically of civil society as a frontier of contact where a politically organized and self-conscious "society" presses against, and sets the bounds of, "the state."[4]

But while definitions of "civil society" in this literature are usually broad and vague, in practice writers move quite quickly from definitional generalities to a much more specific vision that is restricted almost entirely to small, grassroots, voluntary organizations, leaving out of the picture some rather important and obvious phenomena. One is never sure: Is the Anglo-American Corporation of South Africa part of this "civil society"? John Garang's army in Sudan? Oxfam? What about ethnic movements that are not opposed to or prior to modern states, but (as so much recent scholarship shows) produced by them? What about Christian mission organizations, which are arguably more important today in Africa than ever but are strangely relegated to the colonial past in the imagination of much contemporary scholarship? All of these phenomena fit uncomfortably in the state-versus-civil-society grid and indeed cannot even be coherently labeled "local," "national," or "international" phenomena. Instead, each of these examples, like much else of interest in contemporary Africa, both embodies a significant local dynamic and is indisputably a product and expression of powerful forces, national and global.

The state, meanwhile, when apprehended empirically and ethnographically, starts to look suspiciously like civil society. Sometimes, this is literally the case, such as when NGOs are actually run out of government offices as a sort of moonlighting venture. ("An NGO?" a Zambian informant of mine once remarked. "That's just a bureaucrat with his own letterhead.") Perhaps more profoundly, as Timothy Mitchell has argued, the very conception of "state" as a set of reified and disembodied structures is an effect of state practices themselves (Mitchell 1991). Instead, recent work on state practices (e.g., Gupta 1995) suggests that states may be better viewed not in opposition to something called "society" but as themselves composed of bundles of social practices that are every bit as "local" in their social situatedness and materiality as any other.

Such work suggests that, to make progress here, we will need to break away from the conventional division into "vertical" analytic levels that the old nation-building and new state-and-society paradigms share. In the process, we will manage to break out of the range of questions that such a division imposes (how do states rule; what relations exist—or ought to exist—between state and society; how can civil society obtain room to maneuver from the state; etc.), and open up for view some of the transnational relations that I will suggest are crucial for understanding both ends of the vertical polarity. Let us consider what a focus on transnational contexts has to tell us, first about the putative "top" of the vertical topography ("the state") and then about the supposed "bottom" ("grassroots" civic organizations).

"The Top"

If, as neoliberal theories of state and society suggest, domination is rooted in state power, then rolling back the power of the state naturally leads to greater freedom and ultimately to "democratization." But the argument is revealed to be fallacious if one observes that, particularly in Africa, domination has long been exercised by entities other than the state. Zambia, let us remember, was originally colonized (just a little over a hundred years ago) not by any government but by the British South Africa Company, a private multinational corporation directed by Cecil Rhodes. Equipped with its own army and acting under the terms of a British "concession," it was this private corporation that conquered and "pacified" the territory and set up the system of private ownership and race privilege that became the colonial system.

Today, Zambia (like most other African nations) continues to be ruled in significant part by transnational organizations that are not in themselves governments but work together with powerful First World states within a global system of nation-states that Frederick Cooper has characterized as "internationalized imperialism."[5]

Perhaps most familiarly, international agencies such as the IMF and World Bank, together with allied banks and First World governments, today often directly impose policies on African states. The name for this process in recent years has been "structural adjustment," and it has been made possible by both the general fiscal weakness of African states and the more specific squeeze created by the debt crisis. The new assertiveness of the IMF has been likened, with some justification, to a process of "re-colonization," implying a serious erosion of the sovereignty of African states (e.g., Saul 1993). It should be noted that direct impositions of policy by banks and international agencies have involved not only such broad macroeconomic interventions as setting currency-exchange rates, but also fairly detailed requirements for curtailing social spending, restructuring state bureaucracies, and so on. In other words, rather significant and specific aspects of state policy, for many African countries, are being directly formulated in places like New York and Washington, D.C.

Such "governance" of African economies from afar represents, as critics have not failed to point out, a kind of transfer of sovereignty away from African states and into the hands of the IMF. Yet since it is African governments that remain nominally in charge, it is easy to see that they are the first to receive the blame when

structural-adjustment policies begin to bite. At that point, democratic elections (another "adjustment" being pressed by international "donors") provide a means whereby one government can
be replaced by another. But since the successor government will
be locked in the same financial vise grip as its predecessor, actual
policies are unlikely to change. (Indeed, the government that tries
can be swiftly brought to its knees by the IMF and its associated
capital cartel, as the Zambian case illustrates vividly.) In this way,
policies that are in fact made and imposed by wholly unelected and
unaccountable international bankers may be presented as demo-
cratically chosen by popular assent. Thus does "democratization"
ironically serve to simulate popular legitimacy for policies that are
in fact made in a way that is less democratic than ever (cf. chapter 3).

"The Bottom"

Civil society often appears in African studies today as a bustle of
grassroots, democratic local organizations. What this of course ig-
nores, as Jane Guyer has put it, is "the obvious: that civil society
is [largely] made up of *international* organizations" (Guyer 1994:
223).[6] For, indeed, the local voluntary organizations in Africa, so
beloved of civil-society theorists, very often, on inspection, turn
out to be integrally linked with national- and transnational-level
entities (Simone and Pieterse 1993). One might think, for instance,
of the myriad South African "community organizations" that are
bankrolled by USAID or European church groups (Mindry 1998)
or of the profusion of "local" Christian development NGOs in Zimbabwe, which may be conceived equally well as the most local,
"grassroots" expressions of civil society or as parts of the vast international bureaucratic organizations that organize and sustain them
(Bornstein 2003). When such organizations begin to take over
the most basic functions and powers of the state—as they very
significantly did, for instance, in Mozambique (Hanlon 1991)—
it becomes only too clear that "NGOs" are not as "NG" as they
might wish us to believe. Indeed, the World Bank baldly refers to
what it calls BONGOs (bank-organized NGOs) and even GONGOs
(government-organized NGOs).[7]

   That these voluntary organizations come as much from the putative "above" (international organizations) as from the supposed "below" (local communities) is an extremely significant fact about so-called civil society in Africa. For at the same time that international organizations (through structural adjustment) are eroding the power of African states (and usurping their sovereignty), they are busy making end runs around these states and directly sponsoring their own programs or interventions via NGOs in a wide range of areas. The role played by NGOs in helping Western "development" agencies to "get around" uncooperative national governments sheds a good deal of light on the current disdain for the state and celebration of civil society that one finds in both the theoretical and the policy-oriented literature right now.

But challengers to African states today are not only to be found in international organizations. In the wake of what is widely agreed to be a certain collapse or retreat of the nation-state all across the continent, we find a range of forms of power and authority springing up that have not been well described or analyzed. These are usually described as "sub-national" and usually conceived either as essentially ethnic (the old primordialist view, which, as I noted earlier, is far from dead) or, alternatively (and more hopefully), as manifestations of a newly resurgent civil society that has been long suppressed by a heavy-handed state. Yet can we really assume that the new political forms that challenge the hegemony of African nation-states are necessarily well-conceived as "local," "grassroots," "civil," or even "sub-national"?

Guerrilla insurrections, for instance, which are not famous for their "civility," are often not strictly "local" or "sub-national," either —armed and funded, as they often are, from abroad. Consider Jonas Savimbi's UNITA army in Angola: long aided by the CIA, originally trained by China, with years of military and logistical support from South Africa and continuous funding from right-wing U.S. church groups. Is this a "sub-national" organization? A phenomenon of an emerging civil society? What about transnational Christian organizations like World Vision International, which, as Erica Bornstein has recently pointed out, play an enormous role in many parts of contemporary Africa, organizing local affairs and building and operating schools and clinics where states have failed to do so (Bornstein 2003)? Are such giant, transnational organizations to be conceptualized as "local"? What of humanitarian organizations such as Oxfam, CARE, or Doctors without Borders, which perform statelike functions all across Africa?

Such organizations are not states, but they are unquestionably state-like in some respects. Yet they are not well described as "sub-national," "national," or even "supra-national." Local and global at the same time, they are transnational—even, in some ways, a-national. They cannot be located within the familiar vertical division of analytic levels presented earlier. Not coincidentally, these organizations and movements that fall outside of the received scheme of analytic levels are also conspicuously under-studied. Indeed, they seem to have been, until recently, largely invisible to theoretical scholarship on African politics, tending to be relegated instead to the level of "applied," problem-oriented studies.

In all of these cases, we are dealing with political entities that may be better conceptualized not as "below" the state, but as integral parts of a new, transnational apparatus of governmentality.[8] This new apparatus does not *replace* the older system of nation-states (which is—let us be clear—far from about to disappear), but overlays it and coexists with it. In this optic, it might make sense to think of the new organizations that have sprung up in recent years not as challengers pressing up against the state from below but as horizontal contemporaries of the organs of the state—sometimes rivals, sometimes servants, sometimes watchdogs, sometimes parasites, but in every case operating on the same level and in the same global space.

Such a reconceptualization has implications for both research and political practice insofar as these depend on received ideas of a "down there" society and an "up there" state. In particular, I will examine some of these consequences for two sorts of actor with a special stake in the "grassroots": social movements, on the one hand, and anthropologists, on the other.

"GRASSROOTS" POLITICS WITHOUT VERTICALITY?

What does the critical scrutiny of the vertical topography of power mean for progressive social movements that have long depended on certain taken for granted ideas of locality, authenticity, and "bottom-up" struggle? An extremely illuminating example comes out of the practice, and self-criticism, of the South African civic movement. Organized, politically powerful local civic organizations, of course, played a huge role in the struggle for democracy in South Africa. With national political organizations banned, township civics built networks, organized boycotts and demonstrations, educated cadres, and made many townships no-go areas for the white regime's troops and policemen. Civics took up key government functions and sometimes developed remarkably democratic internal institutions. At the height of the antiapartheid movement, the civics were not just protest groups, but something approaching a genuinely revolutionary force—as the apartheid regime itself recognized.

I will here draw on the recent writings of Mzwanele Mayekiso, a township organizer in the Johannesburg neighborhood of Alexandra and a true heir of Gramsci (in an age of many pretenders). Mayekiso sees very clearly the shortcomings of much fashionable celebration of civil society. Simply lumping together everything outside the state may have had its utility in the struggle against totalitarian rule in Eastern Europe. But in South Africa, he insists, it is disastrous. It conceals the diametrically opposed political agendas of distinct and antagonistic social classes. For Mayekiso, the socialist, it makes no sense to allow the Chamber of Mines and the Mineworkers' Union simply to be thrown together as "civil society," in opposition to "the state." Moreover, the unthinking valorization of "civil society" for its own sake contains the risk of "following the agenda of imperialist development agencies and foreign ministries, namely, to shrink the size and scope of third world governments and to force community organizations to take up state responsibilities with inadequate resources" (Mayekiso 1996: 12). Instead, Mayekiso proposes an eminently Gramscian solution: a determination to work for what he calls "working-class civil society." It is this which must be strengthened, developed, and allowed to preserve its autonomy from the state. Mayekiso cites two reasons for this: (1) to build a base for socialism during a period when a socialist state is not yet a realistic expectation; and (2) to serve as watchdog over the state while pressing it to meet community needs in the meantime.

It is useful to keep in mind that Mayekiso is writing from the position of an extraordinarily successful political organizer. The South African civics have been a formidable force to be reckoned with, not only in the antiapartheid struggle, where their organization and political energy proved decisive, but also in their post-independence role. The civics have been successfully transformed from agents of all-out resistance to the apartheid state (aiming, among other things, to make the townships "ungovernable") into well-organized autonomous structures that are ready to lend support to some state campaigns while vigorously attacking and protesting others. SANCO (South African National Civic Organizations, which Mayekiso headed) is today a major player on the national scene and serves as an independent advocate for worker and township interests—all of which makes it at least a bit more difficult for the African National Congress (ANC) government to sell out its mass base.

But the post-independence era has also presented some profound challenges to Mayekiso's Gramscian praxis, which he analyzes with remarkable honesty and clear-sightedness. In particular, Mayekiso has come to recognize that the policies of the new South African government are constrained not only by the balance of forces in South Africa, but also by the forces of transnational capital, which "denude the ability of nation-states to make their own policy." When faced with the threat of a capital boycott, there may be limits on how far even the most progressive South African government can go down the road to socialism. The traditional nationalist approach, based on organizing the masses to put pressure on the government, has no effective response to this situation. Vertical politics seems to have reached its limits.

Such failures of strictly national politics from below lead Mayekiso to a very interesting critical reflection. Recalling the long struggle of the Alexandra Community Organization (ACO) during the apartheid years, he acknowledges that its success grew not simply from its strong base in the community but also from strategic transnational alliances. In fact, he reports, the ACO received *most* of its funds not from the community, or even from within the country, but from international sources. Dutch solidarity groups, U.S. sister-city programs, Canadian NGOs, Swedish official aid, even USAID at one point—all were sources of aid and support for Mayekiso's "local organizing," which (we begin to realize) was not quite so "local" after all (see also Simone and Pieterse 1993). But Mayekiso does not apologize for this. On the contrary, he uses a reflection on the successful experience of the ACO to begin to develop what he calls "a whole new approach, a 'foreign policy' of working-class civil society" (Mayekiso 1996: 283). After all, he says "there is a growing recognition that poor and working class citizens of different countries now have more in common with each other than they do with their own elites" (Mayekiso 1996: 283), while "the ravages of the world economy are denuding the ability of nation states to make their own policy" (Mayekiso 1996: 280). In such circumstances, challenges from below within a vertically conceived national space cannot succeed, but "international civic politics is a real alternative to weak nation-states across the globe" (Mayekiso 1996: 280).[9]

Traditional leftist conceptions of progressive politics in the Third World (to which many anthropologists, including myself, have long subscribed) have almost always rested on one or another version of the vertical topography of power that I have described. "Local" people in "communities" and their "authentic" leaders and representatives who organize "at the grassroots," in this view, are locked in struggle with a repressive state representing (in some complex combination) both imperial capitalism and the local dominant classes. The familiar themes here are those of resistance from below and repression from above, always accompanied by the danger of co-optation, as the leaders of today's struggle become the elites against whom one must struggle tomorrow.

I do not mean to imply that this conception of the world is entirely wrong, or entirely irrelevant. But if, as I have suggested, transnational relations of power are no longer routed so centrally through the state, and if forms of governmentality increasingly exist that bypass states altogether, then political resistance needs to be reconceptualized in a parallel fashion. Many of today's most successful social movements have done just that (as the example of the South African civics in part illustrates). But academic theory, as it does so often, lags behind the world it seeks to account for.

To be sure, the world of academic theory is by now ready to see that the nation-state does not work the way conventional models of African politics suggested. And the idea that transnational networks of governmentality have taken a leading role in the de facto governance of Africa is also likely to be assented to on reflection. But are we ready to perform a similar shift in the way we think about political resistance? Are we ready to jettison received ideas of "local communities" and "authentic leadership"? Critical scholars today celebrate both local resistance to corporate globalization and forms of grassroots international solidarity that some have termed "globalization from below." But even as we do so, we seem to hang on stubbornly to the very idea of a "below"—the idea that politically subordinate groups are somehow naturally local, rooted, and encompassed by "higher-level" entities. For what is involved in the very idea and image of "grassroots" politics if not precisely the vertical topography of power that I have suggested is the root of our conceptual ills? Can we learn to conceive, theoretically and politically, of a "grassroots" that would be not local, communal, and authentic, but worldly, well connected, and opportunistic? Are we ready for social movements that fight not "from below" but "across," using their "foreign policy" to fight struggles not against "the state" but against that hydra-headed transnational apparatus of banks, international agencies, and market institutions through which contemporary capitalist domination functions?

Consider a news article from the *Los Angeles Times* on the worldly engagements of the Zapatistas of Chiapas, Mexico.[10] The Zapatistas, we learn, have become celebrities and have been discovered by the jet set. Oliver Stone was photographed receiving the trademark wool mask and pipe from Subcommander Marcos during a recent visit to the guerrillas' headquarters. Danielle Mitterand, widow of the former French president, recently dropped by. And so on. Most shockingly, Marcos himself has apparently appeared in a fashion spread for the Italian clothing firm Benetton. The subcommander appears in camouflage dress, with the glossy photo captioned: "You have to go to war. But what will you wear? Camouflage visual dynamic: light, photogenic . . . ideal for the soldier who goes from war to war and who doesn't have time to change." Benetton even offered to be the official outfitter of the Zapatistas, but here Marcos drew the line. "Compañeros," he told reporters solemnly (through his mask), "we have decided that it is not suitable to wear sweaters in the jungle."

If this strikes us as funny, it is useful to think about exactly what the joke is here. For at least part of the humor in the story comes from its suggestion that a group of supposed peasant revolutionaries have, in their inappropriate appetite for Hollywood celebrity and Italian clothing, revealed themselves as something less than genuine ("from fighting to fashion"). After all, what would a "real revolutionary" be doing in a Benetton ad or lunching with Oliver Stone? But this reaction may be misplaced. As Diane Nelson (1999) has recently argued, First World progressives need to rethink our ideas of popular struggle and to prepare ourselves to learn from Third World transnational "hackers" with a sense of media politics, as well as a sense of humor—and from movements that offer us not a pure and centered subject of resistance but, like the subcommander, a quite different figure: masked, ambivalent, impure, and canny. Like the South African civics described by Mayekiso, the Zapatistas present us not with authentic others fighting for a nostalgic past, but with media-savvy, well-connected contemporaries finding allies horizontally, flexibly, even opportunistically, but effectively. There is obviously real political acumen in the Zapatista strategy. Celebrity attention and world press coverage may well help to protect Chiapas communities against potential aggression; the cost to the Mexican state of political repression surely rises with the amount of press coverage (and public-relations damage) that it entails. More profoundly, the *image* of destabilization through guerrilla warfare, properly circulated, is perhaps the Zapatistas' most potent political weapon. Capitalism is built on perceptions, and Mexican capitalism is built on an especially precarious set of perceptions—particularly, on the idea that it is an "emerging market" on the path of the "tigers" of East Asia, a carefully nurtured perception that has supported a huge burst of speculative capital investment in the Mexican economy from the United States and elsewhere. The real damage to the Mexican economy (and thus to the Mexican ruling class) may not come so much from the Zapatistas' actual raids as from the effect that the *fear* of such raids has on the Mexican stock market and on the all-important "confidence" (as they say) of the international bondholders who have the Mexican economy in their pocket. A guerrilla war conducted in images on the pages of an international fashion magazine, then, may not be so out of place after all. Indeed, it may well be the most tactically effective sort of warfare that the terrain will support.

The globalization of politics is not a one-way street. If relations of rule and systems of exploitation have become transnational, so have forms of resistance—along lines not only of race and class, which I have emphasized here, but also of gender, sexuality, and so on. Gramsci's brilliant topographic imagination may be a guide to this new political world, but only if we are willing to update our maps from time to time. The image of civil society as a zone of trench warfare between working people and the capitalist state served the left well enough at one moment in history, just as the vision of a self-regulating zone of "society" that needed protection from a despotic state served the needs of an emergent bourgeoisie in an earlier era. But invoking such topographies today can only obscure the real political issues, which unfold on a very different ground, where familiar territorializations simply no longer function. Rethinking the taken-for-granted spatial mapping that is invoked not only in such terms as "the state" and "civil society" but also in the opposition of "local" to "global" (and in all those familiar invocations of "grassroots," "community," etc.), in these times becomes an elementary act of theoretical and political clarification, as well as a way to strategically sharpen—and not, as is sometimes suggested, to undermine—the struggles of subaltern peoples and social movements around the world.

TOWARD AN ETHNOGRAPHY OF ENCOMPASSMENT

Just as a rethinking of the vertical topography of power has special consequences for political practices that depend on unexamined tropes of "above" and "below," it also contains special lessons for forms of scholarship that have traditionally found their distinctive objects in vertically conceived analytic "levels."[11] Working through these conceptual issues, I suggest, might well point in the direction of promising new directions for research. Making verticality problematic not only brings into view the profoundly transnational character of both the state "level" and the local "level"; it also brings the very image of the "level" into view as a sort of intensively managed fiction.

To say this is to point toward an enormous ethnographic project (which, in collaboration with Akhil Gupta, I have only begun to explore): that of exploring the social and symbolic processes through which state verticality and encompassment are socially established and contested through a host of mundane practices (Ferguson and Gupta 2002). On the one hand, such a project would entail the ethnographic exploration of the processes through which (insofar as state legitimation goes smoothly) the "up there" state gets to be seen as (naturally and commonsensically) "up there." The spatialization of the state has usually been understood through attention to the regulation and surveillance of the boundaries of nations, since the boundary is the primary site where the territoriality of nation-states is made manifest. Wars, immigration controls, and customs duties are the most obvious examples. But while this is a rich area of investigation, it is only one mode by which the spatialization of states takes place. The larger issue has to do with the range of everyday technologies by which the state is spatialized, by which verticality and encompassment become features of social life, commonsensical understandings about the state that are widely shared among citizens and scholars. The policing of the border is intimately tied to the policing of Main Street in that they are both rituals that enact the encompassment of the territory of the nation by the state. These acts represent the repressive power of the state as both extensive with the boundaries of the nation and intensively permeating every square inch of that territory. Both types of policing often demarcate the racial and cultural boundaries of belonging and are often inscribed by bodily violence on the same groups of people. Nor is this simply a matter of repressive state power. State benevolence as well as coercion must make its spatial rounds, as is clear, for instance, in the ritual touring of disaster sites by aid-dispensing U.S. presidents. It is less in the spectacular rituals of the border than in the multiple, mundane domains of bureaucratic practice that states instantiate their spatiality. Rituals of spatial hierarchy and encompassment are more pervasive than most of us imagine them to be. An ethnographic focus allows these everyday practices to be brought more clearly into focus (see also Hansen and Stepputat 2001).

At the same time, however, it is part of my argument that new forms of transnational connection increasingly enable "local" actors to challenge the state's well-established claims to encompassment and vertical superiority in unexpected ways, as a host of worldly and well-connected "grassroots" organizations today demonstrate. If state officials can still always be counted on to invoke the "national interest" in ways that seek to encompass (and thereby devalue) the local, canny "grassroots" operators may trump the national ace with appeals to "world opinion" and e-mail links to the international headquarters of such formidably encompassing agents of surveillance as Africa Watch, World Vision International, or Amnesty International. Where states could once counter local opposition to, say, dam projects by invoking a national-level interest that was self-evidently higher than (and superior to) the merely local interests of those whose land was about to be flooded, today "project-affected people" are more likely to style themselves "guardians of the planet," protectors of "the lungs of the earth," or participants in a universal struggle for human rights and to link their local struggles directly to transnationally distributed fields of interest and power. Such rhetorical and organizational moves directly challenge state claims of vertical encompassment by drawing on universalist principles and globally spatialized networks that render the claims of a merely *national* interest and scope narrow and parochial by comparison. The claims of verticality that I have reviewed here (claims of superior spatial scope; supremacy in a hierarchy of power; and superior generality of interest, knowledge, and moral purpose) have historically been monopolized by the state. But today these claims are increasingly being challenged and undermined by a newly transnationalized "local" that fuses the grassroots and the global in ways that make a hash of the vertical topography of power on which the legitimation of nation-states has so long depended.

What this implies is not simply that it is important to study NGOs and other transnational non-state organization, or even to trace their interrelations and zones of contact with "the state." Rather, the implication would be that it is necessary to treat state and non-state governmentality within a common frame without making unwarranted assumptions about their spatial reach, vertical height, or relation to "the local." What is called for, in other words, is an approach to the state that would treat its verticality and encompassment not as a taken-for-granted fact, but as a precarious achievement—and as an ethnographic problem. Such a project would be misconceived as a study of "state–society interactions," for to put matters thus is to assume the very opposition that requires interrogation. Rather, what is needed is an ethnography of processes and practices of encompassment, an ethnographic approach that would center the processes through which the government of the conduct of others (by state and non-state actors) is both legitimated and undermined by reference to claims of superior spatial reach and vertical height.

Such a view might open up a much richer set of questions about the meaning of transnationalism for states than until now have been asked. In this perspective, it is not a question of whether a globalizing political economy is rendering nation-states weak and irrelevant, as some have suggested, or whether states remain the crucial building blocks of the global system, as others have countered. The central effect of the new forms of transnational governmentality, if my argument is correct, is not so much to make states weak (or strong) as to reconfigure the way that states are able to spatialize their authority and stake claims to superior generality and universality. Recognizing this process might open up a new line of approach into the ethnographic study of state power in the contemporary world.

Chrysalis

THE LIFE AND DEATH OF

THE AFRICAN RENAISSANCE

IN A ZAMBIAN INTERNET

MAGAZINE

The African Renaissance did not last long. Its dates can be roughly established as 1997–99. But if its significance was less epochal than its title would imply, it was all the same a key moment in the process through which Africa has come to find its place in a "new world order" of formal democratization, economic liberalization, and global economic integration. In the midst of a historical moment that combined aggressive neoliberal economic restructuring (under the sign of structural adjustment) with political democratization and the advent of multiparty elections, the theme of "Renaissance" flagged an optimistic discourse of legitimation that for a short time spread widely, both internationally and among certain African elites (especially in the Anglophone south of the continent).

For a few brief months, the "African Renaissance" seemed to be everywhere. It was Thabo Mbeki, then deputy president of South Africa, who first introduced the idea of a "Renaissance" in 1997. But similar new themes of "Afro-optimism" seemed to be cropping up all over at about the same time. In a June 1997 speech to the Organization of African Unity (OAU), for instance, U.N. Secretary-General Kofi Annan argued that Africa was entering a "new era" based on "democracy, human rights, and sustainable development"—a "third wave" (after the "first wave" of struggle against colonial domination, and a "second wave" marked by civil wars, undemocratic rule, and economic stagnation). This "third wave" would finally bring the peace and prosperity that had eluded so many post-independence African nations. Ugandan President Yoweri Museveni advanced similar arguments, widely circulated in and out of Africa, to the effect that a democratic and market-friendly Africa, led by a new generation of responsible pragmatists, was finally ready to turn the corner and enter a new era of peace and prosperity.

In March 1998, the "Renaissance" went global. President Clinton led a 1,000-strong delegation to Africa to celebrate the new, democratic, and free-market regimes that, in his view, pointed to a rosy African future. "Africa's accomplishments," Clinton effused, "grow more impressive each month." A few months later, the IMF declared that Africa was indeed in the midst of an "economic Renaissance." As a result of the implementation of "good economic policies," performance in Sub-Saharan Africa had "improved markedly in the last few years" and was "enormously encouraging."[1] Major international news magazines picked up the buzz, running glowingly hopeful cover stories on a "new Africa" that had left behind its bad habits of corruption, socialism, and blaming the West, an Africa finally ready to move ahead with democracy and free enterprise. Academics joined in the fray, dusting off their old paradigms of "political development" and "nation-building" and heralding the late but welcome arrival of democracy in Africa.

But the "Renaissance" seems to have faded as suddenly as it had originally appeared. In the face of a staggering burst of bad news, political and economic, the new Afro-optimism has quickly withered. The glowing magazine stories about a new, reemerging Africa have disappeared, and the continent seems to have resumed its familiar place in the world's media as the source of lurid tales of warfare, hunger, and suffering.[2] The term "Renaissance" is rarely applied to Africa today (outside of South Africa, where it continues to enjoy the patronage of Mbeki) without a certain grim irony.

How are we to account for the abrupt abandonment of such a well developed and elaborately promoted ideological program? No doubt part of the answer is to be found in the inconveniently timed eruption (or intensification) of a chain of civil and interstate wars across much of the continent, with the Democratic Republic of the Congo (DRC) perhaps forming the epicenter. One might point, as well, to the continuing poor economic results across the continent, even in many countries that took extreme measures to liberalize their economies and were identified as exemplary in the "Renaissance" discourse (see UNCTAD 2000). The worsening HIV/AIDS epidemic, too, casts a heavy shadow over any attempt to generate "Afro-optimism."

But such empirical developments can provide only a partial answer to our question. After all, elite ideologies of legitimation — from the Soviet "workers' paradise" to George W. Bush's "compassionate conservatism" — have often coexisted happily enough with empirical facts and conditions that thoroughly contradicted them. Perhaps as important as any political or economic adversity has been that many of the new African elites who originally promulgated the "Renaissance" talk seem themselves to have lost faith in it. In this essay, I seek to shed light on how and why that may have happened by looking at an ambitious on-line publication in Zambia that briefly sought to reinvent Zambian nationalism for the neoliberal age.

As will be shown in the next section, the internet magazine *Chrysalis* was the project of a tiny, highly educated elite. It certainly did not represent the views of "ordinary Zambians" (whoever they might be). What is more, it was an abortive project, consisting of just seven issues in the space of about a year before publication was suspended indefinitely in August 1999. But since my interest here is in a failed elite discourse, both the elite focus of the publication and its ultimate abandonment are very much to the point. For what *Chrysalis* shows, I suggest, is nothing less than why and how a key sector of the new Zambian elite came to lose faith in a neoliberal national project that seemed briefly vital in the immediate post-democratization years.

For many, in and out of Africa, the liberation of South Africa brought with it the hope that a "new South Africa" might help to inspire a new Africa. The advent of democratic rule in South Africa in 1994 seemed to be part of a wider trend toward more democratic and accountable government all across the continent. In this way, the success of the antiapartheid struggle could be rhetorically associated with newly restructured political and economic regimes elsewhere in a "democratized," post-structural-adjustment Africa. It is evident that this association entailed a creative suppression of some significant contradictions—how else could the ANC's often radically socialist liberation struggle serve as a banner for IMF-style market liberalization? But it was through just such finesses that the discourse of the "African Renaissance" became possible.

It was Thabo Mbeki, then deputy president and today the president of South Africa, who first articulated the "African Renaissance" theme. In a series of speeches delivered in 1997–98, he gave a name, and an inspirational rhetoric, to an emerging world view among new South African elites that combined pride in the struggle for liberation and the achievement of democracy with the advocacy of neoliberal, "free-market" economic policies (Barrell 2000).

Much of Mbeki's program for "Renaissance" was a recycling of familiar African nationalist themes. His speeches were studded with celebrations of the achievements of ancient African civilizations, along with tributes to the struggle against colonialism and the search for national identity and national liberation. Many of his programmatic goals, as Howard Barrell (2000) has pointed out, simply articulated an aspiration to such uncontroversial public goods as might be espoused by almost any modern democratic politician. What a "new Africa" needed was democracy, peace, education, good government, economic prosperity, progress against disease, and so on. Who could disagree?

Yet Mbeki had something more original to offer than just the denunciation of dictatorships or the formulaic calls for African progress and democracy. For what was most distinctive in Mbeki's new rhetoric was something much more specific and, indeed, controversial: a frank and unblinking African self-criticism, including the blunt implication that African problems were largely the result of misgovernment by African elites. In a major statement on 13 August 1998, Mbeki openly denounced "the petty gangsters who would be our governors by theft of elective positions, as a result of holding fraudulent elections, or by purchasing positions of authority through bribery and corruption." It was no longer useful, he suggested, to seek to locate the blame for African ills simply in the misdeeds of the colonizing powers. "The thieves and their accomplices, the givers of the bribes and the recipients, are as African as you and I. We are the corrupter and the harlot who act together to demean our continent and ourselves," he said. "Africa cannot renew herself," he continued,

> where its upper echelons are a mere parasite on the rest of society, enjoying a self-endowed mandate to use their political power and define the uses of such power that its exercise ensures that our Continent reproduces itself as the periphery of the world economy, poor, underdeveloped and incapable of development.[3]

Mbeki's was a powerful call, specifically directed toward African elites and intellectuals, not only for "good government" and democracy, but for a kind of elite self-renewal, a re-devotion to the ideals of democracy, patriotism, and national service.

Crucially, Mbeki's rhetoric of renaissance fused this call for political and moral reform with one for neoliberal economic restructuring. As he said at the African Renaissance Conference he organized in Johannesburg in September 1998, "We cannot win the struggle for Africa's development outside of the context and framework of the world economy." Thus, "fundamental to everything we may say about these matters [is] that we have to attract into the African economy the significant volumes of capital without which the development we speak of will not happen." In the same speech, he also spoke about the dangers of "the market" and criticized a tendency to treat "the market" as "the modern God . . . to whose dictates everything human must bow in a spirit of powerlessness." But Mbeki (a master of the fine art known as "talk left, act right") left no doubt that new economic policies for a new Africa should "seek to create conditions that are attractive for domestic and foreign investors, encourage the growth of the private sector, reduce the participation of the state in the ownership of the economy and, in other ways, seek to build modern economies."[4] A trained economist himself, Mbeki (along with his finance minister, Trevor Manuel) has since pursued policies in South Africa that have been described as "a self-imposed structural adjustment programme . . . fairly ruthlessly applied" (Barrell 2000).

In Mbeki's vision of the African Renaissance, then, the neoliberal economic policies associated with structural adjustment could be rhetorically linked with such things as African patriotism, elite self-cleansing, good government, and national liberation. Instead of a set of policies forced down the throats of national governments by foreign banks, "market reform" could be presented as part of the project of a new, morally cleansed African elite seeking to complete a nationalist project sadly betrayed by statist and socialist post-independence governments and their corrupt, parasitic elites.

This line of argument was an especially attractive one in Zambia in the 1990s. Zambia had been led to its 1964 independence by Kenneth Kaunda and his United National Independence Party (UNIP) under a program of African nationalism. In 1969, the party took a turn to the left, as Kaunda sought to institutionalize his version of African socialism (which he called "Humanism") through nationalization of major industries (including the all-important mining industry) and the gradual creation of a host of state-owned "parastatal" corporations. The nationalized parastatals came to monopolize almost the entire economy, which remained heavily dependent on the export of copper. In 1973, a new constitution inaugurated the "Second Republic," making Zambia a one-party state in which "the party and its government" exercised complete control over the formal political process in a type of monopolistic, single-party, patronage-based regime familiar from elsewhere on the continent.

During the early post-independence years, the economy enjoyed high growth rates, and urban workers in particular benefited from a general rise in wages (especially the powerfully unionized workers of the mining sector), the dismantling of the color bar, and the expansion of basic social, educational, and health services. Starting in the mid-1970s, however, and accelerating into the 1980s, the national economy headed into a tailspin from which it has yet to recover. The economic deterioration—largely due to deteriorating terms of trade for Zambia's copper industry (which dominated the national economy) and a consequent debt crisis (see Ferguson 1999)—left UNIP, and President Kaunda himself, ever more unpopular. As a tide of "democratization" washed over Africa in the wake of the end of the Cold War, catalyzed by a new interest on the part of international lenders in "governance" issues, dissatisfaction with the Kaunda regime came to be focused on an emergent alternative political party, the Movement for Multiparty Democracy (MMD), led by the trade unionist Frederick Chiluba. The MMD advocated not only "democracy" and new leadership, but also the aggressive liberalization of the economy, including the full privatization of the mines and parastatals. When multiparty elections finally came to Zambia, the MMD easily defeated the unpopular UNIP, and Chiluba was inaugurated president of the "Third Republic" in 1991.

In the final years of the Kaunda regime, the coming of democracy had seemed to promise an almost millenarian deliverance from the misery and humiliation of economic collapse. The MMD slogan's "The Hour Has Come!" appeared to promise more than a simple change of government. It seemed to suggest that the mere fact of elections might bring a momentous transformation. If it was bad government and lack of democracy that had kept Zambia down for so long, it seemed plausible enough that the arrival of democracy might itself put Zambia back on track toward its rightful— and mysteriously stalled—"emergence" as a modern and prosperous nation.

When the opposition MMD did come to power in 1991, it quickly set to work distancing itself from the old-style African socialist ways of its predecessors. In place of a statist nationalism, the MMD promised privatization and market efficiency; in place of anticolonial diatribes, it offered a language of accountability, renewal, good government, and "African responsibility for African problems." Ideological and generational differences were also marked by stylistic ones (see Hansen 2000: 92–96). In place of the safari suits and African prints that linked many of the Kaunda old guard to the "old days" of the anticolonial struggle and early independence years, the new elites preferred designer-label business suits and cell phones. The "new culture," as it was called, was business-friendly, future-oriented, youthful, and technocratic. Through good government, privatization, generational succession, and information age technology, the "new culture" seemed to promise, Zambia was finally ready to get "up to date."

In practice, the new elites of the Chiluba era turned out to be a good deal more like their predecessors than they were supposed to be. And their economic program, it is fair to say, has had little success in reversing the downward spiral of deindustrialization and pauperization that had marked the 1980s. On the contrary, total GDP (in constant prices) actually shrank slightly during the 1990s (IMF 1999: 5), while poverty levels continued to increase, afflicting by the end of the decade some 73 percent of the population by official estimates, with over 50 percent of Zambian children malnourished or stunted (Zambia 2000: 2–4).

But during the first few years of this process, the promised economic turnaround could plausibly appear, to those who believed in the magic of "transition," to be just around the corner. The architects of structural adjustment had promised, after all, that once the initial pain of market liberalization was over, vigorous economic growth would swiftly follow. With the new hopes raised by Mandela's inauguration in 1994 in South Africa, it seemed to many in the mid-1990s that "the time had come" and that southern Africa was finally ready to "take off." Zambia in particular was tapped by the World Bank and other international observers as a model of the new, democratic, neoliberal African state. The 1994 World Bank poverty assessment on Zambia confidently reported that, "as a result of the recent reforms, the economic decline has been halted and growth is expected to resume" (World Bank 1994: i). With the privatization of the mines scheduled to be completed by 1997, at the latest, the new Zambian economy was supposed to be poised for a successful "transition."

By 1997, not only were the mines beginning to be privatized, but promoters of the "transition" model could finally point to an uptick in GNP (6.5 percent for 1996—though this was arguably due more to unusually good rains than to any macroeconomic policies), and the "turnaround" could be imagined to be under way at last (IMF 1997: 4). Of course, the economic crisis had hardly gone away, and most of the indicators that were being hailed in 1997 went flat, or even back into decline, in the years that followed (as discussed later). But for a moment, at least, Zambia's young, market-friendly elites could imagine that they were on the verge of something new.

It was in this context—and just as the global hoopla about the "African Renaissance" was in full swing—that the first issue of *Chrysalis* appeared in 1998.[5] As the magazine's editors declared in their opening editorial, "About *Chrysalis*" (September 1998):

> *Chrysalis* is the voice of a new generation of Zambians: confident, proud of their heritage and possessing the collective will and capacity to build our country to take its rightful place in the pantheon of sovereign nations.
>
> The first thing we ought to point out about *Chrysalis* is that it is fundamentally and unashamedly a Zambian magazine. . . . For too long Zambia has been interpreted, or more accurately misrepresented, by others who never stopped to look and see, or listen and hear, the extraordinary richness of Zambianness. Simplistic views of a people and culture are bad enough in themselves. They are particularly pernicious, though, when that people begin to view themselves through that narrow lens.
>
> *Chrysalis* seeks to celebrate Zambia, Zambianness and all things Zambian. It is a platform to tout Zambian achievements and achievers. *Chrysalis* is a mirror to reflect us to ourselves.

The stated aims of the publication were to promote and build a new Zambian identity and to form and inspire the emergence of new leadership. The name *Chrysalis* was chosen because

> it seemed to capture the essence of what we felt about Zambia's place in the world, and in her own history. The chrysalis (or pupa) stage in the life-cycle of a butterfly is the seemingly passive stage between the larva and the imago. It is an intermediate stage of development. The words "seemingly passive" are instructive. We are of the opinion that Zambia is merely in its chrysalis stage of development, and there is much going on inside the cocoon.

The writing style was witty and casually erudite, with lighthearted references here and there to figures such as Franz Kafka, Isaac Newton, Jean Piaget, Aleksandr Solzhenitsyn, and Vilfredo Pareto. It was also laced with playful irony and self-deprecating humor. In one story, for instance, after the protagonist exchanges some words with his mother as he is leaving the house, the author inserts the following parenthetic note: "You may wonder, gentle reader, why I, a 28 year old, still live with my mother. Well, keep wondering."[6] Part of the playful pleasure of the publication, too, came from shattering the pious clichés of three decades of official nationalism; a good deal of the magazine's humor came from the explosive joy of pointing out the potentially embarrassing truths (whether about Zambia's politicians, living conditions, standards of spoken English, or national character) that had in an earlier era been officially concealed or ignored.

Although *Chrysalis* was often playful and humorous, it was, at its heart, a very serious project. The ambition of the editors and journalists who made up *Chrysalis* was nothing less than to remake the nationalist project and to reform the Zambian national culture in such a way as to make possible the dramatic new stage of development to which the chrysalis metaphor pointed. Those who participated in this venture were a well-placed and well-connected lot, who included among their numbers some of the most educated and ambitious of the younger generation of Zambia's elite. For all of the joking, the project was neither trivial nor inconsequential.

The writers and editors of *Chrysalis* appear to have been mostly young, male, highly educated, computer literate, and strikingly transnational. To judge by their self-identifications (many articles included short "about the author" paragraphs), the contributors to the magazine were university graduates, technocrats, and would-be capitalists; many were described as professionals employed in Zambia's tiny information-technology sector. Most of the writers knew one another and—according to one reader's comment—had been educated at a handful of elite secondary schools known for providing high-quality, "European"-style educations.[7]

It is also possible to draw some conclusions about the readership of the publication, thanks to the existence of a "guestbook" in which readers were encouraged to sign their names and register their reactions to the publication. It is impossible to say just how many of the magazine's readers actually signed the guestbook. But the 224 different individuals who did make entries to the guestbook (many of whom made several entries over a period of many months and often wrote at some length) give us a very interesting window into the audience for this publication and the reactions of its readers. What is more, many guestbook entries were reactions not only to the magazine's articles, but also to other guestbook entries, which gives an intensely interactive quality to the entire text.

According to the information contained in the guestbook entries, *Chrysalis*'s readers were almost entirely university-educated Zambians, mostly young and male, and mostly living abroad. The editors and article writers seem to have been based in Zambia (though many of them, too, had recently been abroad for university education). The readers, by contrast, were spread around the world but heavily concentrated in the Anglophone countries of the First World. Only 46 of the 224 guestbook signers reported residing in Zambia. In contrast, 76 signed in from the United States and 51 from the United Kingdom or Ireland. The following is a breakdown of the guestbook signers by country or region of residence:

United States: 76
Canada: 7
Britain and Ireland: 51
Other Western Europe: 13
Eastern Europe: 4
Oceania: 5
Zambia: 46
Republic of South Africa: 6
Botswana: 4
Other Africa: 1
Other: 5 (3, Japan; 2, Israel)
Not Stated: 6
Total: 224

It is obvious that the discussions of such a narrow and atypical group tell us very little about how Zambians in general have thought about the recent crisis. But they may tell us a great deal about the efforts of some of Zambia's new elites to remake a national identity that would conform to the economic and political conditions of the new times. They may also perhaps help us to understand why it has been so difficult — and not only in Zambia — to develop viable national identities and ideologies under conditions of actually existing neoliberalism.

THE *CHRYSALIS* PROJECT: A NEW CULTURE FOR A NEW ZAMBIA

The opening article of the inaugural issue of *Chrysalis*, Chanda Chisala's "The Chrysalis Generation" (September 1998), elaborated on the chrysalis metaphor. The author, identified as a "Lusaka entrepreneur and erstwhile biochemist," noted that Zambia's geographical shape has been likened to both a butterfly and a question mark. But, Chisala argued, it was really shaped more like a fetus. A fetus, like a chrysalis, represents "the stage that comes before full activity in a creature's life-cycle." The fetus/chrysalis represents "the stage at which Zambia is today. The stage immediately preceding full activity: full activity in business, full activity in development, full activity in a previously atrophied economy." The older generation, Chisala argued, failed to initiate this developmental dynamic; the members of this generation were those who "see our country as a question mark." They were the "Question Mark Generation":

> They see a nation with a lost sense of purpose and a bleak future. They see a nation ridden with many questions and few answers. The picture is depressing. It reminds me of the last time I saw so many question marks on one sheet of paper: in the exam hall, face to face with my lecturer's final attempt to make me fail in life. It was not uplifting.

The "Question Mark Generation" is addicted to questions; its members are full of talk and blame and verbal attacks on their enemies. They look at the younger generation, and "sigh with despair because of the violence and disorder that they see in us. They interpret this as a question mark." But, Chisala argued, the new energy of the younger generation is the energy of a fetus, "the reaction of a creature that has sensed an opportunity to live a higher life, but which it is being denied for unexplained reasons." This new generation, the "Chrysalis Generation," or "CG," is ready to stop talking and blaming, and start acting, setting in motion a whole new way of thinking about Zambia and its problems. The CG

> knows that the practical change will have to begin in a bold transformation of the core processes that direct and govern the way we think. The CG wants to establish new paradigms that will expose the futility of the old paradigms and set a premise on which future dialogue and action will proceed.
>
> The CG is filled with drive and energy. The CG is possessed with a passion for excellence. It is not armed with question marks; it is armed with explosive ideas.
>
> The CG does not fear the active threats of prosperous Western nations or the consequential threats of the dying East. The CG will create its own wealth, fund its own independence and carve out its own niche in the global village of tomorrow.

Chisala ended his inspirational message with the exclamation: "The creature is about to start flying!"

A similarly optimistic generational tone was struck by the other featured article in the first issue, Nick Tembo's "The Verge of a Metamorphosis." Tembo, identified as a "post-information technology age operator . . . gainfully employed in one of Zambia's mining companies," described having grown up believing that the economic problems of Third World nations like Zambia were the result of exploitation by the West:

> Growing up in a business minded family (my grandfather owned a small grocery store and my father used to deal in safety clothing), I vigorously endorsed this point of view and readily accepted Kaunda's one size fits all excuse for our problems: external factors. Besides, if that wasn't enough, two years of civics in junior secondary school provided the last nail in the proverbial coffin—the "west" was definitely the enemy.

But, "ten years and a British university education later," Tembo continued, he had revised his views. Instead of blaming "outside factors," he maintained (like Mbeki) that it was necessary to face the internal causes of corruption and lack of accountability:

> A lot of our politicians blame it all on the policies of exclusion that our colonial "masters" practiced; but there is no escaping the fact that after independence, in 1972 to be exact, Zambia was tipped to be a "third world economic success." 26 years and the Choma Declaration later, look what we've done.

The task of the new generation was to make a break with the old-style attributions of external blame and to take charge of Zambia's future. "We need to pay a little more honest attention to 'history' to help us prosper in the third republic," Tembo wrote. "The Kaunda era is over, eat your heart out Franz Kafka, the 'Z' has got a metamorphosis of its own going on."

Chrysalis contained quite a range of different kinds of articles. A number focused on Zambian national politics and new developments in that sphere. (Several articles, for instance, were devoted to the National Christian/Citizen's Council of Nevers Mumba and the possible presidential candidacy of Anderson Mazoka.) A change of tone was provided in the humorous lifestyle features by Damien Habantu, as well as occasional works of poetry. But *Chrysalis* was not just a general-interest magazine; it was specifically devoted to an ambitious national project. Two intertwined dimensions of this project dominated both the articles and the guestbook commentary of *Chrysalis*. They were: (1) the Zambian economic predicament and possible solutions to it; and (2) the need to identify or invent a viable modern Zambian culture that would allow both national pride and economic progress.

On the economic front, the diagnosis was almost always an inward-looking one. Zambia's economic crisis was a Zambian failure, caused by a combination of inept and corrupt leadership and a lack of dynamism among Zambians themselves. The way forward required thoroughgoing self-criticism, just as Mbeki had suggested. It was not only incorrect policies that were at issue, but a whole way of thinking. Thus, one author lambasted what he called the "old African Chief culture mentality," blaming it for the acceptance of cronyism and nepotism in government.[8] Another launched a blistering indictment of the Zambian education system, describing his own "miseducation" and concluding that "the UNZA [University of Zambia] graduate has become synonymous with the rather insulting word 'half-baked.'"[9] A third claimed that "being Zambian" entailed such characteristics as "taking the worst inefficiency and shoddy service for granted," "accepting misman-agement and misgovernment without a murmur as long as you are getting by on your meagre pay cheque," and "never really getting together to cooperate and make things happen unless of course you just happen to be in town when one of Lusaka's periodic riots occur."[10]

A recurring theme in the discussions about the economic situa-tion was an emphasis on the need for a new attitude that might fos-ter innovation and new thinking. Several writers complained that in Zambia "no one invents anything." This could not be blamed on external conditions, lack of foreign exchange (forex), or the policies of the "gavment" (a vernacular Zambian pronunciation of "gov-ernment"), Chisala insisted, for economic innovation was funda-mentally a matter of imagination and boldness:

> I don't think it took much "forex" or "gavment" to invent some of the simple, commercially successful products of America. How much money did they put in the development of a paper clip, for in-stance? The inventor of the paper clip became a multi-millionaire by simply playing around with a piece of wire. Is there any reason why this invention could not have been made in Zambia (and brought us some forex)? When an apple fell on the head of one certain Euro-pean, he discovered the principle of gravity. Did he need "gavment" to do that? How many mangoes fall on our heads every day and yet this never inspires anything scientific in us. . . . Yahoo.com was in-vented by two American students. It required no money to do the research before they developed the idea. And now it's a billion dollar company. There is absolutely no reason, no reason, why the Yahoo idea could not have been born in Zambia. We are that close, theo-retically, to having a billion dollar company in Zambia. We are just a good idea away! (think about it).[11]

Other authors agreed that radical economic innovation was pos-sible in Zambia (one cited the invention of the typing-correction fluid Liquid Paper in that connection)[12] if only the right attitudes could be instilled. The discussion of the stalled economy in this way very quickly led into discussions of Zambian national character and culture. Again, Chisala led the way. Debt relief, he suggested, was not going to do Zambia's economy any good unless the "internal" problems of Zambia, and of Zambians, were solved. "What needs to change," he insisted, "is really what is inside us. A stronger police force, a greater anti-corruption system, good economic sense in leaders, accountability, prioritisation skill, and so on, are really all external manifestations of the inside." What was really at the heart of the matter, he insisted, was culture. Zambia, he argued "does not have a culture." What Zambia needed, before it could solve its economic problems, was "architects of culture" who would "reengineer our character and restructure our dreams, so that we may begin to possess a violent and aggressive faith and a fervent confidence in our identity."[13]

In this way, the discussion about the national economy quickly became an anguished one about Zambian national-cultural identity. Chisala asked, "What does Zambia stand for? What is the meaning of Zambianness?" He replied that "there is really nothing that we can call Zambianness."[14] From that starting point, he and the other *Chrysalis* authors set out either to identify or to create a viable "Zambianness," without which, they were convinced, the national-developmental progress that they sought would be impossible.

Several articles pointed to language—and especially to certain distinctively Zambian forms of English—as a key attribute of a distinctively "Zambian" national culture.[15] A regular feature of the magazine (and apparently the most popular, to judge by the guest-book commentary) was Mjumo Mzyece's column, "Chrysalis Dictionary of Zanglish."[16] The "dictionary" explained, often with wry humor, the meanings of Zambian neologisms, or of standard English words whose common Zambian use gave them a distinctive meaning. Thus, Mzyece described for his readers what it means for someone to be "movious" (always on the move), or to "feature" at a party (to be in attendance), or to take "tea" ("any hot beverage, be it coffee, milo, cocoa, or, yes, even tea"). A special emphasis was placed on the linguistic black humor of daily life, where people are "surviving" ("what 99.9% or the Zambian population is doing") or suffering from a "slow puncture" (AIDS).

Although the articles on "Zanglish" were often funny (and certainly considered so by the readers), Mzyece was explicit about his serious purpose. "My aim," he declared,

> is not to incite mockery, but rather to inspire mirth, a word whose etymology can be traced back to the Old English word *myrge*, meaning "merry". For better or worse, English is our national language. It is ours. It belongs to us as much as it belongs to the Americans, the English or the Indians. Consequently, we must celebrate and enjoy English as our very own. One of the beauties of English is that it is such an accommodating language. It is a wonderfully absorbent medium. And pliable, too. We must take English and not be afraid or ashamed to remake it in our image, after our own likeness.[17]

The Zambianness of Zambian English was not diminished by the foreign origins of the English language, Mzyece explained. Zambia might import linguistic "raw materials" from elsewhere, but—like Japan in the economic sphere—it fashioned those raw materials into valuable finished products. Zambians should take pride in this talent for inventively reworking English into something new, for here lay their true national distinctiveness. And this was not a laughing matter:

> I use the humor only as an anaesthetic. My real purpose is to somehow infuse you with such enthusiasm for and enjoyment of your Zambianness that you will literally never be the same. I want you to come to the table and partake of something that only Zambians can partake of. . . . Perhaps something really does come out of these writings besides a few laughs. Perhaps something really does change deep down inside.[18]

The importance of Zambian English for the project of reforming a Zambian national identity was also emphasized by one of the magazine's most prolific and original contributors, Nick Tembo. He began by unsparingly severing the link between a Zambian national identity and the "local languages" that would figure in a more "Africanist" construction of Zambian identity (while also revealing the very particular social location of his elite readership). "When was the last time," he asked his readers,

> if ever, [that] you read a book written in a local language? When was the last time, if ever, you wrote a letter to a friend or family in a local language? How do you feel about the fact that you can only, if at all, communicate effectively in English? Can you sing the Zambian "national" anthem in any of the local languages? Go on, try it now and make us laugh.[19]

Tembo went on to lament that "our ancestors let us down" by failing to develop written languages. ("A pity, really—imagine reading the Ngoni people's personal and first hand accounts of the solar eclipse that occurred on the day they entered this region called Zambia. Wouldn't it be thrilling to share Chuma's and Susi's thoughts and emotions as they carried David Livingstone's body to the coast. But alas, it is all lost to us, they never wrote a word.") Of course, it would be possible "to codify our languages and actively update them to suit and match the 21st century, but do we need to? . . . I feel there is very little profit in that. . . . For me, the Z's written history started in 1964 [Zambia's independence] and I find no shame in that." He continued:

> Everybody has to start from somewhere. The British, oops, I'm sorry—fate has dealt us a hand and we must play it as best we can. We must embrace English. We much take it as our own and celebrate it. We should write songs, movies, and books; telling our stories in this beautiful language. In five hundred years the five year olds in this country won't know the difference and they won't care. I think it is our duty to give them art and works that make them proud to be Zambian so that they do not suffer problems of self-doubt. We should make English such a part of their lives, like *nshima* made from maize meal is for most Zambians today, and yet it was introduced to Africa by the Portuguese in the 16th century from Brazil. Hell, if you like, we can even change the name—how does Zanglish sound to you?[20]

What was true of language was even truer of national identity and national culture. Zambia was understood to suffer from a lack that could be remedied not by turning to the ancient African past, but by inventing something new in the present. If Zambia lacked a culture, as Chisala had said, then it was necessary to invent one.

With characteristic boldness and irreverence, Tembo took up the challenge. Zambia, he concluded, needed patriotism. But there was a small problem. "After some intelligent scrutiny, I have come to the conclusion that Zambians have nothing to be patriotic about," he said. Zambia

> is a collection of different peoples forced by the circumstance of British colonization to reside within the same borders (at this point you are yawning, because you have heard this so many times). For reasons too extended to enter into now, this collection of people has developed into a nation of "peaceful" citizens. This had led some people into making the erroneous assumption that Zambians are united. I think not, I say that Zambians are indifferent. . . . This is why our doctors continue to trek to Canada and Australia, this is why our teachers are flocking to Botswana, this is why the students we send abroad aspire to stay there, this is why some politicians are willing to ask the international community to impose sanctions on Zambia at the expense of the people for the sake of their own interests. We need something apart from money to entice the doctors and teachers to stay, we need something aside from threats of legal action to draw our students back home, we need some force other than the armed forces to make politicians consider first the country and then themselves.

The patriotism for Zambia that was needed, Tembo insisted, would not simply come about with the passage of time. "Time, my dear friends, is neutral. . . . A car driven in the direction of Livingstone will not magically arrive in Mbala." Since it is people who make things happen, not time, Zambian patriotism would have to be actively made, not simply awaited. But "since the 'Z' [Zambia] is a falsely created man-made nation, we need to falsely create a passion for the 'Z'. We need to falsely create a nation of patriots."[21]

How could such a "false creation" proceed? Tembo had no shortage of ideas for the "invention of tradition." (One is tempted to suppose that he had read Hobsbawm's famous essay [Hobsbawm 1983]). Zambian children ("like the Americans"), he suggested, should pledge allegiance to the Zambian flag and be educated in democratic civics. Though this might smack of indoctrination, children would enjoy "a fun official induction ceremony into this lovely club Zambia." They should also write essays and be given badges that read, "You want to be cool? Join the 'Z.'"

Zambia also badly needed national customs and traditions that could draw its people together. "I am aware," Tembo admitted, "that typically nations develop traditions slowly over years, but Zambia should reduce that time and invent some public holiday and a custom to go with it. We should invent some outrageous colourful costume and call it the national Zambian costume." The costume could be combined with songs and dances or even a ceremony centered on selling and eating fish ("national fish day"). Tembo's other ideas involved the promotion of national sports teams, the creation of "catchy" patriotic songs (not "serious folk music of the socialist and communist tradition" but "songs in the tradition of 'New York, New York' and 'California, Here I Come'"). National culture had to become youthful, contemporary, and fun so that Zambians would develop a loyalty and patriotism in their youth that might last all their lives—even to the time when they had to choose whether to "trek to Canada and Australia" or "flock to Botswana."[22]

Like Mzyece's discussions of "Zanglish," Tembo's proposals for an invented national culture were offered with wry self-consciousness and rich postmodern irony, but they were no less serious for all that. "A ridiculously funny idea," as he wrote of "national fish day," and yet "many a serious thing can be achieved in jest." At issue was nothing less than a viable national identity for the new Zambia, an identity that might serve as a source of pride and patriotism for Zambians while also giving the "Z" a recognized place among other nations in the wider world:

> Imagine the international attention this [the proposed national costume and national day] would attract, if we sold it abroad as an invented idea which worked. Every year there would be some camera crew or two filming the festivities. Slowly we could carve out an identity in the world. If one said that one was from Zambia, instead of the common, "Where's that, mate?" one could imagine a reply

like "Oh, yes, I have heard of Zambia, that's the country where they wear those crazy hats and have those colourful dances."

Does this trivialize the question of national identity and national pride? "Tough," replied Tembo. "Just get writing and send us a movie script, send us a play, send us a book, write us a song." As Chisala insisted, "What Zambia needs right now are architects of culture. We need prophets who will define a lifestyle for us, and craft a road map for our future."[23]

THE HAM EFFECT

Almost from the start, *Chrysalis*'s future-oriented discussion about national culture was rudely interrupted by "question marks" from the past. Tembo had asked rhetorically in the October 1998 issue whether Africans were suffering under the biblical curse that Noah placed on his son, Ham, a curse that supposedly fated Ham's descendants to be enslaved.[24] His vigorous conclusion was that the situation of Africans had nothing to do with a biblical curse, that slavery had been "made possible by circumstances," and that to dwell on such aspects of history was to risk "unwittingly instilling an inferiority complex in our children—nothing is more effective in killing ambition and drive than self-doubt." Instead, Tembo argued (in keeping with the *Chrysalis* program) that African problems were the result of "the continued influence of the pre-information age financial and political operators" and of an "old African Chief culture mentality" that fostered corruption. These old mentalities were being thrown off, he suggested, by a new, information-age generation for whom "the interests of the chief before the people is not a part of their culture."

But Tembo's article was followed by an outrageous reply by Chileshe Phiri.[25] Phiri turned Tembo's rhetorical interrogation of the biblical curse of Ham on its head and made the explosively simple argument that blacks were indeed biblically cursed and that their problems derived from their consequent inferiority to whites. "The real truth," he wrote, "is that Zambians, and indeed all black people, just seem to have a problem with, well, everything." Black people all over the world, he argued, were less hygienic than whites. They had corrupt politics because their politicians were motivated only by personal gain, while the people "don't believe in anything" and have "an instantistic culture—give me what's mine now, I'll do anything to get it."

The solution, Phiri went on, was "for a black person to become white inside while staying black outside (coconut)." If the readers and writers of *Chrysalis* seemed (in their hygiene, honesty, perseverance, or inventive intelligence) to contradict Phiri's notion of blacks as cursed, he assured them that it was "because you are white—inside. . . . You are sitting there reading this article on the Internet most probably in a white country or in a white company in Zambia. Or you may have been taught by white teachers during your formative years. They are the ones who built the white conscience into you." What is more, Phiri claimed, the same was true of those other blacks outside Zambia who were most often admired for their achievements. Oprah Winfrey had predominantly white audiences; Cuba Gooding Jr. and Quincy Jones had white wives; Michael Jackson had literally become white. Being a "coconut" in this way was not something to be ashamed of. It was the only way forward:

> For some reason, I think we have this curse on us which has affected us in a very negative way and made us fail to invent, innovate, organise, or clean up our world. God seems to have given the white people these gifts and he has opened the way for us by showing us how to become coconuts. Yeah, all of us need to make the English language our very own and teach it to our kids [as argued by Tembo]. And more than that, we have to read white books, see white movies, listen to white music, and so on until we embrace the whiteness and be relieved of our natural curse.

From this point of view, the lack of a distinctive Zambian culture that other writers had identified as a problem was actually a perverse sort of advantage. Zambians, Phiri maintained, spoke a more proper ("white") form of English than other Africans—"Have you ever heard a Zimbabwean say 'sacks' or a Nigerian say, well, anything?" Indeed, due to their lack of culture, Zambians were closer than any other Africans to "becoming white—the key to full liberation, development, and prosperity. . . . You'll see it very soon," Phiri promised, "as younger coconuts, the calibre of the faithful contributors to this provocative magazine and their intelligent readership, become fully-positioned leaders in the nation."

An extremely vigorous debate about Phiri's "Ham Defect" argument ensued in the pages of *Chrysalis*, opening a wide-ranging discussion about the perceived failings and inadequacies of Zambian culture. Over a period of months, this debate came to dominate both the magazine articles and the guestbook commentary. In the process, the positive tone of the "Chrysalis Generation" gradually changed to one of anguished self-examination concerning the supposed inferiority of Zambian/African culture and personality (cf. Ferguson 1997; Simpson 2003).

To judge by the reactions it provoked, Phiri's inflammatory article seemed not simply to offend, but to open a wound. His unvarnished and publicly expressed assertion of Zambian inferiority clearly insulted and injured the pride of many readers. Some were especially upset that such opinions should be aired in a forum that might be seen by foreigners. ("Please Mr. Chileshe Phiri, stop feeding the white people with the stuff they want to hear from black people," read one guestbook entry.[26]) A number of readers, as one might expect, responded by simply condemning Phiri's "mentally colonized" attitude and "slave mentality" and by reviewing the achievements of black people and the historical and political explanations for black subordination.

Interestingly, however, the more straightforward rejections of Phiri's views came from the handful of non-Zambians who participated in the *Chrysalis* discussion (one African American, a Cuban Bahamian, a white American). Many black Zambian readers, in contrast, were in at least partial agreement with Phiri that Zambia was "backward" and that there was indeed something wrong that lay deep in the national character of Zambians. As for Phiri's characterization of the *Chrysalis* writers as "coconuts," the reactions included not only the predictable angry denials, but also moments of self-recognition. As one letter writer put it:

> I seem to know or recognise the names of just about everybody who contributes, edits or writes this magazine. They all went to:

1. Mine Trust Schools
2. Convent Schools
3. Mpelembe Secondary School
4. Hillcrest Secondary School
5. UNZA

In other words, they are all chongololos [a derogatory term for black Zambians who try to "act white"].[27] Some seem to have violently reacted against their "Africanness" (the little they had left), others seem to have also reacted to the other extreme. The rest, well like me they love to carry on the argument. One chap even laughs at his own language—Zanglish. (I understand Mjumo your mum taught me English for three years about 17 years ago. She hated Zanglish! She probably gives him hell over that imaginative and thought-provoking piece of work). The whole works brings back memories. Trust school, Mpelembe and UNZA. I suppose we according to one author are the quintessential "coconuts."[28]

Another article, strongly critical of Phiri, still acknowledged a certain unpleasant truth in his "coconut" charge:

How many of us take being called "Umusungu" [white person] as a compliment? And how many of our parents boasted of their acquaintance with white people? Remember how proudly they introduced you to John? Oh, and the fact that most priests used to be white did not help.[29]

But the replies to Phiri also marshaled strong and angry counterarguments to Phiri's claims of black inferiority. On the matter of hygiene, of which Phiri had made much, one *Chrysalis* author wrote the following effective rebuttal:

I spent the better part of five years in England studying at the University of Manchester from 1993 and I found that there is nothing inherently great or good about white people or whiteness itself. The concept that blacks are dirty people and whites are clean is a fallacy because I saw white people day in and day out spitting on pavements, spraying graffiti onto walls and also throwing litter all over the place. I came across white people who had obviously not bathed in a long time and I discovered that we Zambians (on average) actually bathe more than white people. In my 22 years in Zambia, I have seldom met a normal person who stunk as much as some of the white folks I came across.

In fact, it was "rules of cleanliness," which varied by region, nation, and level of historical development, that accounted for hygiene, and not race (or else, "Why is Finland cleaner than England [when] both countries are full of whites?").[30] Nor was an "instantistic" orientation distinctively Zambian, the writer continued:

> I spent ten weeks in Ocean City, Maryland in USA in the summer of 1995, working in a fast-food restaurant called "Wendy's". Believe me, there is no country greater than the Americans at "instantistic culture". They are the most impatient people on earth but they just target their impatience on things that matter. That is the lesson we have to learn. We don't need to abandon our 'instantistic culture'. We just need to refine it.[31]

Other writers sharply brought into question Phiri's alignment of the white race with civilization and virtue. Chisala, for instance, responded to the suggestion that he needed to "get some white inside" him by reflecting, "Perhaps you're right, Chileshe. . . . White is apparently more developed, after all." He continued,

> But I'll tell you what else white is. White is killing 6 million Jews in a holocaust just because you hate them. . . . White is telling a nation that you want to help them to prosper but refuse to cancel the huge debt they owe you even when you know it's the thing that's killing them; white is demanding that poor countries should open up their markets completely while you continue to protect your own industries against them; white is sentencing a person to death for writing a book against your religious leader. Does that sound like civilisation? . . . White is two kids killing fourteen people in Colorado before killing themselves, for no apparent reason; white is a religious leader taking thousands of followers to a retreat to make them poison themselves to death. These are all whites.
>
> Or were you talking about those whites with a higher intelligence than these? Were you talking about those who have grown up in "white ways"? The elite whites? Okay. White is making a computer virus for no gain but to simply destroy the computers of many

people who receive your (Melissa) mail. That's productive, huh? Or are these not high enough in the white community to represent the white community? Okay, then we'll go to the highest white in the white community in the world: White is having someone kiss you with their mouth, but not on your mouth, as you make an important telephone call to a Senator in your Oval Office![32] Is that what I should become to be "more civilised"?

No, you mean "white thinking," right? White ideas are obviously always better than black ideas. Here's a small list of white ideas: Fascism, Nazism, Anti-Semitism, ethnic cleansing, Apartheid, and of course, Structural Adjustment Program. No, you mean white behaviour, of course; not white ideas, necessarily. Let's see. White behaviour? The Devil's [Hell's] Angels, the Mafia, English soccer hooligans.[33]

Indeed, Jonathan Sikombe suggested that Phiri was able to idealize whites only because he had not had enough contact with them. Until people like Phiri "face an outright racist, they do not realize that actually whites can be obtuse, dull and backward. Every person has his or her failings and these can be promulgated by an inferior past. We are all imperfect."[34]

The next issue of *Chrysalis* carried a spirited response from Phiri. He acknowledged that black Africans had as much innate intelligence as anyone else but insisted that, even if the historical notables mentioned by some readers such as the Zulu King Shaka, were indeed geniuses, they still failed to bring about "any notable developments in the world" ("Oh, the assegai! I forgot!"). As for contemporary Africans of high achievement such as the Nigerian computer scientist Philip Emeagwali, cited by one writer, Phiri argued that however great Emeagwali's intelligence, "he didn't invent anything while he was in Nigeria. He first went to America, to a white American university and after associating with white people, his intelligence was translated into something useful to society." Knowledge was indeed the key, but whose knowledge? "Not the knowledge of the Bemba or Ngoni traditions and sayings. No! Not that! We must know the white knowledge," he said.

Imagine for a moment that you didn't know any English. You only knew Bemba. No French, no German, just Bemba. Would it be possible for you to become a billionaire? Yes? Did you say yes? You're joking, right? You can't be a billionaire in Bemba! I promise you. You need the English language or some other white language.[35]

The Ham defect, in Phiri's revised formulation, was neither inevitable nor eternal; by pursuing a strategy of emulating white culture as closely as possible, the black man could re-inherit the blessing which Ham originally possessed. "[T]his blessing is higher than anything he can imagine. But the route to our inheritance looks humiliating: it's simply to copy the way of the whites. A man must go down before he goes up."[36]

What emerged in the aftermath of the "Ham Defect" debate was in fact a kind of consensus that qualified Phiri's claims without rejecting them altogether. The suggestion of innate black inferiority that the original "Ham" thesis had seemed to imply was roundly rejected by all. But in its place emerged a widely agreed acceptance of cultural inferiority—a culturalization of the "Ham Defect" (cf. Simpson 2003). In the storm of reaction that followed Phiri's article, it was generally accepted by all commentators that, as Michael Chishala put it, "Black people have failed so far to attain unto the standard of their white counterparts." This was not a matter of any essential or inborn inferiority, but a combination of cultural and circumstantial factors. In Chishala's formulation, these were: (1) a lack of self-esteem; (2) a lack of knowledge or information, and consequently a traditionalistic or backward outlook; and (3) a failure to think in bold and inventive ways.[37] This alternative diagnosis was consistent with the general *Chrysalis* program. Zambian backwardness was real and had to be frankly acknowledged, and a failure of culture was at its root. This failure could be addressed not simply through the imitation of whites, but through the development of national pride and the appropriate application of modern information technology and entrepreneurial attitudes. But the question of "copying" continued to haunt the pages of *Chrysalis*.

Phiri had urged the "coconut" strategy and been rebuked for it. But
other authors, too, repeatedly asserted the inadequacy of Zambian
culture and pointed to the West as a counterexample. Chishala, for
instance, one of the chief critics of the "Ham Defect" thesis, insisted
that it was necessary for Zambia not only to develop its culture,
but specifically to "learn from America," which was so wealthy because it has "a culture that believes in people and their contribu-
tions [and] handsomely rewards individual effort." Thus, it would
be necessary "to foster a culture in Zambians similar to that in
America (as far as making it big is concerned)."[38] Chisala, another
of the sharpest critics of Phiri, also took the United States as an explicit model for the culture he sought to create in Zambia. It was
the "founding fathers" in the United States who had created a culture—even a "cult"—based on deeply held values such as hard work
and freedom. Every successful economy, Chisala insisted, "started
as a cult and still exists as one." For Zambia to develop such a "cult,"
it would, like America, need to have "fathers" who could "reengineer our character and restructure our dreams, so that we may begin
to possess a violent and aggressive faith and a fervent confidence in
our identity."[39]

But if it was generally agreed that in certain respects Zambia
needed to emulate rich Western nations like the United States, a key
question remained unresolved: At what point did emulation become excessive, unnecessary, counterproductive, or even destructive of national pride and valuable traditions? Was it possible for
Zambia to copy only some parts of Western culture? If so, which
ones? And if the future lay in copying, what remained that was distinctive and valuable in things Zambian?

Blind emulation, the *Chrysalis* on-line community seemed to
agree, was not desirable. Zambia had become "a country of the
copy-cat culture," one guestbook commentator complained, and
needed a more positive self-image.[40] Another agreed: Zambians
"should pride ourselves for who we are and not always trying to
mimic others."[41] What is more, the West had negative as well as
positive features. The United States might be rich, one reader ar-

gued, but there "everybody has a risk of getting cancer (it's in the air or food due to high technology)"; Zambia might do better to do without the concrete and skyscrapers and "develop in our own Zambian way."[42] Another suggested that America's "civilization" was really a "Babylon" of "sin," which would soon fall. As for the idea that economic development was to be achieved simply by "following the path of the West," Tembo provided a devastating rebuttal:

> If the UN and the international community could turn a blind eye for about 50 years and allow us to make use of the now internationally illegal press gangs, child labour, a couple of thousands of refugees from the Democratic Republic of Congo as slaves to build our roads and bridges, clean our cities, plough our fields till their backs break and fingers bleed, then we too would develop just like Europe and the US. Why buy expensive tractors, bulldozers, and combine harvesters when we can use slaves? . . . We want to make a little money, why heck, let's invade Botswana and plunder their diamonds and sell 'em. What are they, a population of about 1.5 million? Gee, we could take them easily. When the Europeans plundered Africa they came armed with machine guns and rifles and they took us easily. . . . Maybe we should study history and copy what the Europeans and Americans did to make their regions strong.[43]

Anxieties about the possible dangers of copying Western culture congealed especially around morality and sexuality. If it was on issues of economic prosperity that the argument for following the American path was strongest, it was with respect to questions of sex and morals that the dangers of "copying" appeared most evident. As Chishala put it, there might be much to learn from "white society," but one could not ignore "the obvious fact that whites are also very sexually tolerant and gays, lesbians and the like are free to do anything, not to mention rampant pornography. . . . They have abandoned God in their lives and are heading for a disaster" (Cf. Simpson 2003).[44]

The issue of homosexuality became a special flash point, leading to a vigorous debate, especially in the pages of the guestbook. Damien Habantu started the discussion off with an article in his lifestyle column advocating tolerance. If a man doesn't like women, he argued, "why force the poor guy?" Likewise, if some women preferred women, who could blame them (especially since "a considerable number of Zambian men . . . think monogamy is some type of tree"). If homosexuality is so unnatural, "well then why does it happen?" Live and let live, argued Habantu. "If a man does not interfere with you and yours and he does not make a public nuisance of himself, then let him be."[45]

Habantu's simple plea for tolerance immediately provoked angry objections, mostly in the guestbook commentary. For the most part, the hostility to homosexuality drew on familiar conservative and antimodernist arguments commonly advanced in many other countries. Angry readers invoked the norms of Christianity, "our African traditions," or simply "normality."[46] A number of writers explicitly saw homosexuality (and the suggested tolerance of it) as a consequence of inappropriate "copying" of "the West" or "America," and several were vehemently and even violently homophobic.[47] As one writer insisted, "The developed world such as the United States have their good economy to be proud but for us all we have is our 'rich culture' to be proud of. . . . We don't have to copy all the stupid things that happen in the Western World." Therefore, according to this writer, "the homosexual people and anybody who says anything to encourage them should have his/her leg chopped off."[48]

For the liberals in the debate (who seem to have been about as numerous as the anti-homosexuality writers), the extreme homophobia on display in the guestbook was an embarrassing sign of Zambian backwardness. The debate, as one such commentator put it, was about "whether Zambia joins the family of civilized nations or sticks to primitive values only respected in such non-normal nations as Iran and Afghanistan."[49] Another added: "On the issue of gays, let us follow the trends in the civilised world. (I am not gay, but civilization encourages me to appreciate diversity in orgasmic priorities)."[50]

Homophobes were reprimanded for keeping Africa backward ("You are the kind of backward thinking person that is keeping Africa behind the rest of the world"[51]) and for embarrassing Zambia in the eyes of the "civilized" world.[52] Tolerance, like democracy, was a metonym of membership in the modern world.

Several writers who opposed any tolerance for homosexuality seemed to accept that their own position was in some sense "backward," even as they cast doubt on the morality of being "modern" in this domain. As one of the fiercest opponents of homosexuality put in a guestbook commentary:

> Homosexuality is still a luxury Zambia and Africa cannot afford it right now, maybe in 155 years or so. Or just say as soon as All Africans stop living in round grass and mud houses and every one has access to electricity . . . then John can marry Peter and also Susan can go and stay with Mary. And the good thing is that by then Susan will be able to have her womb and ovaries transplanted into Peter's ass . . . you know just so we do not die out as black people in Africa.[53]

Other writers emphasized that, given Zambia's problems, it was too early to be talking about questions of sexuality. "You people have to be sensible when you talk about what things Africa has to do in order to be with the rest of the world," argued one commentator. "We have way too many problems to resolve than to let this be an issue."[54] Poor countries, the argument seemed to be, were not "ready" for the "luxury" of sexual modernity.

The passionate debate on homosexuality slowly died out over the months that followed. Yet the lingering issue of the attractions and dangers of "copying" continued to hover over the magazine's discussions. Indeed, the debate over the question of "copying whites," together with the associated controversy over homosexuality, ended up taking up the lion's share of *Chrysalis*'s pages—both in the magazine proper and (even more so) in the guestbook commentary. Why is it that a magazine devoted to crafting a new national identity for a new Zambia should have become overwhelmed with these two issues? What is the relation between a project of national-cultural reinvention and the twin specters of the coconut and the homosexual?

The idea of achieving the fruits of development through straightforward cultural mimicry—Phiri's suggested "coconut" strategy—was explosive precisely because it threatened to short-circuit the whole project of national development. The ingenious attempts of the *Chrysalis* authors to devise a new version of Zambianness for the information age were most profoundly challenged, in the

Chrysalis debates, not by any alternative version of national culture, but by the scandalous idea that a national culture was in fact unnecessary. What was the use of speaking Bemba if one was aiming to become a billionaire or to found a Zambian Yahoo.com? Why, by the same token, would one need a national costume, a song, or pride in one's history if the key to success in the global economy was simply mastery of "white" culture? The "chrysalis" of development threatened, in such lines of thinking, to be exposed as merely a "coconut," whose hidden interior contained not a glorious new national character but only a "copy-cat" cultural whiteness.

If the anxiety about "copying" was linked to the danger of such a short-circuiting of the project of national development, it was also bound up with powerful worries over sexuality. For many *Chrysalis* contributors, homosexuality was not simply a social evil but proof of the dangers to the nation of inappropriate "copying" of the West. Several authors specifically identified homosexuality not only as unnatural, but also as a threat to biological and social reproduction. One, as we have seen, even associated it with a concern that "we do not die out as black people in Africa." How are we to understand both the intensity of the concern with homosexuality and its link to concerns over copying, on the one hand, and the reproduction and even survival of a nation, a race, or a continent, on the other?

Understood literally, the idea that a "copied" homosexuality might place either heterosexuality or biological reproduction at risk may seem hard to fathom in a country where both compulsory heterosexuality and very high birthrates seem firmly established. But it may be that the concern with sexuality should be understood in a broader and less literal context, where what is endangered is less biological reproduction than the cultural and social sort. It is impossible to draw firm conclusions based on the limited material available in the *Chrysalis* archive. But if national development (a natural, quasi-biological process of growth and maturation epitomized in the "chrysalis" image) could be short-circuited by "copying"—if the coconut could threaten to make the chrysalis obsolete—then a concern over the reproduction and continuity of "black people in Africa" might be less mysterious. For in a world of excessive and inappropriate "copying," national and cultural reproduction—as well as development—might well appear at risk. What would be the future of "Zambianness" or "Africanness" in a world that seemed to have no use for it?

The years 1998 and 1999 were a time of general disillusionment in Zambia. *Chrysalis* was an attempt to rekindle the sense of hope and high purpose that many had shared at the time of the change of government in 1991. But instead of the long-promised turnaround in the economy that many had expected, the final years of the 1990s brought only a lengthening parade of economic bad news. The pages of *Chrysalis* registered these developments, and the magazine's writers sought to explain and interpret them.

The core MMD policy of privatization proceeded very slowly though the 1990s and produced not a miraculous turnaround in the economy, but a host of major problems and failures. Throughout the period, the mining industry was in free fall as the stalled sell-off of the major mining divisions led to radically slowed production while world copper prices moved mostly downward. Copper output dropped by more than 50 percent from 1991 to 1998 (IMF 1999: table 21), and operations were hampered by what is politely referred to as "asset stripping." The result was that, as the mines sat on the auction block, their value dropped with each passing year. What is more, one large mining division that had been privatized early on, Luanshya, encountered a series of crippling problems. The private Roan Antelope Mining Corporation of Zambia, which took over the Luanshya operations, had been acquired by an Indian-based mining multinational in 1997. But the private firm, meant to be the savior of the Zambian copper industry, was obliged to file for bankruptcy in November 2000 after breaking its promises to retain its workforce and reducing the town of Luanshya to what some called a "ghost town."[55]

Many other industries were also in sharp decline, due to the collapse of state-owned industries and the removal of protective tariffs (see Hansen 2000 on textiles and clothing, for instance). Indeed, manufacturing in general "largely failed to withstand competing imports when the economy was opened up in the mid 1990s," according to a recent Zambian government report (Zambia 2000: 2). Manufacturing employment dropped from 75,400 in 1991 to 43,320 in 1998; mining employment in the same period declined from 64,88 to 39,434 (IMF 1999: table 8). The new industries that were supposed to take up the slack did not materialize, and total paid employment dropped by some 15 percent during the period, while hundreds of thousands of new job seekers in an expanding population were entering the labor market. Even maize marketing, whose great success in 1995–96 had helped give the national-account figures their supposed "turnaround" bump in 1997, was now in decline—against the 668,000 tons marketed in 1995–96, the next two years showed very low figures of just 315,000 and 182,000 tons (IMF 1999: 8).

This relentless procession of economic bad news was duly observed in the pages of *Chrysalis*. The optimism of the opening issues was soon clouded by articles and commentaries that questioned the Chiluba government's policies and cast doubt on the idea that Zambia was on the verge of an economic revival. Instead, Zambia seemed to be, as one guestbook writer put it, "in a state . . . of perpetual doom."[56] Another wrote, "All that I read about seems to be pointing to a deteriorating society; the economy is bad, people are hungry . . . [there are] farmers who are now competing with imported goods, shop keepers been driven out by Shop-Rite [a foreign supermarket chain], criminals now committing day-light robberies, what is going on?"[57] As another commentator put it:

> People are dying every day from starvation and curable diseases, shortage of drugs in hospitals, corruption, unemployment, slave wages, children are denied the right to education, etc. Let's face it, Zambia is a very poor country and we have to accept it. Chiluba has failed, under his rule Zambia will never develop.[58]

In seeking to explain Zambia's economic woes, *Chrysalis*'s authors readily turned, as we have seen, to questions of national character and national culture and to the need for "the right attitude." As the new neoliberal economic policies continued to fail to produce their expected results, this psychologically based approach to economics came increasingly to be applied not only to the past (the supposed mental limitations of the old "Question Mark Generation" discussed in the first issue), but also to the scenarios imagined for the future.

As the months went by, hopeful imagined futures became harder to locate in the magazine. Talk of a general turnaround driven by new economic policies or a rebounding or expanding economy gradually disappeared. Instead, hopes came to focus on the prospects for a "big break" that might come out of the "right thinking" —some great invention or innovation that might suddenly catapult Zambia out of its "Third World" status and into the big time. Thus, Chisala invoked the founding of Yahoo.com, as discussed earlier, insisting that Zambia was just "one good idea away" from having a huge, world-class Internet company.[59] Chishala cited the starting of Globenet, which earned its founders more than $75 million each in the span of forty-eight hours, as well as such inventions as the paper clip and correction fluid for typing as fortune-making ideas that "anyone" might have come up with.[60] As Chishala insisted, "We just need a couple of Zambians, even one, to become a billionaire or do a hit song in America, and other people will slowly begin to believe that they can also do it."[61] Like the unemployed mineworkers I interviewed in Kitwe in the late 1980s, whose economic plans for the future sometimes entailed an unlikely determination to find a million-dollar gemstone in the ground (Ferguson 1999: 156), the *Chrysalis* authors seemed to be replacing their faith in a general societal progression with hopes for a big break that might emerge out of individual ingenuity and luck.

Equally striking in the later issues of *Chrysalis* was a turn away from the early emphasis on self-reliance and a new acknowledgement of the importance of external and structural explanations for Zambia's predicament. In the first issue of the magazine, Tembo had argued forcefully that it was time to stop blaming "the West," "colonialism," or "history" for Zambia's problems. Those problems, he had insisted (in the style of such leading lights of the "African Renaissance" as Thabo Mbeki and Yoweri Museveni), were instead the fault of African elites, and a shift to accountable government therefore promised a whole new world of economic possibilities. By June–July 1999, however, Tembo had changed his mind, and external conditions reentered the picture. If Asia was developing successfully where Africa was failing, he observed, it was not because Asians were so hardworking, but because of enormous investment and intervention by the West "in the efforts to maintain peace after the second world war and to prevent the spread of communism." Zambia had received no such treatment.

> Consider the recently agreed 43 billion dollar IMF bail out of South Korea—corruption or no corruption, we could do a heck of a lot with 43 billion dollars! Hell, with that sort of financial umbrella, Zambians too would walk many miles in the rain and they could praise us for how hard working we are. . . . Don't kid yourself, brother, sure there is a serious need for upright stand up men in our governments, but one would be a liar if one refuses to admit that we need some serious, no-nonsense cash to enable us to enter and compete favourably in the already existing financial global jungle.[62]

At the same time, an ironic dark humor was gradually taking the place of the earnest idealism of the early issues, as the hopeful proposals for putting the nation on a new footing gave way to increasingly cynical and self-deprecating jokes about a nation of "10 million layabouts who owe the world 700 dollars per head, i.e. 7 billion dollars."[63] The final entry from the magazine's chief editor, Tonto Nkanya, complained about the way that rich nations, with their own problems of discrimination and corruption, feel free to lecture Zambia on such things as "good governance and gender equality." The solution?

> Because we are poor, we don't get the chance to point out that these particular emperors are butt naked. What we need to do is get either economic might or military might. Look at how China gets away with human rights abuses because of its economic muscle. Look at Russia getting admitted to the G8 group of nations because of its nuclear arsenal. As I see it, we have two options: either get rich quick or build a nuclear bomb.
>
> J. Robert Oppenheimer proved that a "nuclear device" can be built by a relatively small group of brilliant men (and women, of course) in a relatively short space of time. Turning round a national economy is a much longer term option.
>
> I vote for a bomb.

Please send your applications to tnkanya@hotmail.com. Only revolutionaries need apply. Ph.D. in nuclear physics desirable.[64]

VERGE OF A METAMORPHOSIS,
PART V: THE DREAM BECOMES NIGHTMARE

By the time *Chrysalis* produced its final issues, its tone and purpose had changed dramatically. Instead of a forum for planning a new Zambian future, it had become a venue for reflecting on what was understood as a continuing national failure. The dream, as Tembo put it, had become a nightmare. "What happened to the 'LIGHT AT THE END OF THE TUNNEL?'" asked a contributor to the guestbook in April 1999. "It does not take one to go to college to see that the light has been turned off. It is terrible to be without the light, even worse still to be in the dark tunnel."[65]

Tembo had inaugurated the magazine with an opening essay called "Verge of a Metamorphosis," in which he traced his vision for the new Zambia that would emerge from the "chrysalis." Additional installments followed until the last contribution, titled "Verge of a Metamorphosis, Part V," appeared in June–July 1999.[66] There, Tembo laid out his understanding of the changing meaning of the "metamorphosis":

> There is a certain silence in the country. Production, for most if not all of the major components of Zambia's economic engines, has dwindled; optimism and morale with it. I could claim to be clever and say that I always did tell you that we were on the verge of a metamorphosis, but I have to confess that for a little while there, I actually believed that we were about to soar and fly to new economic heights. However, reality will not let me disappoint. Reality is helping deliver the promise of a metamorphosis, only now the expectant dream is as we speak turning into a nightmare.

Tembo went on to speculate that the continuing economic crisis might well result in "a little civil war." Because of "massive retrenchments (from recently privatised parastatals) and general country wide unemployment," he wrote, we literally have armies of idle, able bodied young men sitting around doing nothing, and worst of all, starving. And when you have plenty of tinder, all you need is one little match for a fire. One wealthy disgruntled "element" and we could have ourselves a little civil war. Plenty of pawns out there roaming the streets just waiting to be used.

Tembo continued by reflecting on the rapid expansion of urban poverty and unemployment and the new phenomenon of massive numbers of "street kids," now chased from the streets by private security guards armed with batons and Rottweilers. His final appeal, so unlike his initial clarion call for "metamorphosis," was for charity:

> People, wherever you are, forget all the silly posters telling you not to give money to beggars and all of that. Most of these people have very little legal alternatives. Please give as much as you can. Set up many foundations and give. Open soup houses like Al Capone and feed your friends. Remember, by a chance of birth it could have been you. Like Bill Cosby says, "If you can't send you, send money!" If you don't know where to send it, ask us at *Chrysalis*, we will tell you. I must say though, a little 43 billion dollars [a reference to the IMF bailout of South Korea, as discussed earlier] could sure come in handy right now—I wonder if Bill Gates is interested in buying a country?[67]

Along with the general disillusionment over the continuing economic crisis, there were also hints of a more specific disappointment over the failure of the *Chrysalis* elites, with their specific program for democratic accountability and cultural renewal, to make any real headway with the governing Chiluba regime. As its corruption and ineptitude grew, the regime seemed to move further and further from its ideals. As one poignant letter put it:

> The tragedy of it all, was to see your most cherished ideals and values swept away by the rough tough miners boys who really run the country. They won in the end. We ended up on the Internet. (The Kantanshi and Chamboli [mine townships] boys can use the Internet too. They laugh at us I am sure. We complain about them. They go on doing whatever it is they do).

In short, as far as the "Z" is concerned, we are obsolete. Your "mu-zung [white] manners" will get you nowhere. This is the real world. Kermit just got mugged by Tona on Sesame Street.

I have just about given up. Maybe if I wake up from this nightmare I might wake up white.[68]

If there were still some attempts to push the sorts of forward-looking arguments for political and economic reforms that marked the early issues, they were accompanied by an evident lack of con-viction. Brian Mulenga, for instance, published an article titled "Zambia's Development: The Missing Keys" in the final issue of the magazine. The article gave a diagnosis of the technical reasons for the economic crisis ("poor management and a lack of capital") and articulated a list of conventional neoliberal remedies for these. (The "pillars" of Mulenga's plan were: "1. Low taxes; 2. High re-wards for success; 3. Investment in infrastructure; 4. Minimizing the cost of doing business in Zambia; 5. Revival of the agricultural and mining industries; 6. A small and efficient government bureau-cracy; 7. Decentralization of government.") But the careful reader would have contrasted this "can-do" technical plan for economic revival with Mulenga's own guestbook comment of 9 April 1999, which took a very different tone:

I am one person who really wonders whether my country is really worth it. Tell somebody the truth and they lock you up and try you for treason. If Zambia persists in behaving suicidally (i.e. its leader-ship), I think it's best we vote with our feet or plane tickets or what-ever. After all we are the Zambians, if we go away they would not have anyone to misgovern, starve, rob, cheat and lie to. I am really ashamed of being Zambian at this point in our largely forgettable, nay, best forgotten, history. 35 years after independence one wishes one's forefathers had not run away from the slave traders and you had been born American, Surinames, Jamaican, Arab (check out the number of very dark negroid types calling themselves Arab) any-thing but Zambian. We deserve the apology of government we have endured since independence. Our capital city looks like a trash heap. One begins to think we are cursed. The only thing I am proud of in this country is Mosi [the national beer]. But then again going by the evidence it seems we are not capable of organising a booze-up in a brewery. To paraphrase another contributor there are 10 things that embarrass me: 1. Zambia 2. Zambia 3. Zambia 4. Zambia 5. Zambia 6. Zambia 7. Zambia 8. Zambia 9. Zambia 10. Zambia.[69]

Man, this country deserves a break.[70]

Many other commentators in *Chrysalis*'s later months alluded, as Mulenga had when he suggested "voting with our feet," to the emigration of large numbers of Zambia's educated elite middle-class. Indeed, several readers writing from abroad acknowledged their own unwillingness to return to Zambia, and their own sadness and guilt over this fact. But as a number of writers observed, it was not surprising, given the deteriorating conditions of life in Zambia, to see "the cream of our country," as one put it, "leave for green pastures to feed on."[71]

Under the circumstances, it is perhaps not surprising that after the August 1999 issue, *Chrysalis* stopped being updated, and came to an effective end—one more in a long list of abandoned projects in the Zambia of the 1990s. ("Just so Zambian," commented a reader in one of the last entries to the guestbook, "to start something and not follow through."[72]) Internet publishing has continued in Zambia, of course, and some of the *Chrysalis* contributors have continued to be active in it. The political magazine *Zamzine*, for instance, was active for a number of months after *Chrysalis* closed and featured some of the old *Chrysalis* columnists, along with current political news and interviews (though it now also seems to have ceased being updated). The irreverent *DaZed* has picked up some of *Chrysalis*'s old turf in its emphasis on questions of humor, satire, and style. But the remaining Zambian Internet publications are special-purpose publications aimed at particular domains; none has the sense of urgent national purpose and high mission that the early issues of *Chrysalis* displayed.

Among *Chrysalis*'s last words, appropriately, were these, penned by an anonymous contributor described only as "the Zambian" in a short contribution at the end of the final issue:

I always chuckle about the fools at the IMF and World Bank who thought 7 billion dollars would be paid back. I mean, ever lend . . . 20,000 [kwachas] to a Zambian? More like donated 20,000 because you never saw any of it again. To quote Winston Churchill, "never did so many owe so much to so few".

God save Zambia.

P.S. Will the last guy out of this place turn out the lights?[73]

At one level, the collapse of the *Chrysalis* project must be read against a deteriorating economic situation of unusual severity, with specific roots in the particularities of the Zambian context. One certainly should not generalize the Zambian situation to that of Africa as a whole. But if Zambia's situation is extreme, it is not unique, for it is not only in Zambia that the briefly optimistic discourse of African renaissance and renewal has been abandoned or forced into crisis. It is possible that that the sad story of *Chrysalis* might help to shed some light on why that is so. For one of the things that became clear during the magazine's brief span of publication was that the new economic realities that were supposed to set the stage for a new, democratic nationalism in fact served to undermine conviction in the very idea of the nation, both as an economic and social unity and as a cultural source of value.

The most obvious irony of the whole "Renaissance" program was that it promoted "African responsibility" at the same time that neoliberal economic restructuring was making clear the extent to which African economies were in fact at the mercy of overwhelming market forces (e.g., the price of copper) and supra-national institutions (e.g., the IMF), over which those who were being styled as newly "responsible" African elites in fact had little or no control. Under the circumstances, the idea of "African responsibility for African problems" began to sound rather hollow. At the same time, however, the cultural basis of traditional African nationalism (e.g., pride in African traditions, languages, history, etc.) was being undermined with equal effectiveness by the perception that "success" was defined in terms of a global market, and not (as it might have been in the 1960s or 1970s) as the continuing development of a nation. If Zambian success hinged less on the old idea of the development of a national economy than on global market opportunities, new technological innovations, or grabbing a piece of the information-technology pie (e.g., a Zambian Yahoo.com), then ancient traditions and local languages could only appear useless, or worse ("You can't be a billionaire in Bemba! I promise you!"). With the cultural as well as economic center of gravity understood to lie in a "white," non-African elsewhere, and with elite options for exit and mobility higher than ever before (thanks in part to the increasing economic integration of the neoliberal world order), it is hardly surprising (at least in retrospect) that a culturally based movement of national renewal should have been a short-lived one. With the national economy spiraling out of anyone's control, and Zambian identity going through its own, equally dramatic crisis, those who could were turning to individual and familial strategies of economic and spatial mobility (cf. chapter 7).

In the program for an "African Renaissance," neoliberal restructuring had been ideologically linked with elite patriotism and nationalist renewal. But actually existing neoliberalism—at least, in Zambia—has left little place for an elite-led movement of national-cultural metamorphosis and rebirth. Instead, as even the idealistic young authors of *Chrysalis* were forced to acknowledge, the times have become much more conducive to individualized strategies of escape and exit. Under the circumstances, the Zambian "chrysalis," like many another developmentalist project on the continent, never really had much of a chance.

Of Mimicry and Membership

AFRICANS AND THE "NEW WORLD SOCIETY"

In August 1998, two dead boys were found in the landing gear of a plane landing in Brussels. Identity documents showed that the boys were Guineans and that their names were Yaguine Koita and Fodé Tounkara. Koita was 14; Tounkara was 15. With the bodies was found the following letter:[1]

Conakry, 29/7/98
Your Excellencies, members and officials of Europe,[2]

It is a distinctive honor and privilege to write this letter to talk to you about the aim of our trip and our suffering—we the children and the youth of Africa. We put our trust in you.

First of all, we bring you our greetings—the sweetest, the most adorable and respectful greetings of life. To this end, please be our support and help, we the people of Africa. Otherwise whom shall we turn to for help?

We beseech you, come to our rescue. Think of your love for your beautiful continent, your people, your family, above all the love of your children that you love so dearly like life. Moreover, think of the love and kindness of the creator "God", The Almighty who has given you the good experiences, wealth and power to build and organize your continent so well that it has become the most beautiful and admirable of them all [?].[3]

Members and officials of Europe, we are appealing to your gracious-

ness and solidarity to come to our rescue. Please, help us. We are suffer-
ing enormously in Africa. Help us, we have problems and those prob-
lems include the lack of children's rights.

The problems we have are: war, disease, malnutrition, etc. As for
children's rights, in Africa, and especially in Guinea, we have plenty of
schools, but a great lack of education and teaching. Only in the private
schools can one get good education and good teaching, but it requires
quite a lot of money and our parents are poor, they must feed us [?].
Therefore, we do not have sports facilities such as soccer, basketball, ten-
nis [?], etc.

Therefore, we Africans, especially we the African children and
youth, are asking you to set up a great, effective organization for Africa
so that it might make progress.

And if you find that we have sacrificed our lives, it is because we suf-
fer too much in Africa. We need your help to struggle against poverty
and to put an end to war in Africa. Our greatest wish, though, is to
study, and we ask that you help us to study to become like you in Africa.

Finally, we beseech you to forgive us for daring to write such a letter
to you, important people whom we truly respect. Do not forget that it is
to you that we must plead [?] the weakness of our strength in Africa.

Written by two Guinean children,
Yaguine Koita and Fodé Tounkara

There is a specific sort of embarrassment, as well as a stark horror,
in reading this letter. It is the embarrassment of encountering Africans—in this ostensibly postcolonial era—who humbly beg Europeans to come to their aid and who bluntly ask for help in order
"to become like you." It is an embarrassment that many anthropological fieldworkers in Africa encounter today when they are confronted (as they often are) with informants who oppose the anthropologist's well-schooled anticolonial convictions with their own
nostalgic reminiscences of colonial days or passionate appeals for
salvation from Africa's problems via some imagined "return" of
whites who might "help us to become like you" (cf. Piot 1999: 43–
44; Worby 1992).

But our embarrassment also recalls a much older sort of anthropological squirming associated with the old question of how to

analyze the cultural dynamics of African cities. The pioneering urban studies carried out by the anthropologists associated with the Rhodes-Livingstone Institute in Northern Rhodesia, for instance, reported a very strong interest on the part of urban Africans in acquiring both the material goods and the social manners of the European colonizers. As early as 1941, Godfrey Wilson documented in the mining town of Broken Hill a widespread fascination with the acquisition and display of fine, European-style clothes, often in the form of elaborate formal wear, tuxedos, and so on. A key focus of social life were dance clubs, in which couples eagerly competed in ballroom-style dancing, in full evening dress, often before European judges (Wilson 1941). J. Clyde Mitchell and A. L. Epstein would later extend the analysis, linking the emulation of white cultural forms to a status hierarchy within black society in which whites formed a "reference group" against which black status was measured (Mitchell 1956; Mitchell and Epstein 1959). But the Rhodes-Livingstone anthropologists were shocked to find themselves bitterly criticized a few years later by Bernard Magubane (1969, 1971), who found the focus on black imitation of whites to be insulting and suggested that the Rhodes-Livingstone ethnographers were in fact practicing a form of colonial racism. Blacks were not imitating whites, Magubane suggested, but simply doing what they had to do to survive in a repressive colonial regime. If some blacks did eagerly seek to imitate white ways, Magubane argued, they were victims of a pathological colonial psychology, not examples of successful urban cultural "adaptation." Magubane's critique on this point recalled Franz Fanon's by then influential critique of the mentally colonized African whose internalized self-hatred was manifested in a perverse attraction for the culture of the colonial master.

The anthropologists were embarrassed. They certainly did not conceive of themselves as colonial racists. But how were they to respond to objections like Magubane's? By adopting a Fanonist line that would leave them in the awkward role of either condemning or pitying their informants? By restricting their studies to isolated, rural villages and seeking to ignore the problem of the "Westernized African" altogether? How were they to deal with an object of alterity who refuses to be other, and who deliberately aims to spoil his or her own "authenticity"? What does one do with the cultural other who wants "to become like you"?

THE ANTHROPOLOGY OF IMITATION

As Homi Bhabha (1994) has insightfully shown, mimicry was an ambiguous presence in the cultural politics of colonialism. At one level, colonial rulers explicitly aimed to "civilize" their subjects and to mold them in the image of Europeans. Natives who imitated the colonizer were in this sense part of the colonial plan. But colonial imitation always threatened to become excessive and uncontrolled and thereby to unsettle the boundaries and relations of authority between settler and native on which the colonial order depended. The uncanny presence of the "civilized native" destabilized colonial identities and presented a specter that haunted the colonial subject. What happened when natives became *too* "civilized"? Or "half-civilized"? What if their mimicry were really parody? When did respectful imitation give way to "cheeky" back talk? And how could the "not white/not quite" be accommodated within the binary model of power and identity on which colonial institutions and colonial subjectivities alike relied?

But mimicry raised a problem for anthropologists that in some ways was quite different from the problems it raised for the colonial administrator or settler. For one thing, anthropologists generally kept their distance from the "civilizing" project of colonial governments and missionaries, finding their distinctive professional mission in studying (and often "respecting") forms of social and cultural difference that the "civilizers" were necessarily determined to destroy. For another, many anthropologists—at least, in southern Africa—took political stances against the social segregation of the colonial order that colonial officials and settlers were so concerned to maintain and police. Indeed, as we move into the latter part of the century, social anthropologists in southern Africa increasingly occupied an explicitly anti-imperialist and nationalist political position. Under such circumstances, mimicry became scandalous for reasons different from those suggested by Bhabha. For the scandal of Africans who "want to be like the whites"—first for African cultural nationalists, and later for anti-imperialist anthropologists—was not that they blurred or destabilized colonial race categories, but that they threatened, by their very conduct, to confirm the claims of the racist colonizer: that "African" ways were inferior to "European" ones. For the late-twentieth-century anthropologist, the native who wanted to "become like you" had become not menacing, but embarrassing.

The dominant anthropological solution to the embarrassment of African mimicry, I suggest, has been to interpret colonial- and postcolonial-era imitations of Europeans as some combination of parody and appropriation and to insist that such "mimesis" is therefore in fact a gesture of resistance to colonialism. Perhaps the central ethnographic text in the elaboration of this solution has been Jean Rouch's remarkable film *Les maîtres fous*. The film records a ritual of possession that took place in Ghana in 1953, in the context of a cultural movement known as Hauka. The Hauka movement originated in Niger in the late 1920s, when Songhay people began to dance and become possessed by the spirits of French colonial administrators. Their rituals of possession, which later formed the subject of Rouch's film, involved an enacted mimicry of the white officials, along with other signs of possession such as frothing at the mouth, bulging of the eyes, contorted movements, and the breaking of dietary taboos. The movement was suppressed by colonial officials, first in Niger, and later in the British territories like Ghana, to which it spread via Songhay migration.

Anthropological interpretations of the Hauka movement have seen it as an exemplary instance of cultural resistance through parody and appropriation. By mocking Europeans, Hauka members denaturalized and contested their authority; by seizing on white cultural forms and ritually stealing their powers, they appropriated colonial power within the terms of their own cultural system. Against the conservative ideological view of colonialism that would see Africans as being "civilized" by being taught superior European cultural forms, the anthropologists seized on Hauka as an illustration of the defiance and autonomy that may be present even in the very act of imitation.[4]

A similar approach to mimicry has been developed by Jonathan Friedman in relation to the question of certain urban cultural practices in Brazzaville, Congo. Friedman reports (in an account that is substantially derived from Gandoulou 1989) that young men in Brazzaville aggressively sought out "Western" status items, especially fashionable Parisian clothes, and sought to display them competitively in a performance called "La Sape." They also sought to acquire the appearance of Europeans, deploying in this project certain skin-lightening creams. But, Friedman tells us, these men were not in fact doing anything that might be described as "Western." On the contrary: They were working within an indigenous cosmology within which "life force" could be extracted from powerful others by a kind of sympathetic magic. Only the cultural materials here were really drawn from the West—the cultural project (appearances to the contrary) was in fact "entirely African" (Friedman 1990, 1992, 1994, 1995; cf. Ferguson 1999: 280, 290).[5] Again, anthropological otherness is salvaged, as what appears to be a practice of cultural assimilation is reclaimed as an appropriation of Western goods and signs within the terms of an "indigenous" cultural logic. The young men in their Paris fashions superficially appear to be acting Western, but at a deeper level, the cultural analyst unearths a logic that is "authentic" and "entirely African."

As I have noted, such ingenious analyses have helped anthropologists of Africa to contain the otherwise scandalous implications of imitation and to recuperate it as a practice that is both culturally authentic and politically resistant. But I suggest that it would be difficult to fit the letter from the two young men found dead on the plane into this scheme of interpretation. Their gesture is neither a parody of the West nor an attempt to appropriate its goods or "magic" for use in a non-Western cultural world. In their desperate voyage, the boys were attempting a literal, bodily crossing of the deadly gulf dividing the West and Africa—to puncture the very boundary that is upheld in cultural analyses like Friedman's. And whatever they may have meant when they appealed to Europeans to "help us to become like you," they were certainly neither joking nor mocking.

This was also the case, I would suggest, with a great deal of colonial-era mimicry, most of which does not fit the paradigm of *Les maîtres fous* very well at all. There is much that might be said about why urban Africans in the Northern Rhodesia of the late 1930s should have been so interested in ballroom dancing and formal eveningwear. But the Rhodes-Livingstone anthropologists were right about at least one thing: When urban Africans seized so eagerly on European cultural forms, they were neither enacting ancient African tradition nor engaging in a parody of the whites. Rather—as Wilson, at least, recognized—they were asserting rights to the city (cf. Caldeira 2001; Holston 1999), and pressing, by their conduct, claims to the political and social rights of full membership in a wider society.

As Wilson noted in 1941, the acquisition and display of European clothes and other goods was the only domain available in colonial society in which Africans could assert their claims to "a civilized status, comparable to that of the Europeans." Urban Africans did not want to be regarded as "decorative barbarians" but as "civilized men." They wanted, that is, to be full and equal citizens of a modern urban society. If they enthusiastically adopted elaborate forms of European dress and manners, it was to press their claim "to be respected by the Europeans and by one another as civilized, if humble, men, *members of the new world society*" (Wilson 1941: 19–20; emphasis added).

This crucial claim to membership is denied by interpretations like Friedman's, which would suggest that such urban Africans were only performing modernity to appropriate its magic for use within an indigenous cultural order. But the most vital political question raised by practices of colonial emulation did not concern the incorporation of Western symbolic materials into African local cultural systems (though this was surely happening, in various ways and in many settings) but, rather, the place Africans were to occupy in a *global* sociocultural order, their status in a new "world society"—a point that both Wilson and his informants seem to have understood very well.

With that question in mind, let us now return to anthropology's favorite film on colonial mimicry, Rouch's *Les maîtres fous*.

There is no doubt that such a complex and vivid film as *Les maîtres fous* can be interpreted in many different ways. But for many anthropologists it seems that the central meaning of the film, and its great virtue, is that (like that other great anthropological favorite, *Trobriand Cricket*) it takes the scandal of mimicry ("We want to be like you") and reinterprets it as an ironic cultural practice that is both culturally defiant (thus resistant and subversive) and authentically other (since it mimes Western forms only to appropriate them within a fundamentally non-Western cultural order). "They appear to want to become like you," the film seems to tell us, "but (thank goodness) they really don't. In fact, just the opposite!"

Anthropological accounts of the Hauka movement, on which Rouch's film was based, emphasize the way that the imitation by entranced African dancers of European authority figures embodied themes of mockery, parody, laughter, and anticolonial resistance. Far from being a symbolic capitulation or attempt at assimilation, the mimicry of Hauka is interpreted by anthropologists as an active and ingenious form of resistance through which an indigenous culture has sought to resist the culture of the West and to protect its own autonomy. As Paul Stoller concluded his 1984 article: "The European will remain in the Republic of Niger, and so will the Hauka, forever resisting through mockery the influences of foreigners and forever protecting those values which are central to the cultural identity of the Songhay" (Stoller 1984: 185).[6]

Michael Taussig's influential account of Hauka (Taussig 1993) follows Stoller's analysis closely. Once again, celebration of cultural resistance is explicit. The "mimesis" of the Hauka movement, Taussig assures us, was a powerful form of resistance, a veritable subversion of the colonial order. He quotes Stoller's characterization of the movement as "an intolerable affront to French authority" as well as Finn Fugelstad's description of it as "open dissidence" and a "total refusal of the system put in place by the French" (Taussig 1993: 240). Rouch's cinematic reproduction of this practice of subversive mimicry, in Taussig's analysis, was doubly subversive. "The Hauka were jailed in 1935 for mimicking the white man who possessed their very bodies, and Rouch's film was banned in the

162   Of Mimicry and Membership

1950s for mimicking that mimicking" (Taussig 1993: 243). Indeed, Taussig claims, this subversive representation was so threatening to colonial authority that the film was banned by the British government.

Taussig's reflections on the uses of mimesis are undoubtedly illuminating. But his account of the reception of Rouch's film departs in telling ways from other published sources. Taussig follows Rouch in claiming that the film was considered so dangerous that it had to be banned because of the threat it posed to colonial authority—specifically, "the insult to the Queen and her authority" is identified as the cause of the banning.[7] Other published accounts of the banning tell a rather different story. Fritz Kramer's account (Kramer 1993: 137) reads as follows: "The film . . . shocked African students and such anthropologists as Marcel Griaule at its premiere in the Musée de l'Homme; they condemned the film as 'racist' and demanded it be destroyed. The film was banned in the British colonies." According to the film critic Mick Eaton, when the film was shown in Paris in 1954, it was widely criticized. "Black students in the audience accused Rouch of reinforcing stereotypes of 'savagery', and the film was banned throughout Britain's African colonies because of its 'inflammatory' content" (Eaton 1979: 6). Stoller is a great admirer of the film, but his frank account of the controversy (Stoller 1993: 151–53) makes clear that it was strongly praised from the start by white critics but widely condemned and deplored by African scholars, students, and directors, who argued that the film perpetuated "a racist exoticism" (Stoller 1993: 153).

What all of these accounts show is what Taussig's account conspicuously sidesteps: that the film was banned not because it was bravely subversive of the colonial order, but because it was regarded by Africans as racist. Why did African students find the film racist? And what are we to make of the fact that the film that is today the paradigmatic exemplar for anthropological understanding of mimicry was in its time regarded by educated Africans as so deeply offensive that it should be destroyed?

African students said the film represented Africans as savages, who only "aped" European cultural forms for their own "tribal" reasons. What they feared, we may suppose, was that Rouch's representation of the Hauka could, by implication, style *all* African performances of modernity as mere savage aping—superficially modern but in fact in the service of deeper levels of "primitive," "tribal," or magical thinking. As in Wilson's day, educated Africans were very attentive to the dangers of being cast as "decorative savages" whose essential "Africanness" was only superficially covered with the trappings of the civilized.[8] How did a representation such as Rouch's (of "tribal" Africans seeking magical results by play-acting as Europeans) position these Parisian students, whose own claims to membership in a modern world hinged on a real, and not pretended, mastery of modern social and cultural forms? The African students, I would suggest, saw—as Wilson had a generation earlier—that, within the cultural politics of the colonial order, imitation was less about sympathetic magic and accommodating white power within indigenous cultural orders than about claims to membership within modern society and negotiations of the rights proper to such membership.

The point here is not that Rouch's (or Stoller's) interpretation of the Hauka was incorrect or that mimicry does not often involve themes of parody, appropriation, and resistance. Surely it does. Indeed, the chief lesson of recent scholarship on the topic would seem to be that mimesis may trouble cultural and racial boundaries in complex, subtle, and sometimes counterintuitive ways (cf. Bhabha 1994; Schwartz 1996; Siegel 1997). Clearly, mimicry can mean many things. But the determination of some anthropologists to find cultural difference lurking even under what most appears to be "the same" has led them to force-fit practices of apparent imitation or assimilation within a Hauka-like scheme of cultural difference and appropriation. The danger is precisely the one the African students so swiftly identified: By taking the extraordinary figure of the Hauka as a paradigm for understanding African gestures of similitude with "Europeans," we risk misreading (as magical appropriations and resistances by a localized "African" cultural system) practices that are better understood in the context of the politics of membership in the "world society" of which Wilson spoke. The consequences of such a misunderstanding, as I hope to suggest in the next section, are perhaps even more consequential today than they were in the time of Rouch's film.

The topic of cultural mimicry has been deeply bound up with discussions of the social dynamics of the colonial era. But how does an approach to mimicry as "cultural resistance," as a parody or appropriation by the colonized of the colonizer, come to terms with the cultural politics of the postcolonial world? The separate cultural worlds and simple colonial binaries that such interpretations depend on are harder and harder to locate in an age of global cultural flows and transnational organizational forms. What becomes of mimicry in a transnational, postcolonial age?

The most developed answer to this question comes in the final pages of Taussig's book on mimesis and alterity (Taussig 1993). Cultural-reproduction technologies and transnational cultural flows, he writes, have in recent years fundamentally reconfigured the binary that gave form to colonial mimesis. "From the mid-point of the twentieth century with the final dissolution of colonial controls there emerged a sort of reversal of contact, a 'second contact', with the birth of a radically different border between the West and the rest, between civilization and its Others." Today, this border has been "punctured porous by the global market and multinational corporations, together with desperate emigration from the south" (Taussig 1993: 251). Under such circumstances, the border becomes "increasingly unreal, micromental, and elusive" (Taussig 1993: 252). With the global free flow of images, and the new forms of copying unleashed by communications technologies, mimicry is unhitched from its old colonial binary, and a new form of human capacity emerges that is "potentiated by postcoloniality"—that is, "to live subjunctively as neither subject nor object of history but as both, at one and the same time." Thus, "mimetic excess" is set loose upon the world to work its uncanny magic and to undermine the naturalness of all of our social and cultural arrangements (Taussig 1993: 255).

Taussig is surely right that at least some sorts of cultural products and images today travel the globe with unprecedented ease. In this (cultural) sense, North–South borders have indeed become remarkably porous, as contemporary anthropological fieldworkers often note when they arrive at their far-flung destinations only to find informants wearing Hard Rock Cafe T-shirts or asking knowledgeable questions about Michael Jordan. But in other respects, the border that Taussig refers to between the First and Third Worlds is harder to describe as porous or ephemeral. Consider, for instance, labor markets. How is it that, in a world where borders have been "punctured porous," the most poorly paid workers in America earn at least fifty times the hourly wage earned by a comparable worker in Zambia? Or immigration, where the "desperate emigration" to the rich countries that Taussig invokes as evidence of the unreal and phantasmic nature of the border is in fact sharply checked by a host of very real institutional and economic barriers (from border police and passports to the—for most Africans, prohibitive—costs of air travel) that do not appear in his account.

It is perhaps significant here that while Taussig's analysis ends by invoking migrant crossings that "puncture porous" and render "unreal" the borders that guard the First World, my account begins with a *failed* crossing that dramatizes their deadly solidity. The border that the two boys on the plane encountered, and against which they directed their final testament, was anything but "unreal" or "elusive." The accelerated cultural connections and globalized flows of images and goods described by Taussig are indeed important, but they are only part of the story. For what is most striking in the recent history of much of Africa is not the breakdown of boundaries, but a process in which economic decline and political violence have produced new political and economic exclusions that distance Africa from the rest of the world and destroy the sense of connection with, and membership in, an imagined world community that so many Africans experienced during the early years of independence. The combination of an acute awareness of a privileged "first class" world, together with an increasing social and economic disconnection from it, is a contemporary African predicament that I have elsewhere described as "abjection" (Ferguson 1999).

To speak of the political and economic borders of a postcolonial world often characterized by its cultural free flows is to reintroduce the question of institutionalized forms of social and economic *membership* into our discussions of contemporary global modernity. The question of membership was explicit in Wilson's day:

The color bar made the racialized exclusions of the modern social order explicit and obviously political. But in an era of political independence, where explicit racial hierarchies are illegitimate and inequality is naturalized by being culturalized and spatialized, an anthropological insistence on interpreting gestures of similitude in terms of parody and magic has the effect of obscuring the continuing claims of Africans and others to full membership rights in a world society.

A similar danger is introduced by treating the question of modernity in exclusively cultural terms and thus too easily including within an analytical "modernity" people who are quite distinctly *excluded* from the political and economic conditions of life that are normally characterized as "modern." One can well understand the urge to de-provincialize the notions of modernity at work in the variously Eurocentric versions of modernization theory that dominated social theory through most of the late twentieth century. And there is certainly a good deal to be gained by contemplating the "alternative modernities" that may contest dominant Eurocentric cultural practices in the name, not of tradition, but of different configurations of the modern (Appadurai 1996; Hannerz 1996). But what is lost in the overly easy extension of an ideal equality to "modernities" in the plural are the all too real inequalities that leave most Africans today excluded and abjected from the economic and institutional conditions that they themselves regard as modern.

When Charles Piot concludes his insightful recent book by insisting that the marginalized people of Kabre, Togo, are "part of the modern world," for instance, and that their rural villages are "a site . . . of the modern, one that is as privileged as any other" (Piot 1999: 178), we contemporary anthropologists may respectfully nod our heads. Who are we to say that they—in their distinctive mode of engaging the modern world—are any less "modern" than we? Surely Piot is right to historicize local cultural practices that are too often understood as timeless and to show their connection to a modern history of slavery, colonialism, capitalism, and state formation (all of which he does very effectively). Describing African societies as "modern" in this sense is to work against generations of exoticizing and primitivizing constructions of an essential and "traditional" Africa. But to say that people live lives that are structured by a modern capitalist world system or that they inhabit a social landscape shaped by modernist projects does not imply that they enjoy conditions of life that they themselves would recognize as modern. Indeed, if we consider modernity, as many Africans do, not simply as a shared historical present, but as a social status implying certain institutional and economic conditions of life, it becomes immediately evident that the Kabre do *not* inhabit a site that is "as privileged as any other."[9] Where the anthropologist extends the label "modern" to the impoverished African as a gesture of respect and an acknowledgment of coeval temporality, African urbanites who believe their lives will not be "modern" until they have running water and a good hospital may find the gesture an empty one (see also chapter 7).

With such considerations in mind, let us return to the letter with which I began. Let me be clear from the start that I take this letter as an *event*, an occasion for reflection on a broad set of issues, rather than as ethnographic *evidence* in the traditional sense. I will not try to contextualize this letter in a traditional anthropological style by seeking to reconstruct the lives and social backgrounds of the authors and understanding the local circumstances out of which their extraordinary appeal emerged.[10] Such an approach would certainly be possible and no doubt useful in some ways. But surely what is most striking in this letter is precisely its determination to refuse the sort of localization that anthropologists habitually force on their subjects and to speak not for this or that local person in this or that circumstance, but for "Africa" as a whole. "We Africans," the letter's writers say. "We, the African children and youth." Let us read these two young men as they meant to be read: as unknown authors of a message in a bottle, an urgent message (delivered at some cost) whose finders might learn from it something not about the authors, but about the needs of "Africa" and its youth and the responsibilities of the "members and officials of Europe." Let us read this letter, in short, *not* as an ethnographic text, but precisely *as a letter*—a letter that demands not a sociological analysis of its authors but a response.

Read in this spirit, what are we to make of the final plea of these the two young men? What are they asking for? Let us read carefully here. When they speak of wanting "to become like you," they are referring to the overcoming of specific "problems," which they identify as war, sickness, malnutrition, lack of education, lack of sports facilities, and lack of children's rights. The "help" they request is thus a commitment to address a set of specific institutional and economic needs. It is neither cultural nor racial resemblance that they are seeking but help in a "struggle against poverty and war" and, thereby, an institutional and economic convergence with a "well constructed and organized" First World.[11] "We want to study," they say. We want health care. We want well-nourished children. It is in these—quite specific—respects that they seek "to become like you." By phrasing their demand for new political and economic conditions as a wish "to become like you," they simultaneously appeal for what they call "solidarity" and attempt to invoke a principle of responsibility via moral and political connection.[12] Their desperate communicative gesture seeks to create neither magic nor parody, but solidarity.

It is also significant that they address the "members and officials (*membres et responsables*) of Europe" in a language that seems to insist on the responsibilities they understand to go with a higher status. Given the combination of abject pleading and the assertion of responsibility, it is hardly surprising that the two address the "members of Europe" explicitly as children. Not only does this evoke parental responsibility (and with it all the well-worn clichés of colonial paternalism); it also suggests the romanticized, ideal international community often evoked through images of "children" and "the youth of the world" (Malkki 1994, forthcoming). The idea of an international bond through youth might also account for the otherwise anomalous references, in a letter that speaks of such grave matters as war, disease, and malnutrition, to such things as soccer, basketball, and tennis—all conspicuously "international" sports through which even the least-well-off Africans can (if basic facilities are provided) imagine themselves as part of a wider world.[13]

We are now in a position to read this letter alongside another one: an article by an anonymous Zambian journalist published in the July 1999 edition of an Internet magazine in the form of an open "Letter to America."[14] The following is an abridged version:

Dear America,

I know you've heard it many times by now: your policy in dealing with international crises is very selective. Europe is more important than Africa, Bosnia is more important than Rwanda, Kosovo than Sierra Leone. What you have not been told yet is what we, the Africans living in Africa, think about not only your actions, but your motives and the underlying principles of your heart.

Your selectivity reveals four realities about the Western world to us: global racism exists and it determines international policy, capitalism is above compassion, the African debt is a deliberate strategy, and finally, democracy is not practised by its preachers.

Racism, the greatest killer of the human race since time immemorial, is still the strongest force. . . .

The irony of the Kosovo crisis is that it was caused by racism (at the ethnic level) and it was saved by racism (at the international level). NATO has shown that it has a colour, it is not as colourless as it presents itself to the world. It has a face and its face is pigmented: it is white. It has shown that the fact that whites rule America and other NATO countries is a significant fact and it does determine what happens to non-white "nations" in times of crisis. . . .

America and her partners practice a racism/tribalism that is worse than that of Serbians against ethnic Albanians, or Tutsis against Hutus. She does not use guns and machetes, she uses the greatest weapon of mass destruction ever invented: the international credit (debt) system. She wields this weapon against all the people that it hates. And the ones at the top of the list, apparently, are Africans.

America, World Bank, NATO, or whatever name you choose to disguise yourself in, it is clear that you do not care about Africa. If you admit this it will be easier for us. At least Milosevic has admitted his hatred for "the lower class" and Hitler never pretended about his anti-Semitic feelings. These evil men will at least be respected for their honesty. It is better to be killed by a man who calls himself your enemy than by one who pretends to be your friend.

After we finish counting the mass graves caused by Milosevic, let us count the graves caused by the USA and the other super-rich nations of the world. Milosevic will seem like a saint when we count the victims of the latter. The graves caused by the gruesome effects of the debt held against Africa are all around us: children die every day of easily cur-

able diseases simply because there is no money in African nations. It has to go to servicing the debt we owe our masters. . . .

Debt reduction is not enough for Africa. Neither is debt cancellation enough. We must fight for compensation. They are the ones who owe us money. . . .

The amount of money they owe us has to be calculated and all African nations must receive the average amount. They owe us for taking some of the strongest men among us to go and work in their plantations. How much has that affected our productive output up to this day?

They owe us for the unfair dealings they did with our unsuspecting chiefs (a gun for miles of land). They owe us for taking the rich minerals out of our land with no permission and with no tariffs. They owe us for brainwashing us to their stupid religions that taught us that poverty was a way of pleasing God and that there is another world after death where things would be better for us, thus taking from us our will to fight for the things they were stealing from us (after all, we'll find better things in the other world!)

So, should they reduce our debt? Should they cancel our debt? No. There is nothing to reduce or cancel here. We owe them nothing; they owe us big time. They are the ones who should be begging for debt reduction from us. They owe each African nation hundreds of billions of dollars. This is not a joke. I propose to African professors that they should sit down and calculate the exact figure so we could present it to them officially. I estimate they owe Zambia in particular about 600 billion dollars (with interest), but we should calculate the exact figure, to four decimal places. . . .

Finally, the present crisis has revealed that there is no democracy in the developed world, or it means something other than what they tell us. Democracy is when the people rule. When the voices of the majority rule. Well, the earth consists of more people in Third World countries than in developed ones and they have unanimously decided that the debt against them should be cancelled. That should be done immediately if the people rule the world, or is democracy just an American idea, to be practised only within the confines of their borders? And even then, their own people believe that they should cancel our debt and that they should intervene fairly in global issues everywhere. They don't listen to them either. Is that democracy?

But let me not allow these closing sentiments to cloud the real call of my article: we want our money back. We need compensation for what has been stolen from us. If we do not fight for it we will be betraying the people that have died because of it. We will be betraying the African slaves, the freedom fighters, the men, women and children that have died from disease and poverty, and the millions who will die today. It's a debt we can not forgive.

At first glance this letter is as different from the first as it could be. In Fanonist terms, the difference is total. One affirms African pride and mounts an attack on the latter-day oppressor; the other defers and shuffles in a humiliating appeal to a superior. One places the blame for African poverty and suffering squarely on the neo-colonial exploiter; the other praises "Europe" and appeals pathetically for paternalistic neocolonial benevolence. One rouses us in our accustomed anthropological anti-imperialism; the other makes us squirm.

Certainly, the *mood* of the "Letter to America" is almost the opposite of that of the two young men who died on the plane to Brussels—angry rather than beseeching, militant instead of supplicating, proud in preference to humble. Evident, too, is a sharp difference in the idiom in which its demands are couched. While the letter from the Guinean boys suggests a relation with "Europe" that is familial and hierarchical and appeals to the responsibilities of a paternalistically conceived superior, the "Letter to America" is frankly confrontational and almost litigious. Its language is not that of familial responsibility but of tort and reparation.[15]

Yet the appeal to which the "Letter to America" gives voice is in other ways remarkably similar to that in the letter found on the plane. Both are letters self-consciously addressed to "the West,"[16] and both insist on a continuing connection and an ongoing moral responsibility on the part of an imagined set of responsible "members" there who might receive the letters. Both letters seem to say (albeit using very different rhetoric): "Pay attention! Our problems are not ours alone. You have responsibilities here which you must not ignore." Both are responses, in different keys, to a condition of perceived expulsion and abjection from an imagined "world."

For all the militancy of his rhetoric, let us note, the author of the "Letter to America" is not calling in the old nationalist style for kicking out the whites or for foreign corporations to keep their hands off of Africa. Indeed, a central grievance is not the presence of white intervention, but its absence: Why are NATO troops in Kosovo but not in Rwanda? The letter demands neither an end to exploitation nor an expulsion of white settlers; it demands an acknowledgement of a debt. It is a right to be connected, noticed, and attended to that is claimed, not a right to autonomy or independence. And while the letter denounces in the strongest terms the burden imposed on Africa by debt, its solution is not to repudiate the debt or to appeal for its cancellation. It is to recognize its true nature. "Should they cancel our debt? No!" To cancel the debt would be to declare the accounts settled and walk away, but accounts are not settled so easily. "They owe us big time."

In this connection, it is worth noting that the first letter also appeals not for the cancellation of debt, but for the creation of a new level of engagement with Africa. Those who discussed the letter in Europe in the days following its discovery tended to assimilate it to the issue of debt relief; indeed, the letter was cited in this connection by actors as diverse as the radical Jubilee 2000 campaign for Third World debt cancellation and IMF President Michael Camdessus himself (who reportedly read the letter aloud to the IMF and World Bank Assembly on the occasion of announcing the Cologne Initiative for the reduction of debt to the poorest countries).[17] But Koita's and Tounkara's letter makes no mention of debt and does not ask for forgiveness. Instead, it calls for the creation of a "great effective organization" that might allow Africa to "progress" toward the same condition and status as the "members of Europe." In this it is much like the "Letter to America" (which, to my knowledge, IMF officials so far have not ventured to read aloud at any meetings).

With respect to the question of membership, then, the two letters are not so different. Both make implicit claims to the rights of a common membership in a global society (a society in which Zambia and Rwanda should enjoy rights no less than Bosnia or Kosovo). Both refuse the idea of a separate Africa with its own separate problems. In their different ways, both make the same paired claim to global status and recognition that Koita's and Tounkara's expatriated countryman, the cultural critic Manthia Diawara, recently voiced in explaining "our [Africans'] desire to be modernized. . . . [W]e . . . want access to education and material wealth; and we are tired of being ignored by the world" (Diawara 1998: 58).

Both letters also share a widespread contemporary recognition of the limitations of the nation-state as the object of appeal or redress. Neither letter addresses itself to a national government, in an implicit recognition of the global roots of the economic crisis they lament. The Fanonist remedy for the problem of colonial inequality, after all, was national independence, but the authors of these letters, like so many others in Africa today, seem to have lost faith in any redemption at the national level. Instead, they "jump scales" (Smith 1992) and seek to appeal to—or, perhaps, even to conjure into being—a global entity or authority ("Members and Officials of Europe"; "America, World Bank, NATO, or whatever name you choose to disguise yourself in") that might be able to address global inequality directly (cf. Ferguson and Gupta 2002). Their appeals are perhaps motivated by an awareness of emergent "global" institutions and ideologies that address the question of rights, but they go far beyond any such empirical referent to imagine a global authority endowed with both an ability to grant rights and a global sense of responsibility or conscience toward which a moral appeal might be directed.

In invoking, however wishfully, such a supranational moral order, the authors of these letters make a challenging claim: that a meaningful solution to the African crisis requires a recognition of a kind of global, supranational belonging, the sort of moral and political recognition of Africans as "members of the new world society" that Wilson had already anticipated in 1941. Such membership is understood to entail a set of claims to social and economic rights that go far beyond those associated with decolonization and national-level political democracy. The young men who died on the plane are quite specific about what is required: education, health care, peace, food, children's rights. Wanting Europeans "to help us to become like you"—today, as in Wilson's day—is neither a mocking parody nor a pathetically colonized aping, but a haunting claim for equal rights of membership in a spectacularly unequal global society. Like the angry "Letter to America," the gentle last words of these two young men make a moral claim to something like global citizenship. In so doing, they appeal poignantly, desperately, for a "graciousness and solidarity" that are, in the West as presently constituted, chillingly absent.

Decomposing Modernity

HISTORY AND HIERARCHY AFTER

DEVELOPMENT

Africa always seems to come to the question of modernity from without. Generations of Western scholars have regarded Africa as either beyond the pale of the modern (the savage heart of darkness that lurks beyond the edges of the civilized world) or before it (the "primitive," "traditional" place that is always not yet in the time of the up-to-date present). Today, scholars who are critical of the evolutionist timelines and static essentialisms of older moderniza-tion paradigms struggle to redescribe Africa as within the modern. Seeking to de-provincialize the notion of the modern and to sever its automatic connection with the West, they prefer to locate con-temporary African social realities within a broader, pluralized idea of the modern as constituting an "alternative" modernity.[1]

Is the idea of "alternative" or "multiple" modernities a useful one? What is at stake in the assertion that African societies are "less modern" than North American and European ones, and what is accomplished by the contrary claim that they are instead only dif-ferently modern ("alternatively")? What are the implications of the different sorts of answers one might give to the question of Africa's relation to "modernity"?

I raise this issue not to attempt to lay down the law on how to think about modernity, but to foreground an important dimension of the discussion that I think has not received enough attention.

In the course of foregrounding this dimension, I will deliberately ignore or move into the background other important dimensions of the discussion. If the picture sketched here seems exaggerated and one-dimensional, then, it is by design.

It should also be noted that I treat "modernity" not as an analytic term to be defined and applied but as what anthropologists call a "native category"—in this case, a native category shared by an enormously heterogeneous population of natives. As vague and confused as the term undoubtedly is when considered as an analytical tool, it remains the center of a powerful "discourse of identity" (as Mary Louise Pratt [2002] has termed it) and a keyword that anchors a host of discussions in and out of the academy about an emerging global social order.

THE TIME OF MODERNIZATION

Let us begin by going back to the days when people thought they knew what they meant by modernity: the years following World War II, the days of decolonization and "emerging nations," modernization theory and "nation-building." At the end of empire, a story about the emergence of "new nations" via processes of "modernization" or "development" provided a new grid for interpreting and explaining the world's inequalities. As the "backward nations" advanced, in this optic, a "modern" form of life encompassing a whole package of elements—including such things as industrial economy, scientific technology, liberal democratic politics, nuclear families, and secular world views—would become universalized. In the process, poor countries would overcome their poverty, share in the prosperity of the "developed" world, and take their place as equals in a worldwide family of nations.

This vision, so crudely sketched here, amounted to a powerful political and economic charter. With the world understood as a collection of national societies, global inequalities could be read as the result of the fact that some nations were farther along than others on a track to a unitary "modernity." In this way, the narrative of development mapped history against hierarchy, developmental time against political economic status. With the progressive nature of

FIGURE 2. THE TIME OF MODERNIZATION

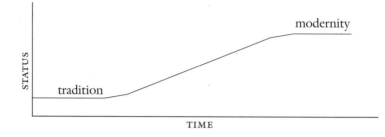

historical time taken for granted, nations could anticipate their inevitable, if gradual, rise in the global order through a natural process of development.

The diagram in figure 2 is painfully simple, but its virtue is to allow us—even to force us—to apprehend this sense of time *analytically* as composed of two dimensions (the two axes, labeled "time" and "status").[2]

If "backward nations" were not modern, in this picture, it was because they were not *yet* modern. Modernity figured as a universal *telos*, even for the most "traditional" of societies. The extent to which societies differed from the modern (and—implicitly or explicitly—Western) ideal neatly indexed their "level of development" toward that ideal.

The effect of this powerful narrative was to transform a *spatialized* global hierarchy into a *temporalized* (putative) historical sequence. Poor countries (and by implication, the poor people who lived in them) were not simply at the bottom, they were at the beginning. One implication of such a scheme, of course, was that postcolonial nations were condemned to live in the "not yet" shadow land of other societies' already realized history, as belated arrivals to a Eurocentrically conceived modernity (Chakrabarty 2000). But another clear implication of the modernization story (one that doubtless accounts for its remarkable appeal to so many citizens of the new nations) was that history—the passage of developmental time —would in the nature of things raise the poor countries up to the level of the rich ones. For those at the bottom of the global hierarchy, the message was clear: Wait, have patience; your turn will come.

This picture is perhaps so familiar as to appear banal. But before my argument can proceed, it is necessary to take this only too familiar narrative and make it strange. To do this, it will help to look briefly into the past, to a time when such a progressive temporalization of human and societal difference was not at all commonsensical.

Nineteenth-century schemes of social evolution, as anthropologists know well, relied on a temporalization of spatial and societal difference that was very close to that found in mid-twentieth-century modernization theory. This was the key device that marked the social evolutionism of our discipline's founding fathers, conventionally recognized as Lewis Henry Morgan in the United States and Edward B. Tylor in Britain. In their speculative schemas of human history, "primitive" societies revealed the earliest history of the human species, while more "advanced" societies showed intermediate stages in a universal human journey from (to use Morgan's categories) the various "statuses" of "savagery" through "barbarism" and finally to "civilization."

However familiar such conceptions may have become, it is worth recalling that in the nineteenth century, they were radically new. As students of the history of anthropology have long observed, the idea of social evolution entailed a radical break, as well as a certain continuity, with older, theological conceptions of a "Great Chain of Being."[3]

The idea that the various creatures of the world formed a great and continuous chain, ranked from highest to lowest, is an idea that Arthur Lovejoy (1936) famously traced from ancient Greek philosophy all the way to the eighteenth-century European philosophers. According to the principle Lovejoy termed "plenitude," a perfectly created world would necessarily contain all possible types of being within it. These various types of being could be ranked—according to their degree of "perfection," as Aristotle would have it, or according to their distance from God, as later Christian theologians would prefer. Man, having been created in God's image, was clearly "higher" in this sense than the "lesser" creatures. But nonhuman creatures themselves were ranked according to the same principle. Thus, a dog or a horse was higher than a rat, which in turn was higher than a frog or a worm, and so on. And, of course,

FIGURE 3. THE GREAT CHAIN OF BEING

God
|
Angels
|
Man
|
Animals
lion
dog
rat
frog
worm
|
Plants
|
Inanimate Matter

for medieval thought, Man was not the only sort of being that was close to God. A variety of types of angels (themselves arranged in a "celestial hierarchy") continued the chain of being upward, providing a continuous series linking the lowest forms of creation to Man and, ultimately, to God (see figure 3).

In keeping with such thinking, the various types and conditions of human being also found their place in a natural hierarchy of being. The religious hierarchy itself, of course, took this form, with church offices ranked (like the angels) from high to low. But so, too, did relations among different religions. Christians were understood to be closer to God than adherents of other religions, while "savage" pagans were clearly understood to inhabit the lowest of human conditions. The different social estates were also understood as distinct cosmological conditions that could be ranked by their distance from God. Thus, the serf's obligations to his master, like the wife's submission to her husband or a child's to its father, was but another form of the legitimate hierarchy that linked Man and God.

As racial thinking emerged in its modern form in eighteenth- and nineteenth-century Europe, the supposed racial "types" of homo sapiens were fitted into a similar scheme. The doctrine of polygenism held that the different "races" were created separately by God and that they held, by nature and divine plan, different ranks in the overall scheme of things. Opponents of such views often held that "inferior" races were not an original creation but, rather, the result of a fall from grace—sometimes understood through the biblical story of Noah's curse on his dark son, Ham. In this alternative view, racial difference was a result of history, but it was a history understood as a fall from an original state of grace. Later variations on this theme notoriously introduced the idea of racial degeneration, a kind of biologicized version of the Fall (see Gould 1996; Mosse 1978).

What is worth underlining in all of this is that such hierarchical rankings of different forms of human and nonhuman being were *not* understood as forming a historical or evolutionary progression. It is all too easy for modern eyes to look at figure 3 and see in it a primitive evolutionary schema. But the conception was actually a very different one. As Lovejoy insists, if God's creation was perfect and complete (and how could it have been otherwise?), then it was also timeless and immutable. The principle of plenitude, he noted, was "inconsistent with any belief in progress, or, indeed, in any sort of significant change in the universe as a whole. The Chain of Being, in so far as its continuity and completeness were affirmed on the customary grounds, was a perfect example of an absolutely rigid and static scheme of things" (Lovejoy 1936: 242).

If some form of temporality did enter into a specifically human history, it was decidedly a nonprogressive one. Whether in the form of the fateful expulsion of Adam and Eve from the Garden of Eden or the degeneration of pagan races, the dynamic was that of the Fall. It is for this reason that the transformation of the Great Chain of Being from a timeless ranking to a progressive temporal sequence (a transformation Lovejoy traces to the eighteenth century) was a true intellectual break. Not only did such a shift make possible the Darwinian idea that new species might emerge, via chance variation and natural selection, from older ones; it also licensed the key social-evolutionist idea that "primitive" people might represent earlier "stages" of a universal human history, and that historical time was, in the nature of things, progressive.

DEVELOPMENT AND ITS AFTERMATH

If the move from a Great Chain of Being to a temporalized evolutionary progression was a sort of epistemic break, the shift from nineteenth-century evolutionism to late-twentieth-century modernization constituted a break of a quite different sort. It entailed not a revolutionary new notion of time but, instead, an insertion of an only too familiar evolutionist temporalization of difference into a quite specific political and historical moment. In the context of decolonization, the development story was no abstract scientific theory. On the contrary, it provided a vital, necessary narrative that could serve both as a charter legitimating and justifying the abrupt withdrawal of the colonial powers and a blueprint for the "nation-building" and "economic-development" programs of the new, post-independence elites (Chatterjee 1986; Cooper 1996, 1997). I will return to this point shortly.

It has been widely observed that developmentalist models have in some measure lost credibility in recent years. Some scholars have interpreted this conjuncture as the advent of a new, hopeful "post-development" era (e.g., Escobar 1995; Rahnema and Bawtree 1997; Sachs 1992). Such formulations should give us pause, not least because such "era" thinking is itself so closely tied to a developmentalist conception of history. But the more fundamental problem with such claims is that they are not quite true—or, at least, they are not true everywhere. The claim that "development" is over would surely sound strange to many people in, say, South Korea or China, who seem to take both "development" and its promises very seriously indeed (and not without reason). A more precise way of posing the problem might be to say that while developmental narratives have hardly disappeared, they have undoubtedly lost much of their credibility for certain people in certain places. This way of putting it underlines a fact that seems quite crucial to grasping the specificity of the present: The loss of credulity toward narratives of social and economic development has occurred not universally, but in specific ways and in specific *places* (i.e., there is a *regional* specificity to this loss of credibility).

Critical social scientists are familiar enough with the intellectual and explanatory failings of developmentalist evolutionary narratives. Modernization theory suggested that the different elements of "modern society" formed a necessary package. The implication was that things like industrial economy and modern transportation and communications necessarily brought with them political democracy; a transition from extended to nuclear families and from communal to individual identities; the rise of bounded, monadic individuals; the secularization of world view; the rise of scientific rationalism and critical reflexivity, etc. Critical ethnographic studies have shown the need to take apart that package. It is now well established that so-called traditional elements can fit together with the various elements of an archetypal modern industrial society without any necessary contradiction. Thus, we have become accustomed to accounts of industrial workers with so-called extended family structures, or transnational business executives who fear witches, or white-collar workers who fly in jet airplanes to visit their matrilineal clan elders. Anthropologists of Africa no longer regard such juxtapositions as entailing any "contradiction" or "lag." Modern Africa is today understood as a place of bricolage and creative invention, where bits and pieces of what used to be called "Western modernity" are picked up, combined with local resources, and put back together (see Comaroff and Comaroff 1993; Donham 1999; Hansen 2000; Meyer and Geschiere 1999; Piot 1999; Werbner and Ranger 1996).

But the developmental narrative is increasingly visible as a failure not only in the domain of academic theory but also in practical economic terms. The basic premise of postwar developmentalism, of course, was socioeconomic convergence. But no one talks about African economic convergence with the First World any more. On the contrary, the economic gap between the richest and the poorest countries — as measured in such standard terms as G D P per capita — is in fact growing rapidly (see Easterly 2001), and most African countries are much farther from economic parity with the First World than they were twenty or thirty years ago. (Indeed, many are worse off even in absolute terms.) This may not be the "End of Development," as some have perhaps overreached in claiming. But the absence of economic convergence in Africa and some other parts of the world is indisputable, even as living standards have risen sharply in some other parts of the former "Third World," sustaining continuing dreams of an ascent to "First World" levels of wealth and security. If "development" is over in some places, it is not in others.

The logical consequence of this, and a crucial one, is a splitting of the world into places that are offered a role in the convergence narrative (e.g. Poland, Turkey, or the handful of neoliberal success stories of East and Southeast Asia, where people still speak unselfconsciously of "transition" and readily imagine an ultimate convergence with the economic standards of the First World) and others that are tracked into that vast, nonconvergent holding tank that Manuel Castells (2000) has called the "fourth world." (Many former Soviet areas seem now to be in the position of anxiously awaiting the news about which tracking they will receive.) Most of Africa is at the far extreme of the nonconvergent, where developmentalist narratives of convergence have the least plausibility.

For this reason, the deployment of the idea of alternative modernities in Africa has a rather different significance than it has had in Asia. East and Southeast Asian versions of alternative modernity have mostly argued for the possibility of a parallel track that is economically analogous to but culturally distinctive from the West. Broadly, the idea has been that it is possible to achieve a First World standard of living while retaining "Asian values," maintaining a more restricted notion of individual rights, or avoiding "the West's" perceived moral vices (see, e.g., Ong 1999). But in Africa, where the idea of economic convergence has lately lost so much plausibility, pluralizing the concept of modernity has been attractive for very different reasons. Academic and nonacademic understandings of African societies and cultures have long misunderstood Africa's difference from the West as anachronistic relic; as somehow not really of the present; as a symptom of backwardness and incomplete development—in short, as "tradition" (cf. Fabian 1983). In the face of this, there is certainly something very appealing, and undoubtedly correct, about emphasizing the modernity of African society and culture and its status as coeval with the West and part and parcel of the modern. In this spirit, it has been very useful for Peter Geschiere (1997), for example, to insist on the "modernity of witchcraft," much as it was helpful for Paul Gilroy (1993) to identify slavery and its aftermath as unfolding within, rather than outside of, the modern.

Yet I want to argue that the alternative-modernity formulation misses what may be most important about the current mutation in the meaning of "modernity" for Africans. To understand why this might be, it will be helpful to return to the old modernization narrative and ask what it is at stake in the current collapse of that narrative.

MODERNITY: FROM *TELOS* TO STATUS

The modernization narrative was a story not just about cultural difference, but also about global hierarchy and historical time, and it combined these three elements in a unique and powerful (if ultimately mistaken) way.

Figure 2 shows the timeline of development and its two dimensions. As time moves forward, status in a global system rises. History and hierarchy are indissolubly bound to each other, and a movement forward in time is also—necessarily, so long as the developmental timeline holds—a movement "upward" on the scales of development and modernity. This story about history and hierarchy encoded a set of factual claims (about the relation between social, cultural, and economic change) that turn out to be mostly wrong. But it also encoded a set of political promises (in the context of decolonization and national independence) that remains quite important.

Anthropologists today are eager to say how modern Africa is. Many ordinary Africans might scratch their heads at such a claim. As they examine the decaying infrastructure, non-functioning institutions, and horrific poverty that surround them, they may be more likely to find their situation deplorably *non*-modern, and to say (as Zambian mineworkers used to sigh to me, ruefully shaking their heads): "This place is not up to date!" Of course, the two claims have different referents. The anthropologists refer to cultural practices and their previously unappreciated historicity;

hence, Africa is modern, not "traditional." But Africans who lament that their life circumstances are not modern enough are not talking about cultural practices. They are speaking instead about what they view as shamefully inadequate socioeconomic conditions and their low global rank in relation to other places. These questions of status and standard of living were squarely addressed by the developmental timeline narratives, if only in the form of a promise: "If you are dissatisfied with your conditions, just wait; your society is moving forward and moving upward." Today, they are more often evaded—by culturally minded anthropology and neoliberal economics alike.

Under the circumstances, it is not surprising that some contemporary Africans seem to feel a sort of nostalgia for the modern. In my own research in Zambia, for instance, mineworkers did not say, "We are modern, but in our own, alternative, way!" or even, "We have never been modern" (as Bruno Latour [1993] would have it). They said, in effect, "We used to be modern—or, at least, well on our way—but now we've been denied that opportunity." Modernity, for them, was not an anticipated future but a dream to be remembered from the past. The real future was almost universally understood as bleak, even apocalyptic (Ferguson 1997, 1999).

Once modernity ceases to be understood as a *telos*, the question of rank is de-developmentalized, and the stark status differentiations of the global social system sit raw and naked, no longer softened by the promises of the "not yet." The developmentalist reassurance that history would, by its nature, transform status and that Third World people needed only to wait and to have patience and their turn would come, ceases to convince.

I thought of this theme of "patience" recently, when the Swedish anthropologist Mats Utas showed me a photograph from his fieldwork on young men in the Liberian civil war. The photograph showed a young man standing at a roadblock, waving an assault rifle in the face of a driver who had been stopped. The young man with the rifle wore a T-shirt, on the back of which were written the following English words: "Patience my ass!"

In a world where developmentalist patience has little to recommend it, the promise of modernization increasingly appears as a broken promise, and the mapped-out pathways leading from the Third World to the First turn out to have been bricked up. The status categories of the contemporary global order, when de-temporalized in this fashion, may even come to resemble the fixed status categories of the pre-independence era, when the color bar segmented the social world into a rich, white, "first-class" sector and the poor, black, "second-class" world of the "natives."

To be sure, there are those who manage to live a "first-class" life even in the poorest countries, enjoying fully "modern" standards of living even in the midst of general deprivation. And unlike in colonial times, these lucky few today include not only white expatriates, but also the considerable numbers of local elites who have found great wealth, and not only poverty, in the wide open spaces of neoliberal Africa. Yet the fact remains that the new rich of today do not, for the most part, seem to be understood as early examples of a soon-to-be generalized societal destination (as the new elites of the 1960s often were). On the contrary, today's success stories are more likely to be seen as proving the power not of education and developmental uplift, but of luck, ruthlessness, or even criminality (on new "figures of success" in contemporary Africa, see Banégas and Warnier 2001). If they enjoy, as few of their compatriots can, a "modern" way of life, it is not because they are farther along, but because they are on top.

Modernity in this historically specific conjuncture appears not (as it does to many contemporary anthropologists) as a set of wonderfully diverse and creative cultural practices, but as a global status and a political-economic condition: the condition of being "first class." Some people and places have it; others don't. The key issues are of membership and rank. Such a conception directly opposes the anthropological urge to construct a plurality of cultural alternatives while refusing to rank them. Hence, two questions arise: How does one term yield two such different discussions? And why are the anthropologists so out of step with the locals on the meaning of modernity?

To answer this question, it may be useful to think a bit more about what sorts of thinking are possible and necessary in the aftermath of the modernization story.

Let us return to figure 2, the time of modernization, and let us take seriously the idea that this picture is in some sense falling apart. What does it fall apart *into*? If it falls apart, what are the *parts*? We might think of this as analogous to the chemical process of decomposition. The word "decomposition" suggests death and decay, but in fact it is a more basic sort of operation. In a laboratory, for instance, a chemist might perform a "decomposition" of a compound by "cracking" it (normally through the application of heat), thereby "decomposing" it into its constituent elements. A similar conceptual operation is called for if we are to understand the "decomposition" of the developmentalist timeline of modernization. As the mythical coupling of historical time to societal location in a spatialized global hierarchy breaks down, it becomes necessary to take the two axes of the diagram and peel them apart, cracking the compound and releasing the elements that the developmentalist timeline for so long fused into a single figure. When such a "decomposition" is performed on the modernization narrative, what does the decomposition yield? It yields two elements, deriving from the two axes of the graph.

The first element comes from the horizontal axis of the diagram in figure 2, which may now be understood simply as history. With the time axis now unhinged from questions of status, history is not a teleological unfolding or a gradual rise through a hierarchical progression but simply a movement through time (no longer a passage through various "stages of development"). Such a de-developmentalized notion of history no longer has modernity as its *telos*. Insofar as different societies share the modern world, in the new conception, they negotiate modernity in different ways, through a variety of coeval paths. Hence, we come to speak not of sequential stages of modernization, but of a variety of "alternative modernities." With social and cultural difference no longer serialized, modernity is plural, history is contingent; the telos is gone. The key themes here are plurality, fragmentation, and contingency.

But there is also—less remarked—a second axis in the diagram. This is the axis of hierarchy. But with the idea of temporal sequence removed, location in the hierarchy no longer indexes a "stage of advancement." Instead, it marks simply a rank in a global political economic order. Insofar as such ranks have lost any necessary relation to developmental time, they become not stages to be passed through but non-serialized statuses that are separated from each other by exclusionary walls, not developmental stairways. Modernity in this sense comes to appear as a standard of living, as *a status*, not a *telos*. The global hierarchy is thereby de-developmentalized and appears as static, without the promise of serialization. Key questions here are not about development and sequence, but about edges, walls, and borders.

The first axis (de-developmentalized time) yields a non-serialized, coeval cultural difference. This is the element of the decomposition that the anthropologists relish, the terrain of "alternative modernities." They are not wrong. We are right to see cultural differences as non-serial and contemporary, as "coeval," in Johannes Fabian's (1983) sense, and to de-developmentalize our understanding of them. This is the terrain of hybrids and bricolage, of creative invention and emergent new possibilities. It is also an area in which a great deal of exciting and valuable work has recently been done.

But what about the second axis? Here, our decomposition yields a second, less benign residue: nonserialized, coeval, but ranked political-economic statuses. If the first axis (once unhinged) shows us a modernity that is newly understood as plural, the second shows us a different understanding of modernity in which, no longer promised as a *telos*, it has come to be simply a status—a standard of living to which some have rights by birth and from which others are simply, but unequivocally, excluded.

As understandings of the modern have shifted in this way, the vast majority of Africans denied the status of modernity increasingly come to be seen, and may even (sometimes and in complex ways) come to see themselves, not as "less developed" but simply as less. As people lose faith in developmental time, the global status hierarchy comes to be understood in new and disturbing ways.

Among the emergent possibilities that are beginning to be visible, perhaps the most obvious is an understanding of global statuses as de-temporalized. Rather than the poorest countries being understood as *behind* "the West"—playing catch-up, developing, or emerging—they are increasingly understood as naturally, per-

haps even racially, *beneath* it. This is visible in both popular ideology and some journalistic treatments in the West, which seem
increasingly content to treat the economic woes and humanitarian
crises of Africa as just more evidence of the way "those places over
there" are. But it is also visible in some African self-conceptions,
where the optimistic mood of a developmentalist era has—at least,
in some specific social locations—given way to a much bleaker view
that identifies "Africa" with an unchanging future of hardship and
suffering (see Ferguson 1997, 1999; cf. Simpson 2003).

What is new here is not the existence of negative and even stereotypical images of Africa, for those go back a very long way, but the
fact that such pictures today seem less dependent on a temporal
frame that would fit African troubles into a progressive developmental trajectory. In such de-temporalized visions of Africa as a
land by nature given to poverty, turmoil, and low global status, the
Great Chain of Being threatens to reappear, with the different conditions of different world regions appearing simply as a naturally
or divinely ordained, unchanging order. If the postcolonial condition is, as some have suggested, most fundamentally characterized by a perceived temporal disjuncture (with postcolonial nations
and societies imagined as "behind" or "belated" in developmental
time),[4] then the de-developmentalization of historical time promises to leave postcoloniality itself ironically "out of date," not by
ending or overcoming colonial inequality, but by rendering obsolete that very hope and dream.

But de-temporalized statuses are not the only alternative to the
developmentalist vision of progressive stages. Another possibility
exists, in the form of *nonprogressive* temporalizations. That is, statuses and conditions of peoples and nations may be understood to
change over time, but not in a progressive way.

One version of such a nonprogressive temporalization, of course
(again, a world picture with a long and disturbing pedigree) is
found in the idea of degeneration, where the temporal dynamic
is one not of progress but of decline, decay, and disintegration.
This may be readily observed in accounts of Africa in the genre
we might term "journalistic Malthusianism." Robert Kaplan's *The
Coming Anarchy* (2001) is perhaps the best known (though hardly
the only) example. Kaplan paints a vivid picture of an Africa at the

leading edge of a downward spiral into chaos, poverty, and war that might eventually sweep up the entire planet. This picture is not de-temporalized or static, but neither is it a progress story. The worst off, in such a view, are not the "least developed," those still at the start of their long journey of uplift and improvement. Rather, the worst off are those who are farthest along a very different journey: a downward slide into degeneration, chaos, and violence.

Yet another sort of nonprogressive temporalization of economic distress may be detected in what we might call "apocalyptic tem-poralizations." At a time that more and more people (both in Africa and in much of the rest of the world) reckon world-historical time by referring not to the calendar or the Five-Year Plan but to the Book of Revelation, the question of "development" threatens to be displaced by the question of the "End Times." Many examples of this might be cited. One that particularly struck me was the televised comment of a refugee from the volcanic eruptions sev-eral years ago in Goma, in the Congo. Having lived though geno-cide, civil war, starvation, cholera, and years of life in a refugee camp, the man betrayed little fear in the face of the terrifying vol-cano. After all, he reasoned, "we have read about these things in the Bible. The Lord will be coming for us soon." One should be wary of forcing overly simple interpretations on this sort of ma-terial, but it is perhaps worth suggesting that there may be some relation between the fading credibility of developmental time, on the one hand, and the rise of new spiritualities and their associated temporalities, on the other.[5]

Such new understandings of the temporal dynamics of social and economic well-being (of the relation, that is, between history and hierarchy) may bring with them new strategies through which people seek to secure their own futures. One thing that seems to come up all over the continent in recent years is a shift from a focus on temporal dynamics of societal progress toward a new reliance on individual spatial mobility. How is one to escape the low global status of being "a poor African"? Not through "patience" and the progress of national or societal development, but by leaving, going elsewhere, even in the face of terrible danger (cf. chapter 6). Today, anthropological fieldworkers in Africa tend to be asked not, "What can you do for us?" (that time-honored question), but, "How can

I get out of this place?" Not progress, then, but egress. If escape, too, is blocked, other avenues may involve violently crashing the gates of the "first class," smashing the bricked-up walls and breaking though, if only temporarily, to the "other side" of privilege and plenty. As Achille Mbembe (2002a: 271) has observed, the contemporary African experience is not simply that of economic deprivation. Rather, it involves "an economy of desired goods that are known, that may sometimes be seen, that one wants to enjoy, but to which one will never have material access." The appropriation of goods "through pillage and violent seizure" here finds its logical place alongside a range of "shadow interventions in the phatasmatic realm." Here, the developmental life course is displaced by a life course "assimilated to a game of chance, a lottery, in which the existential temporal horizon is colonized by the immediate present and by prosaic short-term calculations" (Mbembe 2002a: 271). Patience, my ass.

To the extent that the global status system is de-temporalized, or re-temporalized in nonprogressive ways, the nature of the relation between global rich and poor is transformed. For in a world of non-serialized political economic statuses, the key questions are no longer temporal ones of societal becoming (development, modernization), but spatialized ones of guarding the edges of a status group—hence, the new prominence of walls, borders, and processes of social exclusion in an era that likes to imagine itself as characterized by an ever expanding connection and communication (cf. chapter 6; Ferguson 1999: 234–54).

My thesis has been that anthropologists lately have tended to focus on the first axis of the developmental diagram, the first product of modernity's decomposition—a happy story about plurality and non-ranked cultural difference—to the neglect of the second, which yields relatively fixed global statuses and a detemporalized world socioeconomic hierarchy. In this way, the application of a language of alternative modernities to the most impoverished regions of the globe risks becoming a way of avoiding talking about the non-serialized, de-temporalized political economic statuses of our time, and thus, evading the question of a rapidly worsening global inequality and its consequences. Forcing the question of Africa's political-economic crisis to the center of the contemporary discussion of modernity is a way of insisting on shifting the topic toward the second product of modernity's decomposition: the enduring axis of hierarchy, exclusion, and abjection, and the pressing political struggle for recognition and membership in the emerging social reality we call "the global."

Governing Extraction

NEW SPATIALIZATIONS OF ORDER

AND DISORDER IN NEOLIBERAL

AFRICA

Africa's position in the contemporary global economy has appeared to many observers in recent years as one largely defined by exclusion and marginalization. In the wake of the Cold War, aid flows declined, and public payrolls were shrunk by structural adjustment, while the private capital that was supposed to pour into an "adjusted" Africa was nowhere to be found. Yet recent developments appear to demand some revision of this now conventional account. The fact is that recent years have seen quite significant new capital investment in a number of African countries, with much more forecast for the future. According to UNCTAD (2004), foreign direct investment in Africa now runs at some $15 billion per year—small by world standards, but sharply up from less than $2 billion in the low-point year of 1986—and is likely to see significant expansion in years to come. The new investment is overwhelmingly in mineral-extracting industries (the leading Sub-Saharan countries are Angola, Equatorial Guinea, Nigeria, and Sudan) and largely tied to major new oil finds, mainly in deep-water fields off the West African coast. The United States in particular is already heavily dependent on African oil supplies, and one widely cited estimate projects that West African imports will make up fully 25 percent of all North American imports by 2015 (National Intelligence Council 2000: 73). Not unrelatedly, the U.S. military now appears to be giving a new prominence to West Africa in its strategic planning (Barnes 2005). Such new developments challenge the idea that Africa's place in the global economy is defined simply by marginalization or that the continent is simply irrelevant to the wider global economy. They also provide an opportunity to assess the relationship between capital investment and some political contexts that are conventionally considered to discourage it.

It is difficult to write about these new developments in a scholarly way, since there has not yet been very much academic research (and hardly anything that anthropologists would recognize as fieldwork) in the region on either capital investment or the ways in which it is entangled with matters of political order. But focusing on a rich para-scholarly literature (including reports by NGOs, philanthropic aid and advocacy organizations, international organizations, and industry newsletters), and building on the very valuable work that has already been done by other scholars, it is possible to put together a broad, if preliminary, picture of the ways that new forms of capital investment are intersecting with new techniques for establishing selective political order on the continent.[1]

Reviewing a vast geographic area and relying on a limited secondary literature means running a risk that is even greater than usual of not knowing what one is talking about. I hope the risk is justified by what seem to me to be some rather important things that can be learned about both contemporary capitalism and contemporary politics by considering the undoubtedly extreme situations in parts of Africa.

AFRICA'S POVERTY AND ANGOLA'S EFFICIENCY

"Why is Africa so poor?" The World Bank thinks it knows the answer: African economies are stagnant because they fail to attract private investment. They fail to attract private investment because of bad government, corruption, and civil strife. This is intuitively plausible. Does not capitalist production require strong property law, courts, domestic peace, disciplined workers, and so on? And do not badly governed African states—unable to secure either peace or property—create an unfriendly environment for capital investment?

The answer may depend on what sort of capital investment is involved. Many African states have indeed suffered from extremely low capital investment in recent decades. But a number of African mineral exporters, and especially oil producers, have seen a huge recent surge in investment. Such investment is not occurring (as World Bank doctrine would suggest) where what they call "governance" is good and the rule of law is strong. Rather, the countries that (in the terms of World Bank and IMF reformers) are the biggest "failures" have been among the *most* successful at attracting foreign capital investment. African countries where peace, democracy, and some measure of "rule of law" obtain have had very mixed records in drawing capital investment in recent years. But countries with the most violent and "corrupt" states, even those with active civil wars, have often attracted very significant inflows. As William Reno (2001b: 187) has noted, an Organization for Economic Cooperation and Development (OECD) study of investment patterns in developing countries showed that all five top recipients of foreign investment in the period 1994–96 in Africa fell into the study's "most risky" category; the list was headed by such unlikely paragons of "good government" as Angola, Congo/Zaire, and Equatorial Guinea. Indeed, countries with raging civil wars and spectacularly illiberal governments have on a number of occasions proved to be surprisingly strong performers in the area of economic growth, as well. Angola, for instance, actually had one of Africa's better rates of GDP growth during the war-torn (and, in human terms, quite horrific) 1980s, while Sudan's 8.1 percent annual GDP growth rate for the 1990s put it comfortably at the top of the continental pack, notwithstanding one of the most brutal and intractable wars in recent memory (World Bank 2002).[2]

I began to notice such contrasts in the late 1980s while doing anthropological fieldwork in Zambia. Structural adjustment was newly in force, and democracy, privatization, and the rule of law were being promoted as the magical ingredients that would bring economic growth. But as reformers in Zambia moved into the

1990s in pursuit of these goals, the Zambian economy continued to shed jobs, and the promised new flows of foreign capital mostly failed to appear (see chapter 5). While peaceful, democratic, privatizing Zambia was collapsing, however, its neighbor, Angola —with a statist (indeed, an at least nominally Marxist–Leninist) economy, a raging civil war, and what was generally acknowledged to be one of the most "corrupt" and dysfunctional states on the planet—was attracting a veritable flood of foreign investment. Both were mineral-export economies. Zambia was peaceful and its government clearly more respectful of the rule of law. But the advantage, from the point of view of capital investment, plainly went to Angola. The reason, it seemed, was simple: Angola had oil. But Zambia, after all, was also a major mineral-export economy. If Angola had oil, Zambia had copper. Why should oil be so different? I will briefly note a few features of the Zambian mining economy.

The mining industry in Zambia—as in many other regions of Africa—brought with it a far-reaching social investment. On the Zambian Copperbelt, investment in copper mining brought the construction of vast "company towns" for some 100,000 workers— workers who in time came to be skilled, unionized, highly paid, and politically powerful. The mining towns—classic examples of colonial-era corporate paternalism—eventually came to include not only company-provided housing, schools, and hospitals, but even social workers, recreational amenities such as movie theatres and sports clubs, and domestic education programs to make "housewives" and "modern mothers" out of workers' spouses (Ferguson 1999). Here, the business of mining—exploitative though it undoubtedly was—entailed a very significant broader social project. Its presence, as I noted in chapter 1, was socially "*thick.*"

The gaining of independence in 1964 only made that presence "thicker" and more thoroughly bound up with national-level social and political needs. The state depended on maintaining a political base in urban areas, and the powerful Mineworkers Union of Zambia was a force that could not be ignored. Urban wages rose sharply, while educated Zambians began to take on management positions in the industry. A 51 percent nationalization of the copper mines in 1969, promoted under President Kaunda's mildly socialist ideology of "Humanism," further cemented the association of the industry with the nation (Bates 1971, 1976; Daniel 1979). When the industry went into decline, starting in the mid-1970s, all the forms of social "thickness" that older workers later remembered as the gains of this period—higher wages, good social services, powerful unions, and strong nation-state control over national wealth—were identified by the advocates of privatization and neoliberal reform as "inefficiencies" responsible for the industry's decline. (For a discussion of the industry's contraction and its causes and social consequences, see Ferguson 1999.)

In contrast, oil production in Angola from the start has been socially very *thin*.[3] The country is one of the world's leading oil exporters, producing some 1 million barrels per day (projected to rise within the next few years to 2 million barrels per day—substantially more, that is, than the current production of Kuwait). The Angolan government currently receives something on the order of $8 billion of oil revenue each year. Yet nearly all of the production occurs offshore (and increasingly in very deep-water operations), and very little of the oil wealth even enters the wider society. In spite of some twenty-five years of booming oil production, Angolans today are among the most desperately poor people on the planet, and the country ranks near the very bottom of the usual indices of "human development" (161 out of 173 according to the United Nations Human Development Index, as cited in Gary and Karl 2003: 31). In 2000, UNICEF declared Angola to be the worst country in the world into which a child might be born (Blakeley et al. 2003: 4).

The industry imports virtually all of its equipment and materials, even down to the food and water it serves to staff (Blakely et al. 2003: 6–7). What is more, in a highly capital-intensive industry, even many billions of dollars of investment yield few jobs for Angolans. The entire industry—including the parastatal corporation SONANGOL—employs fewer than 10,000 nationals, and there are very few local contractors outside the security business (Le Billon 2001). Much of the skilled labor is provided by foreign workers brought in on short-term contracts (often from as far away as the U.S. Gulf coast). These workers live in a gated compound in Cabinda called Malongo, which is still surrounded by land mines from the war. They come and go from the airport to their compound in helicopters, bypassing the surrounding town entirely (Christian Aid 2003: 21).

The Angolan government is generally recognized as one of the most corrupt in the world (third worst out of 102 in the annual derby run by Transparency International in 2002, as cited in Gary and Karl 2003: 32). Government revenues (which accrue from tax payments, shares of "profit oil" paid to the state oil company, signature bonuses, and other payments) are systematically siphoned out of the public purse. Through a variety of schemes, subtle and not so subtle, uncounted billions have ended up invested in the foreign bank accounts and Mediterranean villas of government elites (see Global Witness 1999, 2002; Hodges 2001, 2003 for detailed descriptions).

In spite of an astonishing revenue stream, the Angolan government is some $11 billion in debt and has such a bad record of repayment that nearly all conventional credit lines have been severed (Global Witness 1999: 6). The government has therefore turned (in defiance of the IMF) to commercial banks issuing short-term, oil-backed loans at very high rates (typically some two percentage points above Libor rates). This has enabled not just the looting of the revenue from current production, but the mortgaging of future revenues for years into the future. Indeed, oil production is now so fully mortgaged that the government in recent years has had very little net revenue. It can pay for its current operations only by taking on new loans (which continue to be offered thanks to the rapid recent increase of new confirmed ultra-deepwater oil reserves). The whole system is underwritten by a system of export-credit guarantees (issued by the United States and other rich nations[4]) that provide an effective taxpayer subsidy to investors' risk.[5]

It is worth emphasizing that this system has developed and flourished in the midst of a prolonged civil war (more or less continuous from 1975 until 2002).[6] With the vast preponderance of production facilities located off-shore, the oil industry was in general well protected from the fighting. During the 1980s, the ironies of Cold War politics saw Cuban troops providing protection for the U.S. Gulf Oil company's coastal facilities in the oil-rich enclave of Cabinda even as the U.S. government was supporting the UNITA rebels who sought to overthrow the "socialist" Popular Movement for the Liberation of Angola (MPLA) government (see Cilliers and Dietrich 2000; Hodges 2001; Le Billon 2001). In 1993, however, opposition UNITA forces captured the oil facilities in the coastal town of Soyo. The Angolan government responded by hiring the now notorious South African private military firm Executive Outcomes, which had previously worked for UNITA, to recapture the facilities. So successful was this operation that the firm was then offered a contract to train the state army and direct front-line operations against UNITA. With Executive Outcomes taking the lead, the balance of power in the war shifted, and the government successfully secured the entire oil region of Angola and much of the diamond-producing areas. The mercenary operation was reportedly funded with state monies that had originally come from a Canadian mining company named Ranger; in turn, the funding firms allegedly received payment in oil and mining concessions (Singer 2003: 108–110). In the wake of the major publicity it received, Executive Outcomes formally disbanded in 1997, but a number of spinoffs rapidly developed in what has become an extremely rapidly expanding industry (Singer 2003: 118; see also Cilliers and Dietrich 2000; Hodges 2003; Le Billon 2001; Reno 2001a, 2001b, 2004).

In the succeeding years, Angola has made expanded use of the device of paying private military firms with shares of future mineral production (see especially Global Witness 1999, 2002). As I will discuss in a moment, both the use of private military forces and their payment with shares in production have become widespread general features of the mineral-extraction industry in Africa, in what has come to be known as the "security-led" approach (Singer 2003: 117). In this and other respects, Angola has been both a pioneer and an influential model.

Outside observers from the IMF and elsewhere always lament the "inefficiency" of Angola's "corrupt" system of government. But for whom is the system I have sketched here inefficient? The oil companies, for their part, seem to be quite satisfied with the existing arrangements. As a recent Economist Intelligence Unit report observed, "The government has *ring-fenced* the oil sector against the inefficiencies of the rest of the economy and relations with the oil companies are generally good" (as quoted in Global Witness 1999: 5). Indeed, industry insiders often compare the "clean" Angolan set-up (where offshore oil is loaded onto tankers without any mainland entanglements) with other contexts where they are dragged into costly and politically damaging disputes over environmental damage, demands for social services, and so on. Of course, this "cleanness" is only relative. Local people in Angola, too, are often adversely affected by oil operations (which are in fact anything but "clean"), and they often attempt to press their social and environmental claims as best they can.[7] But compared with places where oil extraction is much more deeply ensnared in mainland social and political entanglements, the Angolan system must appear a model of efficiency from the point of view of the foreign oil companies. Major commercial banks also seem to have an extremely attractive arrangement, earning exceptionally high rates of interest on short-term loans backed by oil reserves. According to the *Financial Times*, the combination of high interest rates, short maturities, and solid oil backing means that "the banks' appetites for these oil-backed loans are voracious" (as quoted in Gary and Karl 2003: 41). Angolan government elites meanwhile have been nothing if not efficient in growing fabulously rich. If they have a problem at present, it is the awkward post-2002 peace, which removes what had been a very useful justification for disappearing funds, political repression, and widespread hardship among the citizenry.

While the socially "thick" Zambian model failed in the 1980s (for reasons I have analyzed elsewhere [Ferguson 1999]), the radically "thin" Angolan model not only has been sustained but has seen recent massive increases in both foreign investment and production. What is more, the Angolan model now appears to be spreading. This is so for two reasons: first, the discovery of very substantial new oil fields in West Africa, most of them offshore; and second, new innovations in the organization of mining that make some nonpetroleum forms of mineral extraction more "oil-like" in their social consequences. I will say a bit more about both of these.

In some places, the low-overhead Angolan model seems to be going into effect almost automatically. Equatorial Guinea, with a small national population, a predatory and ruthless group of government elites, and vast new oil deposits located entirely offshore clearly appears to be going the Angolan way. Vast amounts of foreign investment have already poured in (over $5 billion in the past five years from the United States alone, according to Ian Gary and Terry Lynn Karl [2003: 38]), and the country has recently seen astonishing annual economic growth rates (65 percent in 2001, for instance). Yet earnings fall mainly to the president and his relatives, and the World Bank reports that "there has been no impact in the country's dismal social indicators" (as cited in Gary and Karl 2003: 41). Fifty-seven percent of the population, for instance, has no access to clean water, and educational expenditures as a percentage of GNP have remained at just 1.7 percent. These early trends may yet be reversed, but at present Equatorial Guinea's future looks distinctly Angolan.

In others cases, however, the tendency toward an Angolan model is much more contested. Nigeria's system of mineral extraction, for instance, certainly has some Angolan features (including massive corruption and substantial insulation of oil production from the wider society). But it has never been quite such a "clean" set-up. Shell Oil's troubles in the Niger Delta are only the best known of a number of incidents in which multinational oil firms have been exposed to costs ranging from sabotage and theft, to bad press, to local demands for social and environmental accountability. As Michael Watts (2004) has recently argued, oil capitalism in Nigeria relies on several different sorts of "governable or ungovernable spaces," each associated with its own forms of conflict and violence. I will not attempt to detail here the complex local and national political struggles that Watts's analysis describes. Instead, I only emphasize that such political complications constitute their own sort of social "thickness"—albeit a form of thickness that often accrues little benefit to the local population—in comparison with the (from industry's point of view) almost ideal "thinness" of the Angolan set-up. The terrestrial political entanglements of the industry have undoubtedly had a very significant effect on the companies' production and profits. Some estimates suggest that militancy and protest in the Niger Delta have cut onshore oil production by a third (Gary and Karl 2003: 27), while attempts by major oil firms to gain good press and better relations with affected communities by bringing "development" in the form of social services (inadequate though they undoubtedly are) are another added "overhead" cost (see Barnes 2005 on the "strategic philanthropy" of the oil industry in Africa). A recent round of violence led the major oil companies to withdraw from the Niger Delta entirely (at least temporarily) with severe losses to production (Watts 2004: 51). Many companies, including Shell, are seeking to move their production entirely to less complicated off-shore sites, in spite of substantially greater production costs (Gary and Karl 2003: 27).

In other African countries with on-shore production, where geologic fate makes it impossible to simply relocate production off-shore, the strategic goal seems to be to endeavor to make on-shore production as "off-shore-like" as possible. This effort (which does not go uncontested) involves the spatial enclaving of production sites with the use of foreign crews of skilled workers and private security forces. Such enclaves of economic investment are inevitably, as Watts (2004:61) has noted, "saturated with all manner of actual and symbolic violence, and the stench of security and surveillance." They are typically tightly integrated with the head offices of multinational corporations and metropolitan centers but sharply walled off from their own national societies (often literally, with bricks and razor wire). Perhaps the most violent form of the project of separating oil production from the local population has been seen in Sudan, where oil concessions have been advertised as existing on "uninhabited land"—land, that is, that paramilitaries have systematically *rendered* uninhabited by driving off its residents (Christian Aid 2001).

In all these cases, we see a continuing tension between the two political and scalar models I have described (the socially thick model of the national development state and the socially thin model of enclave extraction).[8] Land-locked Chad, for instance, is the site of an ambitious World Bank program to reinvigorate the national development model by harnessing new oil revenues to poverty alleviation and the provision of social services. Chad's autocratic government and the continuing specter of civil war lead many observers to doubt the project's viability, but an unprecedented attempt has been made to create institutional and financial structures meant to protect oil revenue from private appropriation and reserve it for specified public goods. It is still too soon to say how this will work out. Jane Guyer (2002) has suggested reasons for hope, amidst many ambiguities and unresolved issues. Tulipe (2004) offers a more skeptical view, highlighting the risk of state crisis associated with a scramble for control of a valuable new "rent." But for all the hope (and hype) that has surrounded the new financial structures, the most telling innovation of the project may be simply that the pipeline was constructed (at great expense) entirely underground. It seems designed to function without interruption even under conditions of civil war. With such forethought in place, a national-level security project may well be (from the point of view of capital) optional.

There are continuing unresolved tensions over all this, and the national development model is not yet dead, in Chad or elsewhere. Indeed, Sudan may yet see a more benign form of oil development in the event of a successful settlement of the war, and even in Angola there are new domestic pressures for a social redeployment of oil wealth in the aftermath of the 2002 political settlement.

But the dominant model that is emerging across the new African oil states does appear to have distinctly Angolan features: not nation-states developing national resources, but enclaved mineral-rich patches efficiently exploited by flexible private firms, with security provided on an "as needed" basis by specialized corporations while the elite cliques who are nominal holders of sovereignty certify the industry's legality and international legitimacy in exchange for a piece of the action.

THE OIL-LIKE FEATURES OF NEW MINING VENTURES

Some forms of nonpetroleum mineral extraction in Africa have in recent years become more "oil-like" for several reasons. For one thing, many forms of mining have become much more capital-intensive over the years. Mining enterprises that employ as many as 100,000 local workers, as Zambia's copper industry used to do, seem to be a thing of the past. Current mining ventures are either very lightly capitalized and relatively low-tech (as in the case of alluvial diamonds and a range of artisanal and "informal" forms of mining of other minerals) or highly mechanized and reliant on much smaller groups of highly skilled workers (often foreign workers on short-term contract), as in the case of Ghana's gold industry (as discussed briefly in chapter 1). In either case, the industry no longer leaves nearly as much of a national-societal "footprint" as it did in the days of company towns, with their massive and regularized work forces.

This disconnection of mining from national-level social and political entanglements has also been facilitated (as has been observed worldwide in a range of other industries) by new sorts of spatial flexibility made possible by developments in communications, air transport, and so on. But perhaps the most striking innovation is in the use of privatized forms of security. The use of private military forces has become routine in many parts of Africa. As P. W. Singer's important survey (Singer 2003: 227) has noted, corporations operating in "weak" or conflicted African states increasingly view security as "just another function they have to provide themselves, comparable to providing their own electricity or building their own infrastructure" (cf. Lock 1998).

If such conditions of political instability impose "inefficiencies" on some sorts of operations, they enable certain economies for others. As Reno has observed, the most successful new mining ventures in Africa have been launched not by the giant conglomerates like the Anglo-American Corporation that built Zambia's "company towns," but by small, "flexible" firms (often of Canadian, Australian, and South African origin), operating in areas that are both mineral rich and weakly governed by national states. In the DRC, for instance, the Canadian mining firm American Mineral Fields (AMF), headquartered at the time in Hope, Arkansas, helped bankroll Laurent Kabila's rise to power as the Mobutu government fell in exchange for the promise of mineral rights. Once in power, Kabila's administration could not or would not enforce AMF's property rights, so AMF reportedly went into partnership with the private Dutch firm International Defense and Security (IDAS), which enabled it to secure "relative local stability" (Peleman 2000; Reno 2001a: 204–206).[9]

Where large and well-known firms might face scrutiny (and damage to their "brand") over such operations, small firms that are flexible enough to adapt to conditions on the ground are often best positioned to take advantage of these situations. "This," Reno notes, "offers investors a chance to use small firms to grab rights to resources, then to sell them to a larger firm," for which the small firm then becomes a "contractor" (Reno 2001a: 207). In this sense, "political instability can be beneficial to some kinds of foreign investors" (Reno 2001a: 205). As he notes,

> This is especially true of enclave mining operations. Neither the miners nor their host governments need to bear the social costs of fostering, regulating, and protecting local markets to generate a profit. They need only directly control a fairly limited piece of ground and secure access to the relevant external market. (Reno 2001a: 205–206)

This is perhaps the principle of deregulation taken to its logical extreme. The results for the great majority of Congolese citizens have been appalling. But the mining firms flexible enough to operate in such an environment are apparently doing very well, finding that the disadvantages of what I have termed "nongovernmental" states (see chapter 1) are compensated by countervailing advantages. As one European businessman in the Congo observed, "The absence of a banking system is far more of an opportunity than a hindrance. You set up your own network and make your own rules. . . . I find it quite inspirational" (as cited in Reno 2001a: 206).

"Security" in such a landscape appears not as a question of national sovereignty, or even "national security," but instead as a privatized and spatially patchworked project. The apparently chaotic and undoubtedly violent surroundings may well discourage traditional investors and "reputable" firms. But for more "flexible" actors, innovations in both mining and private security increasingly allow operations to proceed without the added expense of securing and regulating an entire national space.

If this model of mineral extraction appears to many observers as a disturbing sign of our new times, it is worth remembering that many of its key features are not very new at all. In many respects, colonial-era extraction was always more "Angolan" than national-developmental. In the early colonial period, in particular, private companies with their own private armies (from King Leopold's Congo to the British South Africa Company) pioneered methods for securing economic extraction in the absence of modern state institutions.[10] Parallels can also be drawn with an even earlier, nineteenth-century form of colonialism that relied on commercial alliances to impose profitable forms of order in "unruly areas" (Reno 2004). Here, as in some other respects, the national economy model in Africa appears less a threshold of modernity than a brief, and largely abortive, post-independence project.

CONCLUSION

With respect to the question of sovereignty, it should be underlined (as Reno [2001a] has argued) that the core feature of the "sovereignty" of weakly governed African states today is not actual or effective control over national territories (and still less a monopoly on the legitimate use of violence). Rather, it is the ability to provide contractual legal authority that can legitimate the extractive work of transnational firms. Neither political instability nor even civil war threaten such sovereignty (as long as the government sustains international recognition — normally the more or less automatic reward for holding the capital city). Nor need they threaten the actual work of extraction (at least of concentrated, high-value minerals), thanks to the private-patchwork model of security that is increasingly dominant. Widespread violence and nongovernmental states can certainly necessitate additional security measures, and thus increase expenses. But they may also have offsetting advantages (preventing expensive and entangling social claims and making unnecessary the costs of social thickness). The costs and benefits entailed can be tallied like any other business expenses (the need to build schools and wells in Ogoniland; the need to hire private military forces in the Congo). All told, one gets the sense that the net effect is more or less neutral, meaning that political disorder in itself provides little or no barrier to an expanding industry. As industry executive (and current U.S. vice-president) Dick Cheney put it in a reply to a question about "political volatility" at the 1998 annual meeting of the Panhandle Producers and Royalty Owners Association, "You've got to go where the oil is. I don't think about it very much" (as quoted in Christian Aid 2003:1).

This does not mean that violence and mineral-extracting capitalism must necessarily go hand in hand (as if united by an evil essence). But neither can we simply assume a natural affinity between nation-state-level political and legal order, on the one hand, and an attractive environment for capital, on the other. In many times and places, domestic peace, the rule of law, and strong central nation-state control will indeed be the conditions of possibility for both capital investment and economic growth. But the cases I have discussed here show clearly that in specific industries (especially certain forms of mineral extraction), and with the help of specific institutional innovations (especially the privatization of security), capital investment can be institutionalized in ways that make it possible to cut out the "overhead" of a nation-level societal project and to provide political order "flexibly" on an as-needed basis, to restricted and delimited non-national spaces.

Might this have implications beyond the study of Africa? I suggest that it does. I certainly do not mean to say that extreme cases like Angola can provide any sort of model for the contemporary nation-state in general. State enforcement of property law remains a foundation of transnational capitalism, and most forms of capital investment do indeed, as conventional wisdom suggests, require the legal, disciplinary, and security infrastructure that strong states provide. But there do seem to be specific niches where the Angolan model appears likely to flourish. I am thinking of places where capital investment is very heavily concentrated in mineral extraction, where domestic markets are of little value, and where stable national-level political order becomes difficult or expensive to achieve. In such contexts, political disorder, endemic private violence, and the reliance on a patchwork of privately secured enclaves might well become (as they already have in many African nations) not temporary irruptions, but long-term features of the political landscape.

Writing at the end of 2004, I do not have any more idea of what is going to happen in Iraq than anyone else does, and the contours of a future Iraqi political economy can only be a matter of profound uncertainty. But as a reader of newspapers and student of African politics, I find it difficult to avoid noting certain "Angolan" features that seem to be emerging there.

Most obvious is a widespread reliance (by both private parties and the U.S. government) on what are termed PMCs ("private military companies"—nobody calls them "mercenaries" any more). Indeed, the Angola watcher will have noted that among the "private contractors" killed in recent months were several former members of the apartheid-era security forces of South Africa, one of whom had admitted to crimes in an amnesty application to the Truth and Reconciliation Commission (*New York Times* 2004). PMCs with names like Blackwater, Erinys, and Global Risk Strategies not only guard facilities and private individuals; they escort U.S. convoys through hostile territory and often engage in sustained heavy fighting with Iraqi insurgents, using heavy weapons and even (in at least one case) private military helicopters (*New York Times* 2004). There are sound economic motives at work here. As one industry insider put it, "Why pay for a British platoon to guard a base when you can hire Gurkhas at a fraction of the cost?" (*The Economist* 2004). Such forces are free from the constraints of usual military discipline; what is more, according to the Coalition Provisional Authority, private forces contracted to the coalition are not subject to Iraqi law, either. Such outsourced firepower cuts down on political as well as economic costs. (U.S. news faithfully reports the daily numbers of dead American soldiers, but there is little notice of, or regret over, the casualties taken by Fijian, Indian, or Iraqi "private contractors.")

In another African parallel, U.S. Proconsul Paul Bremer (like many an African strongman) was protected not by his own national army, but by hired guns (*New York Times* 2004). The same arrangement seems likely to be made for designated Prime Minister Ayad Allawi, given the embarrassment that has been caused by his current reliance for security on U.S. military personnel. Indeed, even the security of the "Green Zone" itself (the supposedly secure section of Baghdad that is the core of the U.S. military occupation) has been put out for bidding to private security firms. The figure $100 million has been mentioned (*New York Times* 2004).

Most ominous, perhaps, is that a single private company, a South African firm called Erinys, now commands a 14,000-strong private army charged with guarding Iraqi oil installations (*The Economist* 2004). Like wartime Angola, Iraq currently boasts of continuing oil production in the midst of apparent chaos and war. One can imagine that, under conditions of prolonged civil strife, the private forces guarding the oil installations may well be a more durable contribution to the Iraqi landscape than either the American occupation force or its rhetorical commitment to "democracy" and "nation-building."

In explaining how the central institutions of Iraqi national culture could be burned and looted in Baghdad while U.S. troops stood by guarding the Oil Ministry, Defense Secretary Donald Rumsfeld memorably observed: "Freedom is untidy." The African cases I have reviewed show just how productive such "untidiness" can be in facilitating the flexible and opportunistic forms of deregulated enterprise that flourish under the conditions that Rumsfeld calls "freedom" and that we might instead term "extractive neoliberalism." African politics, so long misunderstood as backward, is starting to look very up-to-date indeed.

Notes

INTRODUCTION

1   It is noteworthy that the term "Africa" commonly appeared in the titles of anthropological works in colonial days—for example, *African Political Systems*, *Seven Tribes of British Central Africa*, *Schism and Continuity in an African Society*. Today, anthropology titles typically use national and regional descriptors while political scientists and journalists speak of "Africa."

2   Political scientists have not been so shy. Recent years have seen a small boom in the publication of books about the "crisis in Africa."

3   On the importance of conceptions of regions in the workings of finance, see Leyshon and Thrift 1996.

4   For a recent account of some of the (very different) ways that the category "Asia" is put to use, see Ching 2001. For a discussion of the history of continental categorization, see Lewis and Wigen 1997.

5   There is very significant variation within "Africa," of course, and not all African countries are doing so badly in "developmental" terms as this might imply. Botswana in particular is often cited as an African "success story" to rebut the claims of so-called Afro-pessimists. The situation in Botswana is indeed far better than that in most of its regional neighbors, but it should be kept in mind that Botswana's development success is decidedly relative. According to the United Nations Development Program (UNDP 2004: 148), most Batswana live on less than $2 per day, and its "human poverty" rank, while at the high end of the Sub-Saharan African range, is still below such iconically poor non-African countries as Bangladesh and Haiti.

6   On Africa's marginalization in the global economy, see also Adedeji 1993: 1–13; Castells 2000; Hoogvelt 1997, 2002; UNDP 2004.

7   Achille Mbembe has provocatively described the term "Afro-pessimism" as a "red flag waved by those afraid of radically confronting the abyss at those wishing to escape the dead end of developmentalism and populist romanticism" (Mbembe 2002b: 635).

8   For critical reviews of the reasoning that led to structural-adjustment programs, see Bernstein 1990; Williams 1994. For a critical analysis of the more recent modifications to the "Washington Consensus," see Fine et al. 2001.

9   For overviews of the adjustment debate, see Mkandawire and Soludo 1999; van de Walle 2001; White 1996. The main strategy of the World Bank and others who would defend structural adjustment has been to identify African "success stories"—countries like Ghana and Uganda that have recently seen better-than-average rates of growth—and to claim that these rates are the consequence of their willingness to accept "adjustment." Nicholas van de Walle (2001: 277), however, has convincingly argued that "across a wide set of policy indicators . . . these two 'success stories' do not appear that different from the African median"; that GNP per capita in Ghana in 1998 was still 16 percent lower than in 1970; and that both countries clearly exhibit the regional trends toward increased "rent-seeking and corruption." It is also worth noting how often the World Bank's "success stories" have been countries whose high growth rates reflect a restoration of normal economic activities following civil wars that temporarily brought much such activity to a halt (e.g., Uganda and Mozambique), and how quickly countries described as exemplary "adjusters" are discovered not to have adjusted after all once their macroeconomic statistics go into decline (Zambia is a clear African case; Argentina is a spectacular Latin American one).

10   For a stimulating discussion of the role of fortified spatial enclaves in new forms of neoliberal urbanism, see Caldeira 2001.

11   Francis Nyamanjoh makes a stimulating argument along these lines, complaining, "We [African creative writers] virtually mimic them [Europeans and North Americans] in all we do, and compel everyone else around us to do the same" (Nyamanjoh 2004: 317). Importantly, Nyamanjoh links his observations about mimicry and mental colonization to a diagnosis of the political-economic and institutional conditions of the publishing industry that make life so difficult for African writers and readers and points to the impressive publication program of the Council for the Development of Social Science Research in Africa (CODESRIA) as a way forward.

12 France (1927 [1894]): 106. On the transformation of difference (including inequality) into a formally equal "diversity" in the system of nations, see Malkki 1994.

1 GLOBALIZING AFRICA?

1 The duplication of the title *Globalization and Its Discontents* may be taken as a small indication of the clichéd monotony of this literature. In fact, four different books have (so far) been published under this title. (The other two are Burbach et al. 1996 and McBride and Wiseman 2000.)

2 For an up-to-date account of the situation in Zambia (from which the cited statistics have been drawn), see Garbus 2003. See also UNAIDS 2004 and UNDP 2004.

3 For a more detailed discussion of the "alternative modernity" question in Africa, see chapter 7. For the lively recent discussion on "African modernity," see Comaroff and Comaroff 1993; Diouf 2000; Englund 1996; Geschiere 1997; Geschiere and Rowlands 1996; Hodgson 2001; Piot 1999.

4 Note that what Easterly means by "the poorest 20 percent" is the poorest nations (whose population amounts to 20 percent of the whole).

5 The very-lightly capitalized "artisanal" gold mining that has also developed in Ghana generates far more employment than the big capital-intensive operations (World Bank 2003: 3). The World Bank report notes, however, that the "developmental" benefits of this are limited by the unregulated and harsh work conditions of the "informal" industry, and by the very high level of environmental damage inflicted by artisanal methods (World Bank 2003: 21–22).

6 Cited in World Bank 2002: 204, table 4–1.

7 See http://www.africa-rainforest.org (accessed 20 December 2004).

8 As quoted in John Mbaria and Paul Redfern, "Kenyan in Row over Congo Elephants," *Horizon* (Nairobi), 30 May 2002; available at http://www.nationaudio.com/news/dailynation/supplements/horizon/06062002/story4.html (accessed 20 December 2004).

9 The interview was with CNN and aired on 6 November 2002. A transcript of the interview is available at http://cnnstudentnews.cnn.com/transcripts/0211/06/i_qaa.01.html (accessed 20 December 2004).

1   I am grateful to Ricardo Ovalle Bahamón for telling me a version of this joke and for a stimulating discussion of its significance in a southern African context.

2   I use the phrase "the Transkei" to refer to the pre-1976 territory in its days as a "Native Reserve." I use "Transkei" when the reference is specifically to the supposedly independent Republic of Transkei.

3   On the economic history of Lesotho, see, in addition to Murray 1981 and Wilson and Thompson 1971 (cited earlier), Leys 1979 and Palmer and Parsons 1977. On the history of the Transkei, see Bundy 1979; Southall 1982; and Wilson and Thompson 1971 for overviews, and Beinart and Bundy 1987 for a stimulating set of more-detailed studies.

4   See Ferguson 1994: 105–107 and the references cited there.

5   See Anonymous 1991 for an excellent account of similar processes in Ciskei.

6   The *National Geographic* maps contained a note in small print observing that the homelands' independence was not internationally recognized. But Transkei and the other "independent" homelands were nonetheless depicted as "countries," each in its own contrasting color.

7   A related argument is made in Köhler 1993.

8   On the imagined international community of nation-states, cf. Malkki 1994.

9   Jean and John Comaroff have written about the closely related contrast among Batswana between *sekgoa* and *setswana*. See Comaroff and Comaroff 1987, 1991.

10   This is an argument that I have developed more fully in other publications. See Ferguson 1999; Gupta and Ferguson 1997a, 1997b.

11   See Gupta and Ferguson 1997b.

12   I developed this section of my argument jointly with Akhil Gupta. See Gupta and Ferguson 1992, 1997a.

13   The parallel conception of both economies and cultures as nationlike is not fortuitous. Both the twentieth-century concept of culture and the modern notion of "the" economy have their roots in nineteenth-century European nationalist thought.

The late-nineteenth-century Shambaai greeting quoted in the first epigraph is cited in Feierman 1990: 46. Lawrence Summers was chief economist of the World Bank when he made his comment (cited in *Economist* 1992: 66). The independence song of the ZANU-PF Ideological Choir, broadcast on ZBC radio on 17 April 1980, is cited in Lan 1985: 217.

1 Relations between Zambia and the IMF were officially resumed only in September 1989. But many of the austerity measures the IMF was demanding (including a 37 percent devaluation of the kwacha, a sharp rise in food prices, and the removal of most price controls) were already being implemented in the months following the visit of an IMF delegation to Zambia in April and May 1989.

2 See, for example, Clark and Allison 1989 for the Zambian case.

3 See, for example, Geschiere 1982, 1988, 1997.

4 Cf., from among a huge literature, Ardener 1970; Comaroff and Comaroff 1991; Crawford 1967; Douglas 1970; Geschiere 1982; Marwick 1982; Middleton and Winter 1963; Turner 1957; van Binsbergen 1981.

5 Comaroff and Comaroff 1990; Ferguson 1985, 1988, 1992; Hutchinson 1992; Moore 1986; Shipton 1990.

6 For example, Feierman 1990; Lan 1985; Packard 1981.

7 See Feierman 1990; Fisiy and Geschiere 1991; Geschiere 1982, 1988; Lan 1985; Marwick 1965; Packard 1981; Richards 1960; van Binsbergen 1981; Vansina 1990.

8 Cf. also Bayart 1986; Feierman 1990; Fisiy and Geschiere 1991; Geschiere 1982, 1988, 1989; Lan 1985; van Binsbergen 1981.

9 For example, World Bank 1989, 1992. Also cf. Carter Center 1991; Hyden and Bratton 1992.

10 Cf. Ferguson 1994: 280–88.

4 TRANSNATIONAL TOPOGRAPHIES OF POWER

1 My analysis of spatial images of the state should be compared with Hansen and Stepputat's stimulating volume *States of Imagination* (2001) on ways of imagining modern postcolonial states, which I encountered only after this article had appeared in its original form. See especially their illuminating discussion of "languages of stateness" (Hansen and Stepputat 2001: 5–10 and the chapters by Sarah Radcliffe and David Nugent). Compare also the related analysis presented in Ferguson and Gupta 2002.

2 Consider, for instance, that Goran Hyden was able as recently as 1992 to speak, in a widely cited and influential article, about local social structures of kin and community as "ascriptive" and as "part of the natural world over which human beings have limited control." The term "primordial" may be problematic, Hyden acknowledges. Instead, he prefers the term "God-given," he says, "indicating that they have a character that does not lend itself to alteration by human beings at will." Such "God-given" structures are opposed to state and civic structures.that are, in contrast, "man-made" (Hyden 1992: 11). The failure to grasp what might be problematic about the term "primordial" could hardly be more complete, but such views continue to be common.

3 Some representative texts include Chazan et al. 1988; Fatton 1992; Harbeson et al. 1994; Migdal 1988; Rothchild and Chazan 1988.

4 For a range of definitional strategies, see the essays in Harbeson et al. 1994, as well as Bayart 1986. For an illuminating critical review of the uses of the "civil society" concept in African studies, see Comaroff and Comaroff 2000.

5 I borrow this evocative term from remarks made by Cooper at the workshop "Historicizing Development," Emory University, Atlanta, 1993. It should be noted, however, that I am connecting the term to larger claims about transnational governmentality that I do not believe Cooper intended in his own use of the term.

6 Guyer's insightful discussion of the significance of the international affiliations of African "civil society" parallels my argument in important ways. The fact that she does not use her observations about the transnational character of Nigerian organizations to question what I have called the vertical topography of power, however, is shown with special clarity in her own definition of civil society as "those organizations created by nonstate interests within society to reach up to the state and by the state to reach down into society" (Guyer 1994: 216).

7 I am grateful to Parker Shipton for pointing this out to me.

8 The concept of "governmentality" and the ways that my use of the concept is linked to various Foucauldian approaches is discussed in Ferguson and Gupta 2002.

9 For a stimulating account of the use of "foreign policy" in support of working-class organization in the United States, see Herod 1994.

10 "Zapatistas in Transition from Fighting to Fashion," *Los Angeles Times*, 21 April 1996, A4.

11 Parts of this section are adapted from a paper co-authored with Akhil Gupta (Ferguson and Gupta 2002). Many of the sentences and ideas in this section should therefore be regarded as jointly authored.

5 CHRYSALIS

1 The comments were made by Alassane D. Ouattara, deputy managing director of the IMF, in a speech given at the Africa–U.S. Economic Conference, Arlington, Virginia, 11 June 1998. The text of the speech, "The IMF's Role in the Unfolding African Renaissance," is available at http://www.imf.org/external/np/speeches/1998/061198 .htm (accessed 8 July 2005).

2 An obituary for the "African Renaissance" that ran in a number of North American newspapers in 1999 gives a good sample of the return (with a vengeance) of such journalistic themes:

> Sudan, the largest nation, is torn by civil war. So, too, Sierra Leone, where drug-crazed rebels chop off the hands and feet of their victims. Eritrea and Ethiopia are warring over a barren border region—"like two bald men fighting over a comb," one wit noted. Tribal warfare rages in Uganda, Guinea-Bissau, Congo Brazaville, and Liberia. Rwanda is a mountain of bones. . . . Many parts of southern Africa are literally going back into the bush. Even once prosperous South Africa is engulfed by waves of violent crime. (*Ottawa Sun*, 1 February 1999, 15)

3 The speech may be found on the ANC's Web site, at http://www .anc.org.za/andocs/history/mbeki/1998/tmo813.htm (accessed 20 December 2004).

4 The text of Mbeki's speech at the conference is posted at the ANC's Web site, at http://www.anc.org.za/andocs/history/mbeki/ 1998/tmo928 (accessed 20 December 2004).

5 *Chrysalis* was posted at http://www.chrysalis.co.zm/chrysalis .html. I have paper printouts of all of the issues of the magazine.

6 Tonto Nkanya, "The Right Stuff," *Chrysalis*, April–May 1999.

7 "Letters—*Chrysalis* et al.," *Chrysalis*, April–May 1999.

8 Nick Tembo, "The Verge of a Metamorphosis, Part II: What about the Ham Effect?" *Chrysalis*, October 1998.

9 Chanda Chisala, "The Miseducation of Chanda Chisala," *Chrysalis*, November–December 1998.

10 A Zambian (pseudonym), "Being Zambian Is a State of Mind," *Chrysalis*, April–May 1999.

11 Chanda Chisala, "Miseducation Revisited," *Chrysalis*, January–March 1999.

12 Michael Chishala, "The Shame Effect," *Chrysalis*, April–May 1999.

13 Chanda Chisala, "Reinventing Zambia: Crafting the Real New Culture (Part I)," *Chrysalis*, August 1999.

14 Ibid.

15 On the significance of language for Zambian national identity, see Spitulnik 1994.

16 Mjumo Mzyece's column appeared in each issue of *Chrysalis*, with the exception of the first issue (September 1998) and the last issue (August 1999).

17 Mjumo Mzyece, "Chrysalis Dictionary of Zanglish," *Chrysalis*, November–December 1998.

18 Ibid., January–March 1999.

19 This assertion drew strong criticism from one guestbook commentator, who replied in Bemba and contradicted Tembo point for point. But other authors and commentators seemed generally to accept Tembo's claim that a Zambianized English, not the "local languages," would be central to the new national culture they sought to form. The Bemba reply to Tembo (where Bemba was clearly used for effect) was the only non-English entry in the entire guestbook (though several English entries threw in the odd local word or phrase, as is common in "Zambian English").

20 Nick Tembo, "The Verge of a Metamorphosis, Part III: What about This Coconut Thing?" *Chrysalis*, November–December 1998.

21 Idem, "The Verge of a Metamorphosis, Part IV: How about Kith and Kin?" *Chrysalis*, January–March, 1999.

22 Ibid.

23 Chisala, "Reinventing Zambia," 141.

24 Tembo, "The Verge of a Metamorphsis, Part II."

25 Chileshe Phiri, "The Ham Defect," *Chrysalis*, January–March 1999.

26 *Chrysalis* guestbook entry dated 13 June 1999.

27 Mzyece explained the term in "Dictionary of Zanglish," June–July 1999, 130.

Chongololos or Chongs are Zambia's equivalent of those movie-star wannabes living in hovels in Los Angeles waiting for their big break. A chong is someone who tries to speak American English better than the

Americans, and British English better than the British (those seem to be the two paragons). And they have the clothes and mannerisms to boot. The operative word is "tries". A chong is someone who tries to be what they are not. A little elocution never hurt anybody, but chongs mix up that word and concept with evolution. The word has an interesting history. It is derived from a television and radio programme from the 70s and 80s called the Chongololo Club. This was a children's wildlife conservation club. Chongololo means "caterpillar". The Chongololo Club had an interesting theme song that was sung in an interesting accent. Well, not so much interesting as posh. You know, plum-in-the-mouth, Received Pronunciation, Queen's English posh. And hence the word Chongololo.

28 Letter to the editor, *Chrysalis*, April–May 1999.

29 Jonathan Sikombe, "Byte Back," *Chrysalis*, June–July 1999.

30 Michael Chishala, "The Shame Effect," *Chrysalis*, April–May 1999. A letter from a reader (Richard Mutemwa, "ByteBack," *Chrysalis*, January–March 1999) argued along similar lines, citing *The Canterbury Tales* in support of the observation, "Whites have never been clean all the time, and neither are they necessarily cleaner than us today."

31 Chishala, "The Shame Effect."

32 The reference is to the revelations, then current, concerning President Bill Clinton's sex acts in the Oval Office with the White House intern Monica Lewinski.

33 Chanda Chisala, "The Ham Defeat," *Chrysalis*, June–July 1999.

34 Jonathan Sikombe, "ByteBack," *Chrysalis*, June–July 1999.

35 Phiri, "The Ham Defence."

36 Ibid.

37 Chishala, "The Shame Effect."

38 Michael Chishala, "Thoughts on Black Development: The Shame Effect, Part II," *Chrysalis*, June–July 1999.

39 Chisala, "Reinventing Zambia." Compare Simpson's thoughtful discussion of the issue of emulating "Europeans" among the students of an elite Zambian secondary school (Simpson 2003).

40 Guestbook entry dated 22 February 1999.

41 Ibid., 27 January 1999.

42 Ibid., 10 April 1999.

43 Nick Tembo, "The Verge of a Metamorphosis, Part V," *Chrysalis*, June–July 1999.

44 Chishala, "The Shame Effect." The same author pointed to the South Africans, who, "in their bid to become white have ended up with one of the highest crime rates in the world (a woman is raped every

45 seconds there!).” It is striking that, in contrast to the familiar racist readings of South African crime as blackness out of control, Chishala understands rape and violence as the result of excessive and inappropriate whiteness.

45 Damian Habantu, “A Matter of Choice,” *Chrysalis*, November–December 1998.

46 Sitali Sichilima, “Human Rights and Human Wrongs,” *Chrysalis*, November–December 1998; guestbook entries dated 1 February 1999, 27 November 1998, 12 December 1998, 11 December 1998.

47 See, for example, guestbook entries dated 27 November 1998, 9 December 1998, and 19 February 1999, which argued that homosexuals were an “infection” and should all be “burnt to death.”

48 Ibid., 27 November 1998.

49 Ibid., 22 January 1999.

50 Ibid., 1 February 1999.

51 Ibid., 10 December 1998.

52 Ibid., 9 April 1999.

53 Ibid., 9 December 1998. The link expressed here between homosexuality and an imagined reproductive failure that might lead black Africans to “die out” recalls similar arguments in Zimbabwe that are skillfully analyzed in Engelke 1999.

54 Guestbook entry dated 11 December 1998.

55 *Times of Zambia*, 4 April 2001, 1.

56 Guestbook entry dated 10 August 2000.

57 Ibid., 9 August 1999.

58 Ibid., 20 July 1999; see also Sikombe, “ByteBack”; Tembo, “The Verge of a Metamorposis, Part V”; and guestbook entries dated 3 June 1999, 14 April 1999.

59 Chisala, “Miseducation Revisited.”

60 Chishala, “The Shame Effect”; idem, “Thoughts on Black Development.”

61 Chishala, “Thoughts on Black Development.”

62 Tembo, “The Verge of a Metamorphosis, Part V.”

63 The Zambian, “The Zambian Dream,” *Chrysalis*, August 1999.

64 Tonto Nkanya, “Editor’s Note: Do as I Say . . . ,” *Chrysalis*, August 1999.

65 Guestbook entry dated 10 April 1999.

66 Tembo, “The Verge of a Metamorphosis, Part V.”

67 Ibid.

68 “Letters—*Chrysalis* et al.,” April–May 1999.

69 A number of other guestbook commentators had offered "10 best lists" about Zambia, which was soon extended to lists of "ten things about Zambia to be proud/embarrassed about." See, for example, guestbook entries dated 3 June 1999, 17 April 1999, and 15 July 1999.

70 Ibid., 9 April 1999.

71 Ibid., 10 April 1999; see also entries dated 9 August 1999, 10 August 2000.

72 Ibid., 8 May 2000.

73 The Zambian, "The Zambian Dream."

6 OF MIMICRY AND MEMBERSHIP

1 The letter was written in a stilted, elaborately polite French, and combined a very formal style with some grammatical errors and a few unclear passages. Transcriptions of the letter in French, as well as translations into English, have appeared in various newspapers and Web sites, often substantially edited as well as "cleaned up" of ungrammatical or unclear usages. The version which appears to be closest to the original hand-written letter is that found in the archives of Radio Belche, which can be accessed via the Internet (http://radiobelche .cediti.be/archives/1999/Conakry.html). Of the English translations I have found, the most complete (though far from literal) is provided on the Web site of the Jubilee 2000 organization (http://www.jubilee2000 uk.org/news/guinea2408.html). I have followed this translation where possible, though I have corrected a number of passages that differ in important ways from the Radio Belche transcription. Where there is real uncertainty about the meaning, I have inserted a question mark (?). I first encountered the letter in a rather creatively edited English translation which appeared in *Harper's Magazine* (No. 1794), November 1999, 22.

2 The original French salutation here was "*Excellences, Messieurs les membres et responsables d'Europe.*" Jubilee 2000 and most other English translations have rendered "*membres*" as "citizens." In fact, the French "*membre*" has a meaning very close to the English word "member" and is quite distinct from "citizen" (*citoyen*). Given my argument, the distinction is a significant one.

3 I have corrected the Jubilee 2000 translation, which gives the second half of this sentence as ". . . the good experiences, riches, and power to build and organize our continent so that it may become the most beautiful and admirable friend of all." This differs from most other published versions I have seen. Compare the Radio Belche transcription: *"toutes les bonnes experiences, richesse and pouvoirs de bien construire et bien organize votre continent à devenir le plus beau et admirable parmis les autres."*

4 It should be noted that Gandoulou's own interpretation of his ethnographic material is rather different (Gandoulou 1989). Like Friedman, Gandoulou emphasizes that the activities of the young *sapeurs* find their meaning principally within local Congolese society. But the move to link the young men's desire for stylish French clothes with precolonial ideas of "life force" appears to be Friedman's innovation.

5 Compare Meyer's and Geschiere's brief but trenchant critique of Friedman's writings on Africa (Meyer and Geschiere 1999: 8).

6 Stoller's later, more extensive treatment of Hauka goes beyond his 1984 article to incorporate sections of Taussig's argument (Taussig 1993) that mimesis constitutes not only resistance but also an "electro-shocking appropriation of European power" (Stoller 1995: 133). But like Taussig, Stoller combines this formula with the key theme of localist cultural resistance, since such magical acts "tap into" white power only "so that it might be recirculated for local uses" (Stoller 1995: 195–96).

7 Taussig is quoting from Rouch's 1977 interview with John Marshall and John W. Adams (Rouch 1978: 1009). But in the same interview, Rouch also noted that African students who saw the film "said it was an affront to their dignity"—a detail that does not appear in Taussig's discussion.

8 Stoller (1992: 151) cites an account in which the late Senegalese director Blaise Senghor described coming out of a Paris theater where the film was being shown, only to find the spectators staring at him, saying to each other, "Here's another one who is going to eat a dog." (The reference is to a famous—or notorious—scene in the film in which the possessed Hauka sacrifice a dog, drink the blood as it flows from its throat, and then cook and eat it.)

9 Piot, of course, recognizes the absence of economic and political "privilege" and does much to analyze its roots and implications. If the Kabre site is "as privileged as any other," for Piot it is only in a theoretical or epistemological sense. But just as there are other connotations of the word "privileged" that are here passed over, so are there other connotations of the word "modern" that are elided in the asser-

tion that Africa is "as modern as any other" place. In both cases, what such happily balanced assertions tend to leave to one side are the unhappily imbalanced relations of political and economic power that are often at the core of African aspirations to "modernity." I discuss this issue at greater length in chapter 7.

10 If one were to pursue such a reading, one could begin with a long feature article written about the two boys in *Paris Match* (August 1999). There we learn a good deal about the boys' lives and circumstances, including that they came from the poor slum neighborhood of Yimbaya adjacent to the airport in Conakry; that they were devoted to education and successful at school, even as they attended terribly inadequate schools; and that Yaguine Koita's mother had already emigrated to France (where the boys hoped to surprise her), while Koita also had an uncle in Germany and another in the United States. The case of Koita and Tounkara is also discussed, and related to the similarly tragic case of a Senegalese teenager named Bouna Wade, in Michael Lambert's poignant short article "The Middle Passage, 1999" (Lambert 1999).

11 It is true, of course, that the blessings of education, health, peace, and prosperity that the letter's authors seem to associate with "Europe" are not as widely distributed as ideological representations would suggest. The Europe that actually exists is no doubt less well "constructed and organized" than might be imagined from afar, and African immigrants there often find very difficult conditions of life, not the paradise that some of them may have expected (see Lambert 1999). But the contrast that the young men draw is not an entirely fanciful one, either. One need only compare a few crude indicators to see that their perception that many fundamental conditions of life are indeed radically better in "the West" than in most of Africa is well grounded in reality. (In Guinea, for instance, GDP per capita is some $530, while life expectancy is only 46.5 years [UNCTAD 2001].) The letter does not seem to suggest that "Europe" is a fantastic utopia, only that it is a place where one might escape poverty and hunger, avoid the ravages of warfare, and benefit from functioning education and health systems. It is perhaps the very extremity of the African situation, in politicaleconomic terms, that makes it such a challenge for the "alternative modernities" discussion.

12 Homi Bhabha (2001) has recently developed a notion of "semblant solidarity" that captures precisely the way that ideas of equality and solidarity may be bound up with the question of resemblance in a political space that is not utopian but "aspirational."

13 Compare the discussion in Malkki 1994 of a young Burundian in a Tanzanian refugee camp who drafted (and then laboriously copied by hand for international distribution) the rules of a new game that he had invented "for the youth of the world."

14 The letter was posted on the *Zamzine* Internet magazine formerly at http://www.zambia.co.zm/zamzine/1999/july/america.htm (accessed 3 March 2000). The letter was signed simply, "By a *Zamzine* writer."

15 As a number of readers have pointed out, I could "do more" with the differences between the two letters, by tracing the links between their different modes of appeal and the different social contexts and conditions from which they emerged—for example, English versus French colonial histories; a language of rights versus a language of hierarchical corporatist integration; teenage schoolboys versus a college-educated adult professional; and so on. Analysis along these lines would make perfect sense in a conventional ethnographic or historiographic project that seeks to "explain" the letters by placing their authors within a local social and cultural context. But as I noted earlier, I here deliberately refrain from such contextualization in favor of a different sort of response to the letters' appeals.

16 That the first letter addresses "Europe" and the second, "America," is perhaps due to the continuing significance of "Anglophone" and "Francophone" spheres of influence in Africa. But it is significant that the letter to the "members and officials of Europe" reads as if it is addressed to all the citizens of the so-called First World, and not only to Europeans, while the "Letter to America" denounces a category ("they," "the USA and the other super-rich nations of the world") that explicitly merges "America" with Britain and other colonizing nations who owe debts from the colonial past. It is also interesting that, while the "Letter to America" begins by addressing "America" as "you," it soon shifts voice to "they," perhaps reflecting an acknowledgment that "America" is not really listening at all and that the actual reader will most likely be Zambian, not American. Like the colonial Indonesian story "Njai Dasima" analyzed in Siegel 1997: 65, the letter seems to be "an attempt at generating a message so highly charged that someone who is not listening will start to listen."

17 This is according to a news report on an Internet news service, available at http://www.users.skynet.be/cadtm/angokin2.html (accessed 23 January 2001).

1 For recent general discussions of "alternative" or "multiple" modernities, see Appadurai 1996; *Daedalus* 2000; Gaonkar 2001; Knauft 2002; Rofel 1998. For the discussion of "African modernity," see Comaroff and Comaroff 1993; Deutch et al. 2002; Diouf 2000; Donham 1999; Englund 1996; Geschiere 1997; Geschiere and Rowlands 1996; Hodgson 2001; Larkin 1997; Paolini 1997; Piot 1999; Pred and Watts 1992.

2 I label the vertical axis "status" to insist on the way in which narratives of modernization encoded claims to a rising standing in the world that involved more than simply questions of income or GNP. I wish thereby to foreground the idea of the tradition–modernity system as what anthropologists call a "prestige system," a matter not simply of "ahead" and "behind" but also of what is known—again, in the language of political anthropology—as "rank." As later discussion will show, I also seek to make connections with what the nineteenth-century social evolutionist Lewis Henry Morgan termed the "*statuses*" of "savagery," "barbarism," and "civilization" and with the idea of a status as a durable, and even "static," condition.

3 On the history of evolutionary thought, see Nisbet 1969, 1980. On the meaning of the "Great Chain of Being" in a colonial context, see Comaroff and Comaroff 1991.

4 See, for instance, Chakrabarty 2000; Gupta 1998.

5 On new forms of Christianity in Africa, see Bornstein 2003; Ellis and Ter Haan 1998; Englund 2000; Meyer 1999; Meyer and Geshiere 1999; van Dijk 1999.

8 GOVERNING EXTRACTION

1 Especially valuable have been Tony Hodges and the Global Witness organization on Angola; William Reno on West Africa and the Congo; and Peter Singer on private military companies. All are cited frequently in this chapter. A more adequate understanding of the inter-relation between processes of enclave extraction and processes of government would properly require extensive ethnographic study, work that in most cases has simply not yet been done (but see Watts 2004, for Nigeria). The highly simplified sketch I present here has its uses (I hope), but it cannot stand in for the detailed ethnographic accounts

that, one hopes, will soon help to give us a more fleshed-out picture of the social and political life of African mineral-extraction enclaves.

2 Cited in World Bank 2002: table 4–1, available at the http://www .worldbank.org/data/wdi2002/tables/table4–1.pdf (accessed 31 October 2002).

3 The description of Angola in the pages that follows does not address the possibility that the peace agreement of 2002 may allow for some rather different dynamics from those I describe. From what I have been able to learn, it seems possible (but very far from certain) that the extreme disconnection of oil production from broader social claims that I describe may in some measure be moderated under conditions of peace, as new domestic and international pressures are brought to bear on the government for financial accountability and the provision of social services. This remains to be seen. For the present, I claim only that my description is broadly accurate for the pre-2002 period. I am grateful to Kristin Reed (currently doing research in Angola) for alerting me to the significance of some post-2002 developments.

4 Including France, Italy, and South Korea (Global Witness 1999).

5 For detailed descriptions of the role of loans in the Angolan system, see Gary and Karl 2003; Hodges 2001, 2003; Human Rights Watch 2001; and especially Global Witness 1999, 2002.

6 Note that my argument on this point is emphatically *not* that mineral resources "cause" war and corruption—the reductionist and ahistorical "resource curse" argument lately promoted by authors such as Jeffrey Sachs and Andrew Warner (1995) and Paul Collier (2000). My argument, rather, is that high levels of violence and disorder (always with their own complex historical causes) are more compatible with certain sorts of capital investment than is usually acknowledged, and that capitalism is flexible enough to adapt to a surprisingly wide variety of environments. This is not to deny, however, that the physical characteristics of particular natural resources may have significant social and political implications. For stimulating reflections on the crucial case of petroleum, see Coronil 1997; Watts 2004.

7 I am grateful to Kristin Reed for pointing this out to me.

8 See Anna Tsing's stimulating article (Tsing 2001) on the articulations of scale-making projects that she playfully refers to as APHIDS (Articulations among Partially Hegemonic Imagined Different Scales).

9 IDAS had already proved its worth in Angola, where it deployed Gurkha mercenaries on behalf on the government in exchange for a

diamond concession on the Angolan–Zairian border (Peleman 2000: 163). Kabila later reneged on his agreement with AMF and tried to make a deal with Anglo-American, but AMF sued its rivals and ended up returning to its "properties," which it is now developing. See Peleman 2000; Reno 2001a.

10 Such historical precedents themselves seem to be present in the fantasies of an African "heart of darkness" that appear to animate investors and soldiers of fortune alike in their African ventures. As Tsing (2001: 186) has noted, the idea that "capitalism" today is characterized by a uniform condition of "space-time compression" is confounded by the apparently anachronistic creation of a very different sort of space proper to the frontier mineral boom, a space that, "far from miniature and easy . . . becomes expansive, labored, and wild, spreading muddy, malarial frontiers."

References

Adams, Jonathan S., and Thomas O. McShane. 1996. *The Myth of Wild Africa: Conservation without Illusion*. Berkeley: University of California Press.

Adedeji, Adebayo, ed. 1993. *Africa within the World: Beyond Dispossession and Dependence*. London: Zed Books; Ijebu-Ode, Nigeria: African Centre for Development and Strategic Studies.

Ake, Claude. 1997. *Democracy and Development in Africa*. Washington, D.C.: Brookings Institution Press.

Amnesty International. 2002. *Making a Killing: The Diamond Trade in Government-Controlled DRC*. 22 October 2002. AI Index: AFR 62/017/2002.

Anonymous. 1991. "Ethnicity and Pseudo-ethnicity in the Ciskei." In *The Creation of Tribalism in Southern Africa*, ed. Leroy Vail. Berkeley: University of California Press.

Appadurai, Arjun. 1996. *Modernity at Large: Cultural Dimensions of Globalization*. Minneapolis: University of Minnesota Press.

Arato, Andrew, and Jean-Louis Cohen. 1994. *Civil Society and Political Theory*. Cambridge, Mass.: MIT Press.

Ardener, Edward. 1970. "Witchcraft, Economics and the Continuity of Belief." In *Witchcraft Confessions and Accusations*, ed. Mary Douglas. London: Tavistock.

Arrighi, Giovanni. 2002. "The African Crisis: World Systemic and Regional Aspects." *New Left Review* 15: 5–36.

Asad, Talal, ed. 1973. *Anthropology and the Colonial Encounter*. London: Ithaca Press.

Auslander, Mark. 1993. "'Open the Wombs': The Symbolic Politics of Modern Ngoni Witchfinding." In *Modernity and Its Malcontents:*

Ritual and Power in Postcolonial Africa, ed. Jean and John Comaroff. Chicago: University of Chicago Press.

Avant, Deborah. 2004. "Conserving Nature in the State of Nature: The Politics of INGO Policy Implementation." *Review of International Studies* 30: 361–82.

Banégas, Richard, and Jean-Pierre Warnier, eds. 2001. Theme issue: "Figures de la réussite et imaginaires politiques." *Politique Africaine*, no. 82.

Barnes, Sandra T. 2005. "Global Flows: Terror, Oil, and Strategic Philanthropy." *African Studies Review* 48, no. 1: 1–22.

Barrell, Howard. 2000. "Africa Watch—Back to the Future: Renaissance and South African Domestic Policy." *African Security Review* 9, no. 2: 82–93.

Bates, Robert H. 1971. *Unions, Parties, and Political Development: A Study of Mineworkers in Zambia*. New Haven, Conn.: Yale University Press.

———. 1976. *Rural Responses to Industrialization: A Study of Village Zambia*. New Haven, Conn.: Yale University Press.

Bauman, Zygmunt. 2004. *Wasted Lives*. New York: Polity Press.

Bayart, Jean-François. 1986. "Civil Society in Africa." In *Political Domination in Africa*, ed. Patrick Chabal. New York: Cambridge University Press.

———. 1993. *The State in Africa: The Politics of the Belly*. New York: Addison-Wesley.

———. 2000. "Africa in the World: A History of Extroversion." *African Affairs* 99: 217–67.

Bayart, Jean-François, Stephen Ellis, and Béatrice Hibou. 1999. *The Criminalisation of the State in Africa*. Bloomington: Indiana University Press.

BCP (Black Community Programmes). 1976. *Transkei Independence*, Black Viewpoint no. 4. Durban: Black Community Programmes.

Beinart, William, and Colin Bundy. 1987. *Hidden Struggles in Rural South Africa: Politics and Popular Movements in the Transkei and Eastern Cape 1890–1930*. Berkeley: University of California Press.

Bernstein, Henry. 1990. "Agricultural 'Modernisation' and the Era of Structural Adjustment: Observations on Sub-Saharan Africa." *Journal of Peasant Studies* 18, no. 1: 3–35.

Bhabha, Homi K. 1994. "Of Mimicry and Man: The Ambivalence of Colonial Discourse." In Homi K. Bhabha, *The Location of Culture*. New York: Routledge.

———. 1994. *The Location of Culture*. New York: Routledge.

———. 2001. "Scrambled Eggs and a Dish of Rice." 2001. Wellek Library Lectures, presented at the Critical Theory Institute, University of California, Irvine, November 2001.

Bhinda, Nils, Jonathan Leape, Matthew Martin, and Stephany Griffith-Jones. 1999. *Private Capital Flows to Africa: Perception and Reality*. The Hague: Forum on Debt and Development.

Biko, Steve. 1978. *I Write What I Like*. New York: Penguin Books.

Blakeley, Amanda, Jorge Araujo, Filippo Nardin, and Eddie Rich. 2003. CSR *in the Oil Sector in Angola: World Bank Technical Assistance Study*. Washington, D.C.: World Bank.

Boli, John, and Francisco O. Ramirez. 1986. "World Culture and the Institutional Development of Mass Education." In *Handbook of Theory and Research in the Sociology of Education*, ed. John G. Richardson. Westport, Conn.: Greenwood Press.

Bornstein, Erica. 2003. *The Spirit of Development: Protestant NGOs, Morality, and Economics in Zimbabwe*. New York: Routledge.

Bundy, Colin. 1979. *The Rise and Fall of the South African Peasantry*. Berkeley: University of California Press.

Burbach, Roger, Orlando Nunez, and Boris Kagarlitsky. 1996. *Globalization and Its Discontents: The Rise of Postmodern Socialisms*. London: Pluto Press.

Caldeira, Teresa P. R. 2001. *City of Walls: Crime, Segregation, and Citizenship in São Paulo*. Berkeley: University of California Press.

Callaghy, Thomas. 1995. "Africa: Back to the Future?" In *Economic Reform and Democracy*, ed. Larry Diamond and Marc F. Plattner. Baltimore: Johns Hopkins University Press.

Carter Center. 1990. *African Governance in the 1990s*. Atlanta: Carter Center.

Castells, Manuel. 2000. *End of Millennium*. London: Blackwell.

Chabal, Patrick, and Jean-Pascal Daloz. 1999. *Africa Works: Disorder as Political Instrument*. Bloomington: Indiana University Press.

Chakrabarty, Dipesh. 2000. *Provincializing Europe*. Princeton: Princeton University Press.

Chatterjee, Partha. 1986. *Nationalist Thought and the Colonial World: A Derivative Discourse?* London: Zed Books.

Chazan, Naomi, Robert Mortimer, John Ravenhill, and Donald Rothchild. 1988. *Politics and Society in Contemporary Africa*. Boulder: Lynne Rienner Publishers.

Ching, Leo. 2001. Globalizing the Regional, Regionalizing the Global: Mass Culture and Asianism in the Age of Late Capital. In *Globalization*, ed. Arjun Appadurai. Durham, N.C.: Duke University Press.

Christian Aid. 2001. *The Scorched Earth: Oil and War in Sudan*. London: Christian Aid.

———. 2003. *Fuelling Poverty—Oil, War and Corruption*. London: Christian Aid.

Cilliers, Jakkie, and Christian Dietrich, eds. 2000. *Angola's War Economy: The Role of Oil and Diamonds*. Pretoria: Institute for Security Studies.

Clapham, Christopher. 1996. *Africa and the International System: The Politics of State Survival*. New York: Cambridge University Press.

Clark, John, and Caroline Allison. 1989. *Zambia: Debt and Poverty*. Oxford: Oxfam Publications.

Clynes, Tom. 2002. "Heart Shaped Bullets." *The Observer Magazine* (London), Sunday, 24 November 2002. 1–10.

Cobbett, Matthew. 1986. "Review Article: A Rural Development Strategy for Lebowa." *Development Southern Africa* 3, no. 2: 308–17.

Cohen, David. 1993. "Forgotten Actors." *PAS News and Events*. Evanston, Ill.: Northwestern University Program of African Studies.

Collier, Paul. 2000. *The Economic Causes of Civil Conflict and Their Implications for Policy*. Washington, D.C.: World Bank.

Comaroff, Jean, and John L. Comaroff. 1987. "The Madman and the Migrant: Work and Labor in the Historical Consciousness of a South African People." *American Ethnologist* 14: 191–209.

———. 1990. "Goodly Beasts and Beastly Goods: Cattle in Tswana Economy and Society." *American Ethnologist* 17, no. 2: 195–216.

———. 1991. *Of Revelation and Revolution: Christianity, Colonialism, and Consciousness in South Africa*, vol. 1. Chicago: University of Chicago Press.

Comaroff, Jean, and John L. Comaroff, eds. 1993. *Modernity and Its Malcontents: Ritual and Power in Postcolonial Africa*. Chicago: University of Chicago Press.

———. 2000. *Civil Society and the Political Imagination in Africa: Critical Perspectives*. Chicago: University of Chicago Press.

Cooper, Frederick. 1996. *Decolonization and African Society: The Labor Question in French and British Africa*. New York: Cambridge University Press.

———. 1997. "Modernizing Bureaucrats, Backward Africans, and the Development Concept." In *International Development and the Social Sciences: Essays on the History and Politics of Knowledge*, ed. Frederick Cooper and Randall Packard. Berkeley: University of California Press.

Coronil, Fernando. 1997. *The Magical State: Nature, Money, and Modernity in Venezuela*. Chicago: University of Chicago Press.

Crawford, J. R. 1967. *Witchcraft and Sorcery in Rhodesia*. London: Oxford University Press for the International African Institute.

Daedalus. 2000. "Multiple Modernities" (special issue), vol. 129, no. 1.

D'Amico-Samuels, Deborah. 1991. "Undoing Fieldwork: Personal, Political, Theoretical and Methodological Implications." In *Decolonizing Anthropology*, ed. Faye Harrison. Washington, D.C.: Association of Black Anthropologists.

Daniel, Philip. 1979. *Africanization, Nationalization, and Inequality: Mining Labour and the Copperbelt in Zambian Development*. New York: Cambridge University Press.

Deutch, Jan-Georg, Peter Probst, and Heike Schmidt, eds. 2002. *African Modernities*. London: Heinemann.

Diawara, Manthia. 1998. *In Search of Africa*. Cambridge, Mass.: Harvard University Press.

Diouf, Mamadou. 2000. "The Senegalese Murid Trade Diaspora and the Making of a Vernacular Cosmopolitanism." *Public Culture* 12, no. 3: 679–702.

Donham, Donald L. 1999. *Marxist Modern: An Ethnographic History of the Ethiopian Revolution*. Berkeley: University of California Press.

Douglas, Mary, ed. 1970. *Witchcraft Confessions and Accusations*. London: Tavistock.

Duffield, Mark. 2001. *Global Governance and the New Wars: The Merging of Development and Security*. New York: Zed Books.

Duffy, Rosaleen. 2000. *Killing for Conservation: Wildlife Policy in Zimbabwe*. Bloomington: Indiana University Press.

Easterly, William. 2001. *The Elusive Quest for Growth: Economists' Adventures and Misadventures in the Tropics*. Cambridge, Mass.: MIT Press.

Eaton, Mick, ed. 1979. *Anthropology—Reality—Cinema: The Films of Jean Rouch*. London: British Film Institute.

The Economist. 1992. "Let Them Eat Pollution," vol. 322, no. 7745, 66.
———. 2004. "The Baghdad Boom," vol. 370, no. 8368, 55.

Ellis, Stephen, and Gerrie Ter Haar. 1998. "Religion and Politics in Sub-Saharan Africa." *Journal of Modern African Studies* 36, no. 2: 175–202.

Engelbert, Pierre. 2002. *State Legitimacy and Development in Africa*. Boulder: Lynne Rienner Publishers.

Engelke, Matthew. 1999. "'We Wondered What Human Rights He

Was Talking About': Human Rights, Homosexuality, and the Zimbabwe International Book Fair." *Critique of Anthropology* 19, no. 3: 289–314.

Englund, Harri. 1996. "Witchcraft, Modernity, and the Person: The Morality of Accumulation in Central Malawi." *Critique of Anthropology* 16, no. 3: 257–79.

———. 2000. "The Dead Hand of Human Rights: Contrasting Christianities in Post-Transition Malawi." *Journal of Modern African Studies* 38, no. 4: 579–603.

Escobar, Arturo. 1995. *Encountering Development: The Making and Unmaking of the Third World*. Princeton: Princeton University Press.

Evans-Pritchard, E. E. 1976. *Witchcraft, Oracles, and Magic among the Azande*. Oxford: Clarendon.

Fabian, Johannes. 1983. *Time and the Other: How Anthropology Makes Its Object*. New York: Columbia University Press.

———. 1998. *Moments of Freedom: Anthropology and Popular Culture*. Charlottesville: University of Virginia Press.

Fatton, Robert, Jr. 1992. *Predatory Rule: State and Civil Society in Africa*. Boulder: Lynn Rienner Publishers.

Feierman, Steven. 1990. *Peasant Intellectuals: Anthropology and History in Tanzania*. Madison: University of Wisconsin Press.

Ferguson, James. 1985. "The Bovine Mystique: Power, Property, and Livestock in Rural Lesotho." *Man* 20: 647–74.

———. 1988. "Cultural Exchange: New Developments in the Anthropology of Commodities." *Cultural Anthropology* 3, no. 4: 488–513.

———. 1992. "The Cultural Topography of Wealth." *American Anthropologist* 94, no. 1: 55–73.

———. 1994. *The Anti-Politics Machine: "Development," Depoliticization, and Bureaucratic Power in Lesotho*. Minneapolis: University of Minnesota Press.

———. 1997. "The Country and the City on the Copperbelt." In *Culture, Power, Place: Explorations in Critical Anthropology*, ed. Akhil Gupta and James Ferguson. Durham, N.C.: Duke University Press.

———. 1999. *Expectations of Modernity: Myths and Meanings of Urban Life on the Zambian Copperbelt*. Berkeley: University of California Press.

Ferguson, James, and Akhil Gupta. 2002. "Spatializing States: Toward an Ethnography of Neoliberal Governmentality." *American Ethnologist* 29, no. 4: 981–1002.

Fine, Ben, Costas Lapavitsas, and Jonathan Pincus. 2001. *Development*

Policy in the Twenty-first Century: Beyond the Post-Washington Consensus. New York: Routledge.

Fisiy, Cyprian F., and Peter Geschiere. 1991. "Sorcery, Witchcraft and Accumulation: Regional Variations in South and West Cameroon." *Critique of Anthropology* 11, no. 3: 251–79.

France, Anatole. 1927 [1894]. *Le Lys Rouge*. Paris: Calmann-Lévy.

Friedman, Jonathan. 1990. "The Political Economy of Elegance: An African Cult of Beauty." *Culture and History* 7: 101–25.

———. 1992. "Narcissism, Roots and Postmodernity: The Constitution of Selfhood in the Global Crisis." In *Modernity and Identity*, ed. Scott Lash and Jonathan Friedman. Oxford: Blackwell.

———. 1994. *Cultural Identity and Global Process*. London: Sage.

———. 1995. *Global System, Globalization, and the Parameters of Modernity: Is Modernity a Cultural System?* Roskilde University, International Development Studies, Occasional Paper no. 14. Roskilde, Denmark.

Gandoulou, J. D. 1989. *Dandies à Bacongo: Le culte de l'élegance dans la société congolaise contemporaine*. Paris: L'Harmattan.

Gaonkar, Dilip Parameshwar, ed. 2001. *Alternative Modernities*. Durham, N.C.: Duke University Press.

Garbus, Linda. 2003. *HIV/AIDS in Zambia: Country AIDS Policy Analysis Project*. San Francisco: University of California, San Francisco AIDS Research Institute.

Gary, Ian, and Terry Lynn Karl. 2003. *The Bottom of the Barrel: Africa's Oil Boom and the Poor*. Baltimore: Catholic Relief Services.

Geertz, Clifford. 1994. "The Uses of Diversity." In *Assessing Cultural Anthropology*, ed. Robert Borofsky. New York: McGraw-Hill.

George, Susan. 1993. "Uses and Abuses of African Debt." In *Africa within the World: Beyond Dispossession and Dependence*, ed. Adebayo Adedeji. London: Zed Books.

Geschiere, Peter. 1982. *Village Communities and the State: Changing Relations among the Maka of Southeastern Cameroon since the Colonial Conquest*. London: Kegan Paul International.

———. 1988. "Sorcery and the State: Popular Modes of Action among the Maka of Southeast Cameroon." *Critique of Anthropology* 8, no. 1: 35–63.

———. 1989. "L'etat en Afrique: Book Review." *Critique of Anthropology* 9, no. 3: 101–3.

———. 1997. *The Modernity of Witchcraft: Politics and the Occult in Postcolonial Africa*. Charlottesville: University of Virginia Press.

Geschiere, Peter, and Michael Rowlands. 1996. "The Domestication of Modernity: Different Trajectories." *Africa* 66, no. 4: 552–54.

Gibbon, Peter. 1993. " 'Civil Society' and Political Change, with Special Reference to 'Developmentalist' States." Paper presented to the Nordic Conference on Social Movements in the Third World, University of Lund, 18–21 August.

Giddens, Anthony. 2002. *Runaway World: How Globalization Is Reshaping Our Lives*. New York: Routledge.

Gilroy, Paul. 1991. *There Ain't No Black in the Union Jack*. Chicago: University of Chicago Press.

———. 1993. *The Black Atlantic: Modernity and Double Consciousness*. Cambridge, Mass.: Harvard University Press.

Global Witness. 1999. *A Crude Awakening: The Role of the Oil and Banking Industries in Angola's Civil War and the Plunder of State Assets*. London: Global Witness.

———. 2002. *All the President's Men*. London: Global Witness.

———. 2004. *Same Old Story: A Background Study on Natural Resources in the Democratic Republic of Congo*. London: Global Witness.

Gould, Jeremy, and Julia Ojanen. 2003. *"Merging in the Circle": The Politics of Tanzania's Poverty Reduction Strategy*. University of Helsinki, Institute of Development Studies, Policy Papers no. 2/2003, Helsinki.

Gould, Stephen Jay. 1996. *The Mismeasure of Man*. New York: W. W. Norton.

Gupta, Akhil. 1995. "Blurred Boundaries: The Discourse of Corruption, the Culture of Politics, and the Imagined State." *American Ethnologist* 22, no. 2: 375–402.

———. 1998. *Postcolonial Developments: Agriculture in the Making of Modern India*. Durham, N.C.: Duke University Press.

Gupta, Akhil, and James Ferguson. 1992. "Beyond 'Culture': Space, Identity, and the Politics of Difference." *Cultural Anthropology* 7, no. 1: 6–23.

———. 1997a. *Culture, Power, Place: Explorations in Critical Anthropology*. Durham, N.C.: Duke University Press.

———. 1997b. *Anthropological Locations: Boundaries and Grounds of a Field Science*. Berkeley: University of California Press.

Guyer, Jane I. 1994. "The Spatial Dimension of Civil Society in Africa: An Anthropologist Looks at Nigeria." In *Civil Society and the State in Africa*, ed. John W. Harbeson, Donald Rothchild, and Naomi Chazan. Boulder: Lynne Rienner Publishers.

————. 2002. "Briefing: The Chad–Cameroon Petroleum and Pipeline Development Project." *African Affairs* 101: 109–15.

Hanlon, Joseph. 1991. *Mozambique: Who Calls the Shots?* Bloomington: Indiana University Press.

————. 2000. "An 'Ambitious and Extensive Political Agenda': The Role of NGOs and the Aid Industry." In *Global Institutions and Local Empowerment: Competing Theoretical Perspectives*, ed. Kendall Stiles. Basingstoke: Macmillan.

Hannerz, Ulf. 1987. "The World in Creolization." *Africa* 57, no. 4: 546–59.

————. 1992. *Cultural Complexity: Studies in the Social Organization of Meaning*. New York: Columbia University Press.

————. 1996. *Transnational Connections: Culture, People, Places*. New York: Routledge.

Hansen, Karen Tranberg. 2000. *Salaula: The World of Secondhand Clothing and Zambia*. Chicago: University of Chicago Press.

Hansen, Thomas Blom, and Finn Stepputat, eds. 2001. *States of Imagination: Ethnographic Explorations of the Postcolonial State*. Durham, N.C.: Duke University Press.

Harbeson, John W., Donald Rothchild, and Naomi Chazan, eds. 1994. *Civil Society and the State in Africa*. Boulder: Lynne Rienner Publishers.

Hardt, Michael, and Antonion Negri. 2001. *Empire*. Cambridge, Mass.: Harvard University Press.

Hart, Gillian. 2002. *Disabling Globalization: Places of Power in Post-apartheid South Africa*. Berkeley: University of California Press.

Hecht, David, and A. M. Simone. 1994. *Invisible Governance: The Art of African Micro-politics*. New York: Autonomedia.

Held, David, Anthony G. McGrew, David Goldblatt, and Jonathan Perraton. 1999. *Global Transformations: Politics, Economics and Culture*. Stanford, Calif.: Stanford University Press.

Herbst, Jeffrey. 2000. *States and Power in Africa*. Princeton: Princeton University Press.

Herod, Andrew. 1994. "The Practice of International Labor Solidarity and the Geography of the Global Economy." *Economic Geography* 71, no. 4: 341–63.

Hibou, Béatrice. 2004. *Privatizing the State*. New York: Columbia University Press.

Hobsbawm, Eric. 1983. "Introduction: Inventing Traditions." In Eric Hobsbawm and Terrence O. Ranger, eds. *The Invention of Tradition*. New York: Cambridge University Press.

Hobsbawm, Eric, and Terrence O. Ranger, eds. 1983. *The Invention of Tradition*. New York: Cambridge University Press.

Hodges, Tony. 2001. *Angola from Afro-Stalinism to Petro-Diamond Capitalism*. Bloomington: Indiana University Press.

———. 2003. *Angola: The Anatomy of an Oil State*. Bloomington: Indiana University Press.

Hodgson, Dorothy L., ed. 2001. *Gendered Modernities: Ethnographic Perspectives*. New York: Palgrave.

Holston, James. 1999. "Alternative Modernities: Statecraft and Religious Imagination in the Valley of the Dawn." *American Ethnologist* 26: 605–31.

Holston, James, ed. 1999. *Cities and Citizenship*. Durham, N.C.: Duke University Press.

Hoogvelt, Ankie. 1997. *Globalization and the Postcolonial World: The New Political Economy of Development*. London: Macmillan.

———. 2002. "Globalization, Imperialism and Exclusion: The Case of Sub-Saharan Africa." In *Africa in Crisis: New Challenges and Possibilities*, ed. Tunde Zack-Williams, Diane Frost, and Alex Thompson. London: Pluto Press.

Hulme, David, and Marshall Murphree, eds. 2001. *African Wildlife and Livelihoods: The Promise and Performance of Community Conservation*. Portsmouth, N.H.: Heinemann.

Human Rights Watch. 2001. *The Oil Diagnostic in Angola: An Update*. New York: Human Rights Watch.

Hutchinson, Sharon. 1992. "The Cattle of Money and the Cattle of Girls among the Nuer, 1930–83." *American Ethnologist* 19, no. 2: 294–316.

Hyden, Goran. 1983. *No Shortcuts to Progress: African Development Management in Perspective*. London: Heinemann.

———. 1992. "Governance and the Study of Politics." In *Governance and Politics in Africa*, ed. Göran Hydén and Michael Bratton. Boulder: Lynne Rienner Publishers.

Hyden, Goran, and Michael Bratton, eds. 1992. *Governance and Politics in Africa*. Boulder: Lynne Rienner Publishers.

IMF (International Monetary Fund). 1997. *Zambia—Selected Issues and Statistical Appendix*. IMF Staff country report no. 97/118, 17 November.

———. 1999. *Zambia: Statistical Appendix*. IMF Staff country report no. 99/43, May.

Kaplan, Robert D. 2001. *The Coming Anarchy: Shattering the Dreams of the Post Cold War*. New York: Vintage.

Kaunda, Kenneth D. 1968. *Humanism in Zambia and a Guide to Its Implementation, Part I*. Lusaka: Zambian Information Services.

————. 1974. *Humanism in Zambia and a Guide to Its Implementation, Part II*. Lusaka: Zambian Information Services.

Keane, John, ed. 1988. *Civil Society and the State: New European Perspectives*. New York: Verso.

Knauft, Bruce M., ed. 2002. *Critically Modern: Alternatives, Alterities, Anthropologies*. Bloomington: Indiana University Press.

Köhler, Gernot. 1993. "Global Apartheid." In *Talking about People: Readings in Contemporary Cultural Anthropology*, ed. Robert J. Gordon and William A. Haviland. Mountain View, Calif.: Mayfield Publishing.

Kramer, Fritz W. 1993. *The Red Fez: Art and Spirit Possession in Africa*. Trans. Malcolm Green. New York: Verso.

Lambert, Michael. 1999. "The Middle Passage, 1999." *Anthropology News* 40, no. 9: 7–8.

Lan, David. 1985. *Guns and Rain: Guerrillas and Spirit Mediums in Zimbabwe*. Berkeley: University of California Press.

Larkin, Brian. 1997. "Indian Films and Nigerian Lovers: Media and the Creating of Parallel Modernities." *Africa* 67, no. 3: 406–40.

Latour, Bruno. 1993. *We Have Never Been Modern*. Cambridge, Mass.: Harvard University Press.

Le Billon, Philippe. 2001. "Angola's Political Economy of War: The Role of Oil and Diamonds, 1975–2000." *African Affairs* 100: 55–80.

Lemarchand, Rene. 1992. "Uncivil States and Civil Societies: How Illusion Became Reality." *Journal of Modern African Studies* 30, no. 2: 177–91.

Leonard, David K., and Scott Straus. 2003. *Africa's Stalled Development: International Causes and Cures*. Boulder: Lynne Rienner Publishers.

Lewis, Martin W., and Kären E. Wigen. 1997. *The Myth of Continents: A Critique of Metageography*. Berkeley: University of California Press.

Leys, Roger. 1979. "Lesotho: Non-development or Under-development: Towards an Analysis of the Political Economy of the Labor Reserve." In *The Politics of Africa*, ed. Timothy M. Shaw and Kenneth A. Heard. New York: Africana Publishing.

Leyshon, Andrew, and Nigel Thrift. 1996. *Money/Space: Geographies of Monetary Transformation*. New York: Routledge.

Lock, Peter. 1998. "Military Downsizing and Growth in the Security Industry in Sub-Saharan Africa." *Strategic Analysis* 22, no. 9 (December).

Lovejoy, Arthur O. 1936. *The Great Chain of Being: A Study of the History of an Idea*. Cambridge, Mass.: Harvard University Press.

Magubane, Bernard. 1969. "Pluralism and Conflict Situations in Africa: A New Look." *African Social Research* 7: 559–654.

———. 1971. "A Critical Look at Indices Used in the Study of Social Change in Colonial Africa." *Current Anthropology* 12: 419–45.

Malan, T., and P. S. Hattingh. 1976. *Black Homelands in South Africa*. Pretoria: Africa Institute of South Africa.

Malkki, Liisa H. 1992. "National Geographic: The Rooting of Peoples and the Territorialization of National Identity among Scholars and Refugees." *Cultural Anthropology* 7, no. 1: 24–44.

———. 1994. "Citizens of Humanity: Internationalism and the Imagined Community of Nations." *Diaspora* 3, no. 1: 41–68.

———. 1995. *Purity and Exile: Violence, Memory, and National Cosmology among Hutu Refugees in Tanzania*. Chicago: University of Chicago Press.

———. Forthcoming. "Children, Humanity, and the Infantalization of Peace," unpublished MS.

Mamdani, Mahmood. 1996. *Citizen and Subject: Contemporary Africa and the Legacy of Late Colonialism*. Princeton: Princeton University Press.

Marwick, Max. 1965. *Sorcery in Its Social Setting: A Study of the Northern Rhodesian Cewa*. Manchester: Manchester University Press.

Marwick, Max, ed. 1982. *Witchcraft and Sorcery: Selected Readings*, 2d ed. Harmondsworth: Penguin Books.

Marx, Karl. 1978. "On the Jewish Question." In *The Marx-Engels Reader*, ed. Robert C. Tucker. New York: W. W. Norton.

Mayekiso, Mzwanele. 1996. *Township Politics: Civic Struggles for a New South Africa*. New York: Monthly Review Press.

Mbembe, Achille. 2001. *On the Postcolony*. Berkeley: University of California Press.

———. 2002a. "African Modes of Self-Writing." *Public Culture* 14, no. 1: 239–73.

———. 2002b. "On the Power of the False." *Public Culture* 14, no. 3: 629–41.

McBride, Steven, and John Wiseman, eds. 2000. *Globalization and Its Discontents*. New York: Palgrave Macmillan.

Meyer, Birgit. 1999. *Translating the Devil: Religion and Modernity among the Ewe in Ghana*. Trenton, N.J.: Africa World Press.

Meyer, Birgit, and Peter Geschiere, eds. 1999. *Globalization and Identity: Dialectics of Flow and Closure.* Oxford: Blackwell.

Meyer, John W., David Kamens, Aaron Benavot, Yun-Kyung Cha, and Suk-Ying Wong. 1992. *School Knowledge for the Masses: World Models and National Primary Curriculum Categories in the Twentieth Century.* London: Falmer.

Middleton, John, and E. H. Winter, eds. 1963. *Witchcraft and Sorcery in East Africa.* London: Routledge and Kegan Paul.

Migdal, Joel. 1988. *Strong Societies and Weak States: State–Society Relations and State Capabilities in the Third World.* Princeton: Princeton University Press.

Mindry, Deborah. 1998. " 'Good Women': Philanthropy, Power, and the Politics of Femininity in Contemporary South Africa." Ph.D. diss., Program in Social Relations, University of California, Irvine.

Mitchell, J. Clyde. 1956. *The Kalela Dance: Aspects of Social Relationships among Urban Africans in Northern Rhodesia.* Rhodes-Livingstone Papers no. 27. Manchester: Manchester University Press.

Mitchell, J. Clyde, and A. L. Epstein. 1959. "Occupational Prestige and Social Status among Urban Africans in Northern Rhodesia." *Africa* 29: 22–39.

Mitchell, Timothy. 1991. "The Limits of the State: Beyond Statist Approaches and Their Critics." *American Political Science Review* 85: 77–96.

Mkandawire, Thandika, and Charles C. Soludo. 1999. *Our Continent, Our Future: African Perspectives on Structural Adjustment.* Trenton, N.J.: Africa World Press.

Moore, Sally Falk. 1986. *Social Facts and Fabrications: "Customary" Law on Kilimanjaro, 1880–1980.* New York: Cambridge University Press.

———. 1994. *Anthropology and Africa.* Charlottesville: University of Virginia Press.

Mosse, George L. 1978. *Toward the Final Solution: A History of European Racism.* New York: Howard Fertig.

Mudimbe, V. Y. 1988. *The Invention of Africa: Gnosis, Philosophy and the Order of Knowledge.* Bloomington: Indiana University Press.

Murray, Colin. 1981. *Families Divided: The Impact of Migrant Labour in Lesotho.* New York: Cambridge University Press.

Musah, Abdel-Fatau, and J. 'Kayode Fayemi, eds. 2000. *Mercenaries: An African Security Dilemma.* London: Pluto Press.

National Intelligence Council. 2000. *Global Trends 2015: A Dialogue about the Future with Nongovernmental Experts.* NIC no. 2000–02. Washington, D.C.: U.S. National Intelligence Council.

Nelson, Diane M. 1999. *A Finger in the Wound: Body Politics in Quincentennial Guatemala*. Berkeley: University of California Press.

Neumann, Roderick P. 2001a. *Imposing Wilderness: Struggles over Livelihood and Nature Preservation in Africa*. Berkeley: University of California Press.

————. 2001b. "Disciplining Peasants in Tanzania: From State Violence to Self-Surveillance in Wildlife Conservation." In *Violent Environments*, ed. Nancy Lee Peluso and Michael Watts. Ithaca: Cornell University Press.

New York Times. 2004. "Security Companies: Shadow Soldiers in Iraq," 19 April, A1, A11.

Nisbet, Robert A. 1969. *Social Change and History: Aspects of the Western Theory of Development*. New York: Oxford University Press.

————. 1980. *History of the Idea of Progress*. London: Heinemann.

Nkhulu, W. L. 1984. "Regional Development in Transkei." *Development Southern Africa* 1, nos. 3–4: 333–42.

Nordstrom, Carolyn. 2001. "Out of the Shadows." In *Intervention and Transnationalism in Africa: Global–Local Networks of Power*, ed. Thomas M. Callaghy, Ronald Kassimir, and Robert Latham. New York: Cambridge University Press.

Nyamnjoh, Francis B. 2004. "From Publish or Perish to Publish and Perish: What the 'Africa's 100 Best Books' Tell Us about Publishing in Africa." *Journal of Asian African Studies* 39, no. 4: 309–33.

Nyerere, Julius K. 1968. *Ujamaa: Essays on Socialism*. New York: Oxford University Press.

Obstfeld, Maurice, and Alan M. Taylor. 2002. *Globalization and Capital Markets*. Working Paper no. 8846, National Bureau of Economic Research, Cambridge, Mass.

Omond, Roger. 1985. *The Apartheid Handbook: A Guide to South Africa's Everyday Racial Policies*. Harmondsworth: Penguin.

Ong, Aihwa. 1999. *Flexible Citizenship: The Cultural Logics of Transnationality*. Durham, N.C.: Duke University Press.

Packard, Randall M. 1981. *Chiefship and Cosmology: An Historical Study of Political Competition*. Bloomington: Indiana University Press.

Palmer, Robin, and Neil Parsons, eds. 1977. *The Roots of Rural Poverty in Central and Southern Africa*. Berkeley: University of California Press.

Paolini, Albert. 1997. "The Place of Africa in Discourses about the Postcolonial, the Global, and the Modern." *New Formations* 31: 83–106.

Peleman, Johan. 2000. "Mining for Serious Trouble: Jean-Raymond

Boulle and His Corporate Empire Project." In *Mercenaries: An African Security Dilemma*, ed. Abdel-Fatau Musah and J. 'Kayode Fayemi. London: Pluto.

Piot, Charles. 1999. *Remotely Global: Village Modernity in West Africa*. Chicago: University of Chicago Press.

Platzky, Laurine, and Cherryl Walker. 1985. *The Surplus People: Forced Removals in South Africa*. Johannesburg: Ravan Press.

Pratt, Mary Louise. 1987. "Linguistic Utopias." In *The Linguistics of Writing*, ed. Nigel Fabb, Derek Attridge, Alan Durant, and Colin MacCabe. Manchester: Manchester University Press.

———. 2002. "Modernity and Periphery: Towards a Global and Relational Analysis." In *Beyond Dichotomies*, ed. Elizabeth Mudimbe-Boyi. Albany: State University of New York Press.

Pred, Allan, and Michael John Watts. 1992. *Reworking Modernity: Capitalisms and Symbolic Discontent*. New Brunswick, N.J.: Rutgers University Press.

Pritchett, Lant. 1997. "Divergence, Big Time." *Journal of Economic Perspectives* 11, no. 3: 3–17.

Rahnema, Majid, and Victoria Bawtree, eds. 1997. *The Post-Development Reader*. London: Zed Books.

Reno, William. 1999. *Warlord Politics and African States*. Boulder: Lynne Rienner Publishers.

———. 2001a. "How Sovereignty Matters: International Markets and the Political Economy of Local Politics in Weak States." In *Intervention and Transnationalism in Africa: Global–Local Networks of Power*, ed. Thomas M. Callaghy, Ronald Kassimir, and Robert Latham. New York: Cambridge University Press.

———. 2001b. "External Relations of Weak States and Stateless Regions in Africa." In *African Foreign Policies: Power and Process*, ed. Gilbert M. Kaldiagala and Terrence Lyons. Boulder: Lynne Rienner Publishers.

———. 2004. "Order and Commerce in Turbulent Areas: 19th Century Lessons, 21st Century Practice." *Third World Quarterly* 25, no. 4: 607–25.

Richards, Audrey, ed. 1960. *East African Chiefs*. London: Faber.

Riles, Annelise. 2001. *The Network Inside Out*. Ann Arbor: University of Michigan Press.

Rofel, Lisa. 1998. *Other Modernities: Gendered Yearnings in China after Socialism*. Berkeley: University of California Press.

Roitman, Janet. 2004. *Fiscal Disobedience: An Anthropology of Economic Regulation in Central Africa*. Princeton: Princeton University Press.

Rothchild, Donald, and Naomi Chazan, eds. 1988. *The Precarious Balance: State and Society in Africa*. Boulder: Westview Press.

Rouch, Jean. 1978. "Jean Rouch Talks about His Films to John Marshall and John W. Adams (September 14th and 15th, 1977)." *American Anthropologist* 80, no. 4: 1005–14.

Sachs, Jeffrey D., and Andrew M. Warner. 1995. *Natural Resource Abundance and Economic Growth*. National Bureau of Economic Research Working Paper no. 5398, Cambridge, Mass.

Sachs, Wolfgang, ed. 1992. *The Development Dictionary: A Guide to Knowledge as Power*. London: Zed Books.

Sassen, Saskia. 1999. *Globalization and Its Discontents: Essays on the New Mobility of People and Money*. New York: New Press.

Saul, John S. 1993. *Recolonization and Resistance: Southern Africa in the 1990s*. Trenton, N.J.: Africa World Press.

Schmitz, Gerald J. 1995. "Democratization and Demystification: Deconstructing 'Governance' as Development Paradigm." In David B. Moore and Gerald J. Schmitz, eds. *Debating Development Discourse: Institutional and Popular Perspectives*. New York: St. Martin's Press.

Schwartz, Hillel. 1996. *The Culture of the Copy: Striking Likenesses, Unreasonable Facsimiles*. New York: Zone Books.

Seligman, Adam B. 1992. *The Idea of Civil Society*. New York: Free Press.

Shipton, Parker. 1990. *Bitter Money*. American Ethnological Society Monograph Series, Washington, D.C.: American Ethnological Society.

Siegel, James T. 1997. *Fetish, Recognition, Revolution*. Princeton: Princeton University Press.

Simone, Abdou Malik. 2001. "On the Worlding of African Cities." *African Studies Review* 44, no. 1: 15–43.

Simone, Abdou Maliqalim, and Edgar Pieterse. 1993. "Civil Societies in an Internationalized Africa." *Social Dynamics* 19, no. 2: 41–69.

Simpson, Anthony. 2003. *"Half-London" in Zambia: Contested Identities in a Catholic Mission School*. Edinburgh: Edinburgh University Press.

Singer, P. W. 2003. *Corporate Warriors: The Rise of the Privatized Military Industry*. Ithaca: Cornell University Press.

Smith, Neil. 1992. "Contours of a Spatialized Politics: Homeless Vehicles and the Production of Geographical Scale." *Social Text* 33: 55–81.

———. 1997. "The Satanic Geographies of Globalization: Uneven Development in the 1990s." *Public Culture* 10, no. 1: 169–89.

Southall, Roger. 1982. *South Africa's Transkei: The Political Economy of an "Independent" Bantustan*. London: Heinemann.

Spence, J. E. 1968. *Lesotho: The Politics of Dependence*. New York: Oxford University Press.

Spitulnik, Debra. "Radio Culture in Zambia: Audiences, Public Works, and the Nation-State." Ph.D. diss., Department of Anthropology, University of Chicago.

Stiglitz, Joseph E. 2001. "Thanks for Nothing." *Atlantic Monthly*, vol. 288, no. 3: 36–40.

———. 2003. *Globalization and Its Discontents*. New York: W. W. Norton.

Stoller, Paul. 1984. "Horrific Comedy: Cultural Resistance and the Hauka Movement in Niger." *Ethos* 12, no. 2: 165–89.

———. 1989. *Fusion of the Worlds: An Ethnography of Possession among the Songhay of Niger*. Chicago: University of Chicago Press.

———. 1992. *The Cinematic Griot: The Ethnography of Jean Rouch*. Chicago: University of Chicago Press.

———. 1995. *Embodying Colonial Memories: Spirit Possession, Power and the Hauka in West Africa*. New York: Routledge.

Taussig, Michael. 1993. *Mimesis and Alterity: A Particular History of the Senses*. New York: Routledge.

Thongchai, Winichakul. 1994. *Siam Mapped: A History of the Geo-body of a Nation*. Honolulu: University of Hawai'i Press.

Tsing, Anna. 2000. "The Global Situation." *Cultural Anthropology* 15, no. 3: 327–60.

———. 2001. "Inside the Economy of Appearances." In *Globalization*, ed. Arjun Appadurai. Durham, N.C.: Duke University Press.

Tulipe, Simon. 2004. "Le bassin Tehadien à l'épreuve de l'or noir: Réflexions sur la 'nouvelle donne pétro-politique' en Afrique centrale." *Politique Africaine*. No. 94: 59–81.

Turner, Victor. 1957. *Schism and Continuity in an African Society: A Study of Ndembu Village Life*. Manchester: Manchester University Press.

UNAIDS. 2004. *2004 Report on the Global AIDS Epidemic*. New York: Joint United Nations Programme on HIV/AIDS.

UNCTAD (United Nations Conference on Trade and Development). 2000. *The Least Developed Countries: 2000 Report*. New York: United Nations Publications.

———. 2001. *Statistical Profile of the Least Developed Nations*. Geneva: UNCTAD.

UNCTAD. 2004. *World Investment Report: The Shift toward Services.* New York: UNCTAD.

UNDP (United Nations Development Program). 2004. *2004 Human Development Indicators.* New York: UNDP.

van Binsbergen, Wim. 1981. *Religious Change in Zambia: Exploratory Studies.* London: Kegan Paul International.

van de Walle, Nicholas. 2001. *African Economies and the Politics of Permanent Crisis, 1979–1999.* New York: Cambridge University Press.

van der Merwe, A. F. 1986. "The Policy Implications of an Appropriate Development Strategy for Southern Africa." *Development Southern Africa* 3, no. 3: 462–65.

van Dijk, Rijk. 1999. "Pentecostalism, Cultural Memory and the State: Contested Representations of Time in Postcolonial Malawi." In *Memory and the Postcolony: African Anthropology and the Critique of Power*, ed. Richard P. Werbner. London: Zed Books.

Vansina, Jan. 1990. *Paths in the Rainforests: Toward a History of Political Tradition in Equatorial Africa.* Madison: University of Wisconsin Press.

Watts, Michael. 2004. "Resource Curse? Governmentality, Oil and Power in the Niger Delta, Nigeria." *Geopolitics* 9, no. 1: 50–80.

Werbner, Richard, and Terence Ranger, eds. 1996. *Postcolonial Identities in Africa.* London: Zed Books.

White, Howard. 1996. "Review Article: Adjustment in Africa." *Development and Change* 27: 785–815.

Williams, Gavin. 1994. "Why Structural Adjustment Is Necessary and Why It Doesn't Work." *Review of African Political Economy* 60: 214–25.

Wilson, Godfrey. 1941. *An Essay on the Economics of Detribalization in Northern Rhodesia, Part II.* Rhodes Livingstone Papers no. 6. Manchester: Manchester University Press.

Wilson, Monica, and Leonard L. Thompson. 1971. *The Oxford History of South Africa.* Oxford: Oxford University Press.

Wolpe, Harold. 1972. "Capitalism and Cheap Labour-Power in South Africa: From Segregation to Apartheid." *Economy and Society* 1, no. 4: 425–56.

Worby, Eric. 1992. "Remaking Labour, Reshaping Identity: Cotton, Commoditization and the Culture of Modernity in Northwestern Zimbabwe." Ph.D. thesis, Department of Anthropology, McGill University, Montreal.

World Bank. 1981. *Accelerated Development in Sub-Saharan Africa: An Agenda for Action.* Washington, D.C.: World Bank.

————. 1989. *Sub-Saharan Africa: From Crisis to Sustainable Growth*. Washington, D.C.: World Bank.

————. 1992. *Governance and Development*. Washington, D.C.: World Bank.

————. 1994. *Zambia Poverty Assessment*, vol. 1. Human Resources Division, Southern Africa Department, Africa Regional Office, report no. 12985-ZA, 10 November.

————. 2002. *2002 World Development Indicators*. Washington, D.C.: World Bank.

————. 2003. *Project Performance Assessment Report: Ghana Mining Sector Rehabilitation Project (Credit 1921-GH) and Mining Sector Development and Environment Project (Credit 2743-GH)*. Sector and Thematic Evaluation Group, Operations Evaluation Department, report no. 26197, Washington, D.C.

Wright, Patrick. 1985. *On Living in an Old Country*. London: Verso.

Zambia (Republic of Zambia). 2000. "Interim Poverty Reduction Strategy Paper." Ministry of Finance and Economic Development, Lusaka, 7 July.

Index

Acquired Immunodeficient
Syndrome (AIDS), 8, 28, 115,
129

Africa: anthropology and, 3, 103,
106, 185; Central, 26–27; children in, 154–55, 168–70, 198;
civilizations in, 116; civil society
in, 91–99, 104–5, 216 nn.4, 6;
clientelism and, 10, 12; conservation of nature and, 42–48;
corruption and, 10, 11, 41, 95,
117, 200, 226 n.6; as "dark continent," 2, 29; democracy in,
84–85, 89, 96, 100–101, 113–
15, 119; development and, 5,
16, 21, 23, 28, 32, 34, 41, 61, 62,
63, 87, 88, 95, 97, 114, 182, 183,
184, 189–90; diseases and, 28,
172; economy of, 7, 8, 9, 35,
41, 77–83, 87–88, 97, 113–15,
117, 118–19, 147–48, 154, 183,
184, 191–93, 194–210; education
and, 28, 102, 174; ethnicity in,
94, 97, 98; Europe and, 172,
174, 223 n.10, 224 n.13; foreign
investment in, 32–42, 194, 195–
96, 203; geography of, 25, 27–
28; globalization studies and,
25–29, 41–42, 48–49; "global
order" and, 5, 173–74, 185–86,
192; governance in, 38–42, 83–
84, 85, 87, 95–96, 97, 102–3, 107,
196; health in, 9, 79, 102, 169;
life expectancy in, 28; literacy
in, 9; local elites and, 10, 19,
29, 113, 115, 117, 118, 121, 154;
modernity and, 32–34, 176–93;
nation-building in, 94–99, 114;
natural resources of, 13, 35–37,
40–42, 119, 145, 15, 194, 202–
7; nepotism and, 95; North,
85–86; political regimes in, 40;
population of, 25; Sub-Saharan,
1, 4, 9, 34, 41, 194; toxic waste
and, 70–71; tribalism in, 94,
95; United States and, 172, 175,
194–95, 224 n.13; usable vs. useless, 39–40; violence in, 9–10,
37, 40–41, 43, 44–45, 102, 192;
the "West" and, 2, 6, 17, 20, 27,
66, 87, 165, 168–75, 176, 184,
189, 223 n.10. *See also* Economy;
Lesotho; Poverty; South Africa;
Zambia

African National Congress (ANC),
105, 116

African Renaissance, 10–11, 113–
19, 147, 153–54, 217 n.2

African Renaissance Conference,
117

Africa Rainforest and River Conservation (ARRC), 44–45
Africa Watch, 111
Agency: African understandings of, 74–75, 82, 88
Alexandra Community Organization, 105
Allawi, Ayad, 209
American Mining Fields, 205
Amnesty International, 111
Anglo-American Corporation, 98
Angola, 28, 41, 194, 210, 226 n.3; civil war in, 102, 199–200; economy in, 35, 36, 198–202; as exemplar, 196, 204, 207, 208. *See also* Popular Movement for the Liberation of Angola (MPLA)
Annan, Kofi, 114
Anthropology: authenticity and, 158, 160; colonialism and, 3, 156–61, 167; concept of culture and, 51, 66–68; critique of modernity and, 32–33, 89, 167–68, 187, 192–93; fieldwork and, 18–20, 26–27, 51, 66–68, 70, 76, 90, 156, 165–66, 186, 195, 196; globalization and, 28, 30, 89; native categories and, 177; studies of mimesis and, 159–64; urban studies and, 157, 161. *See also* Africa; Ethnography; Nongovernmental organizations (NGOs)
Anticolonialism. *See* Postcolonialism
Anti-Semitism, 138, 170
Apartheid, 55–61, 64, 104, 105, 138, 209; struggle against, 116
Appadurai, Arjun, 31
Argentina, 212 n.9
Arrighi, Giovanni, 9
Asia, 25, 29, 30, 31; as compared to Africa, 147–48; East, 108, 184; Southeast, 31, 184

Assimilation, 21, 160
Avant, Deborah, 45
Azande, 74, 82

Bantu, 60
Bantustans, 17, 51–66, 68; usage of name "Transkei," 214 n.2; position of, in South African economy, 61
Barrell, Howard, 116
Bauman, Zygmunt, 29
Bayart, Jean-François, 5, 10, 39, 75
Bemba, 138, 154, 218 n.19
Berg Report. *See* World Bank
Bernstein, Henry, 71, 81, 84
Bhabha, Homi, 21–22, 158, 223 n.12
Biko, Steve, 59–60
Black market. *See* Economy
Black People's Convention, 59, 62
Blair, Tony, 2
Bornstein, Erica, 102
Botha, P. W., 57, 64, 65
Botswana, 1, 52, 57, 131, 132, 210 n.5, 214 n.9
Brazil, 130
Bremer, Paul, 209
British South Africa Company, 100, 207
Bryant, Dave, 44–45
Burundi, 224 n.13
Bush, George W.: compassionate conservatism and, 115

Camdessus, Michael, 173
Cameroon, 31, 75
Canada, 106, 200
Capital flows. *See* Economy
Capitalism, 23, 27, 28, 29, 73, 75, 106, 108, 167, 168, 227 n.10; in Eastern Europe, 82; exploitation and, 75–77; ideology of, 80–81; in Mexico, 108; scientific, 78–82

Nigeria, 28, 41, 134, 138, 194, 202–3, 216 n.6
Nkanya, Tonto, 148
Nongovernmental organizations (NGOs), 13, 14, 38, 44–45, 87, 99, 111–12, 195; bank-organized, 101; Christian, 101, 102; conservation of nature and, 43–46; government-organized (GONGO), 101; international, 101–2, 106; local communities and, 101–2; as object of anthropology, 90; the state and, 40, 102–3
Nordstrom, Carolyn, 15
Nyamanjoh, Francis, 212 n.11
Nyerere, Julius, 75–76

Observer, 45, 46
Obstfeld, Maurice, 34
Ojanen, Julia, 13
Oppenheimer, J. Robert, 148
Organization for Economic Development and Cooperation (OEDC), 196
Organization of African Unity (OUA), 114
Ouattara, Alassane D., 217 n.1
Oxfam, 103

Panhandle Producers and Royalty Owners Association, 208
Pareto, Vilfredo, 122
Phiri, Chileshe, 133–38, 143
Piaget, Jean, 122
Piot, Charles, 167
Poaching, 43; anti-poaching policies and, 44–45
Poland, 184
Pollution, 70–71
Popular Movement for the Liberation of Angola (MPLA), 200
Postcolonialism, 5, 50–51, 94, 119, 120, 156, 165, 178, 190, 215 n.1;

theories of, 66. See also Colonialism
Poverty, 8, 9, 13, 21, 28, 51, 60, 63, 172, 192, 195–204; depoliticizing of, 61, 64–66; global status and, 178; as a social relation, 82–83
Power, 51, 60, 74–75, 99, 111; of chiefs, 73–75; vertical topographies of, 89–112, 216 n.6
Pratt, Mary-Louise, 17
Pritchett, Lant, 35

Rachidi, Hlaku, 62
Racism, 17, 20, 163, 166–67, 170; anthropologists accused of, 157; biblical justification of, 133–34; economic, 170; scientific, 181
Rainforest Action Network, 46
Reagan, Ronald, 58, 81, 91
Relief agencies, 28
Reno, William, 10, 39, 196, 205, 206, 207
Rhodes, Cecil, 100
Rhodesia, Northern, 157
Rhodes-Livingstone Institute, 157
Rights: children's, 174; human, 84, 114, 174; individual, 80
Riots: Copperbelt, 77, 81
Rituals: of possession, 159–61
Roan Antelope Mining Corporation, 145
Roitman, Janet, 40
Rouch, Jean, 159, 161, 162, 163, 164, 222 n.7
Rumsfeld, Donald, 210
Rwanda, 173, 217 n.2

Sassen, Saskia, 25
Save the Children, 47
Savimbi, Jonas, 102
Security forces, 15, 39, 46, 204, 205, 206, 209, 210, 225 n.1
Senegal, 32
Senghor, Blaise, 222 n.8

Tsing, Anna, 226 n.6, 227 n.10
Turkey, 184
Turks: in Germany, 56
Tylor, Edward B., 179

Uganda, 85, 114, 212 n.9
United Kingdom. *See* Great Britain (United Kingdom)
United National Independence Party (UNIP), 118–19
United Nations, 95, 97
United States, 58–59, 106, 110, 122, 194–95, 199–200, 202, 208, 209–10, 216 n.9
Urban studies. *See* Anthropology
Utas, Mats, 186

Vorster, John, 59

Walle, Nicholas van de, 9, 11, 212 n.9
War: civil, 8, 15, 39, 41, 45, 116, 18, 196, 204, 217 n.2, 226 n.6; chronic, 13; guerilla, 107–9
Warlord politics, 10
Watts, Michael, 202, 203
Wealth: kinds of, 72–73; political power and, 74–75; as a social relation, 82
Westernization, 30–32. *See also* Globalization
WildAid, 45
Wilson, Godfrey, 164, 166, 174
Winfrey, Oprah, 134
Witchcraft, 31, 32, 73, 75, 85, 185

Working class, 16, 104, 115, 197, 216 n.9
World Bank, 25, 34, 40, 70–71, 81, 82, 83, 87, 100, 101, 120, 174, 195, 196, 203, 212 n.9, 215; Berg Report and, 78–79, 84; Cologne Initiative and, 173
World Vision International, 102, 111
World Wildlife Fund, 45, 46

Xhosa: "traditional" culture, 57

Zaire, 41, 196, 217 n.2, 222 n.4
Zambia, 6, 19, 20, 28, 35–36, 41, 70, 76, 77, 80–83, 84, 85, 86, 93, 99, 100, 101, 115, 118–19, 166, 169, 171, 173, 185, 212 n.9, 213 n.2, 215 n.1; American culture and, 127, 224 n.13; economic crisis in, 121, 123, 145–47, 198, 201; economic reform in, 121, 126–27, 128, 147–54, 196–97; education in, 122, 123, 126–27; English language in, 128–30, 132, 218 n.19; natural resources and, 145, 150, 197, 205; new culture in, 120–30; patriotism in, 131–32; poverty in, 120; the "West" and, 125, 133–45; young generation in, 121–25
Zapatista movement, 107–8
Zimbabwe, 28, 37, 45, 69, 75, 101, 134

JAMES FERGUSON is professor of cultural and social anthropology at Stanford University. His publications include *Expectations of Modernity: Myths and Meanings of Urban Life on the Zambian Copperbelt* (California, 1999) and *The Anti-Politics Machine: "Development," Depoliticization, and Bureaucratic Power in Lesotho* (Cambridge, 1990; Minnesota, 1994); and with Akhil Gupta, *Culture, Power, Place: Explorations in Critical Anthropology* (Duke, 1997) and *Anthropological Locations: Boundaries and Grounds of a Field Science* (California, 1997).

Library of Congress Cataloging-in-Publication Data
Ferguson, James, 1959–
Global shadows : Africa in the neoliberal world order / James Ferguson.
p. cm.
Includes bibliographical references and index.
ISBN 0-8223-3705-3 (cloth : alk. paper) — ISBN 0-8223-3717-7 (pbk. : alk. paper)
1. Africa—Foreign relations—1960– 2. Africa—Foreign economic relations. 3. Africa—Economic conditions—1960– 4. Africa—Politics and government—1960– 5. Globalization. I. Title.
JZ1773.F47 2006
327.6—dc22   2005028226